Praise for *Paragon o)*

Martin Luther's career as a Reformer has often overshadowed his incisive work as a biblical theologian. This fresh study of his sermons on 1 Peter by Professor Ngien helps to correct that and reveals Luther the exegete at his best. In short, this is a superb examination of Luther's evangelical reflection on the Petrine text.

—Dr. Michael A. G. Azad Haykin,
chair and professor of church history,
The Southern Baptist Theological Seminary

For the great Reformer, 1 Peter was up there with Paul's main letters and John's Gospel (so, his NT prefaces). Thoroughly versed in the best scholarship, and with a thematic approach that moves through the epistle's concerns from pure doctrine to "political theology" (which is what Luther himself was trying to do—i.e., present Christian teaching in an ordered way), this book both helps and invites us to read Luther for himself—on an unfashionable but central biblical book. Ngien begins and ends with the Lutheran insistence that gospel words give life: this seems quite a claim until one remembers that the cross is a passive "work." This book too is that kind of work that is self-effacing, as it allows Luther and the preaching of the cross to speak loud and clear.

—Dr. Mark Warwick Elliott,
professor of biblical and historical theology,
University of the Highlands and Islands,
and Professorial Fellow, Wycliffe College, Toronto

Dennis Ngien makes Luther's sermons on 1 Peter come alive for us as a catechism or teaching that links our everyday lives to Luther's major theological themes (e.g., the performative power of God's Word, justifying faith and works of love, and Christ as gift and example). I recommend this book for anyone who seeks to understand how Luther's hermeneutic principle, the theology of the cross, makes a difference for all aspects of our lives—at home, in the workplace and politics, and in the church.

—Dr. Lois Malcolm, Olin and Amanda Fjelstad
Reigstad Chair of Systematic Theology,
Luther Seminary, St. Paul, Minnesota

Luther's engagement with Paul has been widely researched, but little attention has been given to the Reformer's reception of 1 Peter. With mastery of Luther's texts and a discerning use of a wide range of secondary resources, Dennis Ngien has provided readers with an accessible and robust guide to Luther's understanding of faith and love as the essential shape of 1 Peter. Ngien elucidates Luther's use of this epistle to provide consolation and hope to Christians in times of suffering, as well as strengthening them in their callings in the world. I look forward to using this book in the classroom and beyond.

—Rev. Dr. John T. Pless,
assistant professor of pastoral ministry and missions,
Concordia Theological Seminary, Fort Wayne, Indiana

Before anything else, Luther was a preacher. Dennis Ngien's fine, detailed, and sympathetic study of Luther's sermons on 1 Peter, preached in 1522 as his reforming theology came to its mature form, offers us a rich survey of the key themes of these sermons. This careful and illuminating study from a scholar who knows his field well allows these sermons to speak their wisdom again, outlining a wide-ranging and dramatic view of the Christian life which is at the same time personal, theological, and deeply practical.

—Bishop Graham Tomlin, director of the
Centre for Cultural Witness,
Lambeth Palace, London

If 1 Peter is just as undeservedly underestimated an epistle in the Bible as Luther's sermons on it are within Reformation scholarship, then this book has much to offer to change that shortcoming: a masterful exposition on six major themes by a theologian deeply at home in Luther's theology and Luther scholarship, demonstrating the power and topicality of the Reformer's exegesis of 1 Peter in the light of perennial challenges that Christians face in faith, church, and domestic and civil life.

Dennis Ngien admirably succeeds in showing how Luther's deep theological convictions regarding the primacy of grace over works, which his sermons on 1 Peter present in catechetical and orderly fashion, lead to a wellspring of pastoral wisdom that has much to offer to believers of our time.

—Dr. Dr. habil. Bernd Wannenwetsch,
professor of systematic theology and ethics,
FTH Giessen (Germany), and author of
Political Worship (Oxford University Press, 2004)
and (with Brian Brock) of two volumes of
Theological Commentary on 1 Corinthians,
titled *The Malady of the Christian Body*
(W&S, 2016) and *The Therapy of the
Christian Body* (W&S, 2018)

Once again, Dennis Ngien has persuasively shown that the pastor Luther had matured in his evangelical theology by reading, preaching, and living out the word of God. Indeed, Ngien's careful and thorough study of Luther's sermons on 1 Peter, delivered in 1521 and 1522, helps us to see how Luther translated biblical teaching into primary vocational guidance for everyday Christians.

—Dr. Aihe (Luke) Zheng, academic dean,
International Chinese Biblical Seminary in Europe

Paragon *of* Excellence

Paragon *of* Excellence

Luther's Sermons on 1 Peter

Dennis Ngien

Foreword by Robert Kolb

Fortress Press
Minneapolis

PARAGON OF EXCELLENCE
Luther's Sermons on 1 Peter

Library of Congress Control Number 2023008336 (print)

Cover design and illustration: Joe Reinke

Print ISBN: 978-1-5064-8818-9
eBook ISBN: 978-1-5064-8819-6

Dedicated to

Ronald K. Rittgers,
an erudite Reformation scholar
whose writings benefit
both the academy and the church.

Contents

Acknowledgments

The *Paragon of Excellence* is the fourth of a series of works focused on the reformer's exegetical instruction from which readers can harvest numerous fruits for faith and practice. Luther's sermons on 1 Peter take on a catechetical shape, which aids in the instruction of Christian doctrine and its application to various walks of life, including household living, societal relationships, workplace duties, and religious duties.

This book is dedicated to Ronald Rittgers, whose writings benefit both the academy and the church. His masterpiece, *The Reformation of Suffering: Pastoral Theology and Lay Piety in Late Medieval and Early Modern Germany*, is a priceless resource, one to which my students and I constantly return for aid and direction. I am grateful to Robert Kolb, a world-renowned Luther scholar, for his generous foreword to this volume. Gratitude belongs to several (whose names will not appear here) who have read and commented on every chapter I wrote. This book enjoys warm reception from erudite scholars, including Bernd Wannenwetsch, Graham Tomlin, Luke Zheng, Lois Malcolm, Michael Haykin, Mark Elliott, and John Pless, to whom I am indebted. Thanks to my editor at Fortress Press, Laura Gifford, for her patience and suggestions, which makes a much better production as the outcome. Appreciation goes to the library staff of Tyndale University, for supporting this project, and cheering colleagues and close friends (especially Janet Clark, Arnold Neufeldt-Fast, Jeffrey Greenman, Andrew Stirling, Beth Green, and Ken Gamble), for their ceaseless prayers for me and my work in teaching, service, and scholarship. These significant people teach me faith, hope, and love, and in various ways have become "daily bread" to me, although Christ is "the eternal, living bread."

Dennis Ngien

Reformation Sunday, 2022

Foreword

Exegetes have offered differing explanations of the context and purpose of the first epistle of Saint Peter. In my student days, it was viewed as a baptismal sermon preached on Easter eve at the baptisms of the catechumens and turned into a general letter, a theory that has lost support. What is evident from a reading of the letter, however, is that it offers an overview of Christian teaching, and of the application of faith in Jesus Christ to the daily lives of believers. Whatever its proper genre, it provides a catechism—fundamental instruction in belief and conduct—for Christians in all ages. Martin Luther included 1 Peter in the list of books that he regarded as those that reveal "in masterly fashion how faith in Christ overcomes sin, death, and hell, and gives life, righteousness, and salvation."[1]

Martin Luther continues to make an impact on people around the world in the twenty-first century, above all through his Small and Large Catechisms. He composed them in 1529 after attempting to recruit colleagues to undertake a very necessary task for the reform of the church that the Wittenberg reformers had not yet tackled to Luther's satisfaction, the fashioning of a handbook to enable parents to instruct their children in the faith. Luther's participation in the visitation of Saxon village and town churches the previous year had convinced him to undertake the sorely needed project himself. In late 1528 and early 1529, he preached three more series—in a long succession of such series during his years as an Augustinian brother—of catechetical sermons. With his notes in hand, he then set about to create his "enchiridion" (Greek for "handbook," and the title of late medieval catechisms) for parents, teachers, and pastors to use in instructing the young, and an instructional manual repeating the insights of his catechetical sermons.

Luther had begun to publish sermons or treatises on parts of the catechism a good decade earlier: his *"sermones"*— treatises—on baptism, confession and absolution, and the Lord's Supper, as well as the Lord's Prayer. What is seldom recognized is that his exposition of Peter's first epistle, delivered from the pulpit of the Wittenberg town church from May to December 1522 and published the following year, took the text of this letter and let it serve as a kind of catechism. For the epistle provides an overview of the doctrine and the practice of the Christian faith that Luther had discovered over the previous decade and that guided his reform. In the course of his life, Luther preached a number of weekday sermon series, including treatments of Genesis (1523–1524), Exodus (1524–1527), Leviticus (1527–1528), and Numbers (1528–1529), moving through the texts of these books as he and his colleagues were working on the translation of the Old Testament into German. He also substituted for the pastor of Wittenberg's town church, Johannes Bugenhagen, when Bugenhagen had left the town on missions to aid other towns and territories in their introduction and organization of Wittenberg-type reform. This assignment imposed upon him the necessity of preaching on Matthew (1528–1529, 1530, 1532, 1537–1540) and John (1528–1529, 1530–1532, 1537–1540), for the new ecclesiastical ordinances of Wittenberg mandated weekday series of sermons on those two gospels.

Before these other books, Luther had held the first of these weekday homiletical examinations of books with his weekly treatment of the first epistle of Peter, to which he added sermons on 2 Peter and Jude. These sermons on 1 Peter took place soon after what Munich Reformation professor Reinhard

Schwarz has proposed as the conclusion of the reformer's forming of the core of his theology in 1521 and 1522.[2] Thus, these
sermons on 1 Peter mark an organized attempt to present his
mature reformational theology to the Wittenberg congregation
in a somewhat ordered way. Its catechetical nature made it a
valuable source for such a presentation.

Professor Dennis Ngien has taken Luther's interpretation
of biblical books under the magnifying glass in several studies
that have assessed the reformer's exegetical instruction from
differing angles. His study of Luther's lectures on the lament
psalms focused above all on issues of pastoral care.[3] His analysis of the Christology in his sermons on John examined how
he proclaimed Christ crucified and risen for the comfort of his
people.[4] His comparison of Luther's exegesis of Galatians in his
two lecture series on the epistle with Calvin's interpretation of
the book evaluated how the two reformers treated the heart of
biblical teaching, as it is made concrete in Christian spirituality according to the apostle Paul's exposition of it in addressing the crisis in the churches of Galatia.[5] In this volume, Ngien
identifies one or two of the major themes in each of Peter's five
chapters as focal points for taking a broader look at Luther's
application of these topics in the breadth of his mature theology. His intimate knowledge of Luther's writings allows him to
draw together a coherent picture of Luther's mature thinking
on the basis of his treatment of 1 Peter.

Ngien's sharp ear for the life that Christians lead together
in their congregations; and as they interact with the broader
population in family, workplace, neighborhood, and religious
locations or walks of life; informs Ngien's venture into Luther's
world of thought. The author's rich experience with Luther's
way of thinking and the notes it sounds that play to contemporary questions serve readers well once again as he shows the
relevance of the Wittenberg reformer's insights into Scripture
and the challenges of daily life.

Readers will enjoy this exploration of Luther's way of thinking; his manner of proclaiming the heart of God's biblical message and its implications for the daily life of the Christian in home, economic, and societal life; and the life of the church. For Professor Ngien has again caught the ways in which the Wittenberg reformer engaged Scripture and transmitted its message into pastoral practice and application. The adventure upon which Luther's hearers were taken in exploring the Petrine landscape five hundred years ago finds fresh rehearsal in these pages.

Robert Kolb
Mainz, Festival of Saint Matthew the Evangelist 2022

Introduction

A Statement of Purpose

Martin Hengel describes St. Peter as *"the underestimated Apostle."* Roman Catholics and Protestants alike, he argues, have underplayed "the historical and theological importance of the fisherman from Bethsaida." Most scholars who devote time and attention to Peter do so merely to "harmonize him in his relationship with Paul."[1] More frequently, Peter disappears midway through the book of Acts, never again to resurface as an exegetical priority. Hengel, on the other hand, claims Peter as of central importance to Christian history. This position finds him in a distinguished company. Martin Luther preached a series of sermons on 1 Peter at the Wittenberg town church around 1522.[2] Luther's sermons reflect the significance the reformer places on Peter's epistle, finding resources within it that instruct us in core matters of faith and practice.

First, Luther highly esteems Peter and places him on a par with John and Paul, viewing him also as the master of the doctrine of justification. In the *Prefaces to the New Testament*, Luther ranks St. Peter's first epistle alongside John's gospel and St. Paul's epistles, especially Romans, and considers them as "the true kernel and marrow of all books."[3] These are "the foremost books" because they contain masterful descriptions of how faith in Christ triumphs over sin, death, and hell, and acquires righteousness, life, and heaven.[4] St. Peter's first epistle, for Luther, is "the paragon of excellence,"[5] for it is "the genuine and pure gospel."[6] The gospel, for Luther, is "nothing else than a sermon or report concerning the grace and mercy of God merited and acquired through the Lord Jesus Christ with His death."[7] It is not so much what is written in the books as it is "an oral sermon and a living Word, a voice" that is proclaimed publicly so that people can hear it.[8] In this, Luther underscores both the oral and aural aspects of proclamation. The gospel is "not a book of laws that contains many good teachings. . . . It does not tell us to do good works to make us pious, but it announces to us the grace of God bestowed gratis and without our merit, and tells us how Christ took our place, rendered satisfaction for our sins, and destroyed them, and that He makes us pious and saves us through His work."[9] The "best evangelists," including St. Peter, accentuate the primacy of the words of Christ over the works of Christ. Luther avows that it is better to do without the historical knowledge of the works and miracles of Christ (in the sense of the *fides historica* that was seen as the acknowledgment of facts, just as the devils believe while trembling before God), for they, he claims, "do not help me, but his words give life, as he himself says (Jn. 6:63)."[10] Miracles might cease, but not the word. The Word, apart from which there is no life, is indispensable. Luther writes:

> Now since greater value attaches to the words of Christ than to His works and deeds—and if we had to dispense with one or the other, it would be better for us to do without the deeds and the history than to be without the words and the doctrine—those books that treat mainly of Christ's teachings and words should in all conscience be esteemed most highly. Without them we could not have life.[11]

Second, Luther's sermons on 1 Peter underscore Luther as a theologian of the cross. In his seminal *Heidelberg Disputation* (1518), Luther develops what he labels "the theology of the cross" (*theologia crucis*), his hermeneutical method by which he conceives of the content of the gospel. This disputation, Saleska notes, represents his attempt to abandon "scholasticism's use of syllogism in order to express doctrinal truth and [embrace] paradox as a new way of doing theology. Luther's move can be described as a move from *ergo* (therefore) to *dennoch* (nevertheless). This is true, nevertheless, this is also true."[12] Luther relishes paradox, and his entire theology, Forde writes, "sound[s] the note of contraries."[13] The contraries laid out in his disputation include law/gospel, Christ's/human righteousness, alien/proper work, wrath/mercy, old/new Adam, works/faith, flesh/spirit, sinner/saint, human/divine love, Christ as sacrament/Christ as example, merit/grace, revelation/reason, sin/righteousness, and God as hidden/revealed. These basic elements of Luther's evangelical way of thinking, as propounded in his *Heidelberg Disputation*, are on display in his sermons on 1 Peter. Luther locates the 1 Peter sermons in their historical context, as an early expression of Luther's mature thought.

Third, Luther's sermons reflect, to borrow Kolb's apt description, "an evangelical maturation"[14] distinctive of the reformer's vocation as, in Spitz's phrase, "a care-taker of the soul" (*Seelsorger*).[15] "Above all," Kittelson expands, "the care of souls (*cura animarum*) . . . was the driving force in Luther's personal development and in his career as friar, professor, theologian, and even reformer."[16] Pulpit and lecture podium are precisely the contexts where the process of growth occurs, as Luther seeks how best to formulate his thinking and disseminate it. The movement from text to sermons opens a window into Luther's world of faith and instills in his congregants a love for the pure, genuine word, which is "the good news" St. Peter proclaimed (1 Pet 1:24) by which our faith is nurtured and established.

This book does not provide an analysis of each chapter of Luther's printed sermons on 1 Peter but rather an overview and summary of Luther's thought that is outlined according to the chief themes one can glean from each of Peter's five chapters: the performative power of God's word, Christ as cornerstone, Christ as both gift and example, household holiness, the priesthood of all believers, and the relationship between God's command and secular government. Throughout, Luther's reflections on 1 Peter further develop the foundational pillars of Lutheran theology.

Distinctive Features in Luther's Sermons on 1 Peter

The superscription "an apostle of Jesus Christ" (1 Pet 1:1), with which Peter begins his epistle, defines his office as an emissary who delivered what Christ commanded him to do by word of mouth "to the exiles of the dispersion in Pontus, Galatia, Cappadocia, Asia, and Bithynia" (1 Pet 1:1). Each apostle wrote in his unique literary style but bore the same gospel. The gospel was revealed to the Spirit-filled prophets from whom Peter learned what true faith is, and from him, we learn it so that we know how to preach. What Peter preached are the "genuinely evangelical words" about who Christ is and what he has acquired for us through his blood.[17] The inheritance, "imperishable, undefiled, and unfading" (1 Pet 1:4), that the Father gives us through Jesus Christ proceeds out of his pure mercy, apart from any merits of human works. Accessibility to the Father occurs not through the intercession of saints or Mary but through the mediation of Christ and his precious blood. The cross blotted out sin in exchange for Christ's righteousness. God's separation from us through sin is abolished by his reconciliation to us through righteousness. The accusatory function of the law ceases, and so does the terror of God's wrath. In Christ, we encounter God not as a stern judge but as a friendly father who makes us his children. He issues forth, says Luther, "a new existence," transposing us from the state of Adam and his inheritance to the state of Christ and his inheritance.[18] Together with all the saints, we are partakers of all his inestimable riches without distinction. We have been regenerated to "a living hope" through Christ's resurrection. Believers taste in this life only a tiny portion of the immeasurable inheritance, which awaits its full exposure at the end. Luther writes, "It is still hidden, still covered, locked and sealed up. Yet in a short time it will be revealed and exposed to our view."[19] With St. Paul (who wrote in Romans 8:24 "You are already saved, but in hope; you do not yet see it, but wait for it"), St. Peter exults, "Your salvation is kept in heaven for you, ready to be revealed on the Last Day" (1 Pet 1:4–5).[20] These words St. Peter preached are not "unnecessary words"; they are creative words through which "everything is alive."[21]

Luther's Christology is conceived in terms of the Augustinian Christ as sacrament and Christ as example.[22] St. Augustine's sacrament- and example-Christology were already assumed in his earlier commentary on Galatians, where he avers, "Saint Augustine teaches that the suffering Christ is both a *sacramentum* [gift] and an *exemplum* [example]—a *sacramentum* because it signifies the death of sin in us and grants it to those who believe, an *exemplum* because it also behooves us to imitate Him in bodily suffering and dying."[23] Here in his exposition of 1 Peter 2:21, 3:17, and 4:1, Luther reiterates the Augustinian pair: "For in Scripture the life of the Lord Christ, and particularly His suffering, is presented to us in a twofold manner. In the first place, as a gift," and "in the second place . . . as an example."[24] This line of thinking, Lohse opines, dominates the entirety of Luther's theology.[25] Lage observes the pair in Luther's later writings, citing, for example, thesis 50 of his first *Disputation against the Antinomians* (1538): "We know, and they have learned from us, that Christ became both sacrament and example for us."[26] In his second *Disputation*, Luther continues, "You know that Paul usually joins two things, just as Peter did in 1 Peter 2:21; first that Christ died for us and redeemed us through his blood to purify for himself a Holy people. Thus he shows us Christ as gift and sacrament. Then, they show us as an example we should imitate in His good works."[27] Not only must we preach the expiatory function of the cross, that we might grasp Christ as gift by faith, but we should also perform the exemplary function of the cross with love, that we might imitate Christ as model. The logical order begins with Christ as savior, followed by Christ as model. As Luther declares, "Whoever, therefore, would imitate Christ as He is the *exemplum* must believe first with a firm faith that Christ suffered for him as *sacramentum*."[28] Just as Christ as sacrament precedes Christ as gift, so faith precedes works. Christ as gift "nourishes your faith" and produces sonship, but Christ as example "exercises our works" and expresses sonship.[29] "Faith possesses nothing of its own"; it merely grasps or receives Christ's life and actions.[30] But "our works have something of ours in them"; they benefit the neighbors.[31]

The object of God's justifying action, Hamm writes, is not "the loving person but the sinful person,"[32] who is declared righteous *ex nihilo*, not out of any prior quality or worth but out of pure grace. The simultaneity (*simul*) of sinner and saint in the same person is no contradiction but a contrary of perspective: the law makes a sinner, but the gospel makes a saint, the former leading to the latter. Luther concedes the *simul* to a paradox in which though faith reckons us righteous, no longer in need of cleansing, we in our flesh are impure, still in need of mortification (1 Pet 2:11–12).[33] Contrary to the medieval conception of "faith formed by love" (*fides charitate formata*) that justifies, Luther insists that "faith in Christ alone justifies."[34] Justification occurs through a transformation of the human's relationship with God, not through a transformation of the human in us. Durheim writes aptly:

> When Christ is taken on in faith, the human moves only from *peccator* to *simul iustus et peccator*. This is a change not of the human person but of the human's standing before God (or of the human's relationship with God). It is a change by addition rather than a change by transformation. When the believer is united with Christ, an entirely new aspect of the human

becomes real, namely, the human as someone in and through whom Christ lives.[35]

God's righteousness is ours by faith, that is, to use Hamm's phrase, "by pure receiving,"[36] not by our working. Faith alone that justifies places us outside us (*extra nos*) so that we do not rely on ourselves but completely on God. St. Peter underscores joy as a by-product of, to borrow Hamm's phrase, "a passive stirring of the heart"[37] through the efficacy of God's justifying word and his goodness. This is borne out in his explanation of 1 Peter 2:3, "For you have tasted the kindness of the Lord," where Luther puts the emphasis on the affective dimension of the justified existence, denominated by the experiential language of "taste." To the heart of the one who has tasted God's goodness, Luther writes, "it tastes right; to them, it is sweet."[38] Accordingly, Luther's doctrine of justification is not couched in impersonal or mechanistic terms, devoid of pious emotions—joy, comfort, and peace—created by faith. He does not conceive justification in terms of "the sterile dogmatic vocabulary of a cognitive appreciation for the distinction between law and gospel" but, as Helmer writes, as "the word of justification [that] elicits a joy that 'jumps and skips.'"[39]

Christ is the chief cornerstone in whom we have everything for justification. All our being and actions must correspond to Christ, just as stones set together might construct a wall. Any collision with the cornerstone smashes the wall into pieces, not because of any deficiency in it but because of one's rejection and contradiction of the cornerstone. The priestly ministry of the church has its being in Christ. The rejected stone whom God has made the foundation stone has conquered the enemies of sin, death, and hell. Nothing of our own—no pious acts, no penitential love, no performance of law, and no free will—could supplant Christ; they are chaff in the wind. The conscience terrified by sin, law, and wrath seeks relief by turning outward to Christ, the sole remedy, rather than by turning inward to its own resources. As Kachelmeier writes, "The bad conscience becomes terrified at the sound of God's voice, and there is no place to flee from God's presence. Only Christ fulfils the demands of the law for us. Only in Christ, then, is there peace for the conscience."[40]

Where Christ is eclipsed, the whole world deviates from God's way and lapses into the terror of God's wrath. We acquire holiness, not by any prior action or pious emotions of our own but by Christ's holiness, which is imputed to us if we believe. This is borne out in Luther's explanation of 1 Peter 1:15–16: "But as He who called you is holy, be holy yourselves in all your conduct, since it is written: You shall be holy, for I am holy." Faith distinguishes us as God's holy people: "Just as God, our Lord, is holy, so His people are also holy. Therefore we are all holy if we walk in faith."[41] Holiness is God's by right and nature; holiness is ours by grace. It is not intrinsic but extrinsic to us. Just as our goodness is "a borrowed goodness,"[42] so, too, is our holiness a "borrowed" holiness. The stress on "passive holiness"[43] means holiness is received, not achieved. The stress on "active holiness"[44] means that we are appointed to reflect God's holy character as part of a responsive life of faith characterized by a reverential fear (1 Pet 1:17) of the God of the first commandment.

Luther avers that the Christian life is summed up in this phrase: "Walk in faith and love."[45] The pair of "faith and love" constitutes the shape of the Christian life, that is, vertically before God by faith and horizontally before others by love.[46] "Faith alone" justifies, but good works are the "fruits and signs of faith."[47] Faith that justifies vivifies works as part of the justified existence. Luther stresses the effectual nature of faith: "So faith first makes the person, who afterwards performs works."[48] Freedom that Christ has acquired for us means, in Nessan's words, both "free indeed" and free "in deed."[49] Faith has so radically freed Luther from what he called the state of being "curved in on itself"[50]—that is, idolatry of self—that he is willing to live out his righteous identity by one moral dictum: "I will do nothing in this life except what I see is necessary, profitable, and salutary" to others, freely and joyfully serving them with the abundant goods he has from Christ.[51] Christ's expiatory work is so complete that it has no need of supplementation. It is so efficacious that it changes us into a new person, who then is aroused to works. The order of justifying action is from person to work: the person must first be justified before they can perform righteous work. Iwand captures Luther's point well: "Thus, our works are born out of our condition, and we are not born out of our works."[52] The suffering love of the rejected stone, the crucified Jesus, awakens in us attraction to God and his work, as a bride is drawn to her groom.[53] The impetus to work is not generated by self but by Christ, who dwells in us, and by whose action we act through faith. In all this, believers remain the passive recipients of God's prior act; God remains the active agent of all.

A theologian of the cross dwells not on God's essence, speculating on how God is in and for themself, but on how God is toward us. As Luther avers, "The Lord Christ should not be isolated as existing for himself but should be preached as belonging to us."[54] In Christ, God is known in his coming to us as a father to his beloved child, and thus we have a God we can cling to. God is not hidden in his majesty but, in fact, as "the incarnate, human God,"[55] has stepped out of his naked hiddenness and approaches us in a friendly manner. Christ, for Luther, is "the divine majesty sweetened and mitigated to your ability to stand it."[56] The God who hides in himself is of no concern to us, unlike the God who is "preached as belonging to us."[57] Faith grasps "the God as he is preached";[58] as St. Peter declares, "That word is the good news which was preached to you" (1 Pet 1:25, quoting Deut 30:14).[59] The revealed word leads us away from the wrathful deity of the hidden majesty to the incarnate God whom St. Peter preached as immanently near and kindly disposed to us; in Luther's own words, "as belonging to us." So grasp him not where he is in his impassive, inscrutable nature, which is beyond reach, but in the "incarnate, human God"[60] where God has become, to borrow Mattes's phrase, "a graspable God."[61]

Luther's theology begins with the economic action of the triune God, which is, in Swain's phrase, the "grammar of divine agency."[62] The trinitarian shape and substance of the apostolic proclamation was apparent in 1 Peter 1:2: "chosen and destined by God the Father and sanctified by the Spirit for obedience to Jesus Christ and for sprinkling with his blood." All three persons act as one God, as (to borrow Pannenberg's phrase) "a differentiated unity,"[63] constituting believers as the beneficiaries of "the precious blood of Jesus Christ" (1 Pet 1:19). The prophets had already predicted "the sufferings of Christ and the subsequent glory" (1 Pet 1:22), which were also the subject of the apostolic proclamation. Luther quotes Psalm 22:6, "I am a worm, and no man," to indicate the depth of Christ's self-humiliation; and Psalm 44:22: "We are accounted as sheep for the slaughter," to speak of the suffering of God's people and Christians.[64] For Christ, the road to his glory is through abject humiliation of the cross; likewise, the Christians must also bear the cross, the antecedent to glory. The prophetic language of suffering and subsequent glory is emptied of its force unless "the Spirit of Christ" (1 Pet 1:22) teaches it to our hearts. Likewise, the apostolic language of proclamation yields no fruits unless the Holy Spirit impresses it in our hearts. Luther avers:

> The fact that we have so little understanding of the prophets today is the result of our inability to understand the language. In any case, they spoke clearly enough. Therefore those who are familiar with the language and have the Spirit of God, as all believers do, understand without any difficulty, since they

know the purport of all Scripture. . . . Yet if one of these is
lacking, the Spirit without the language is better than the language without the Spirit.[65]

Preaching, Luther concedes, is "God's speaking to us," albeit
through the voice of a creature.[66] God's word, for him, is "the
inexpressibly precious gift"[67] from which we harvest an inestimable treasure that benefits our soul. In Schwöbel's words: "We
are all God's vocabulary."[68] "The words of God," for Luther, "are
realities, not bare words."[69] Whatever God pronounces will of
necessity occur, for the same word that spoke the world into
being now says, "You are justified." Creation and justification,
Cortez explains, are "new realities" that God's word brings into
being.[70] God can accomplish what he says. Parallelism occurs
between God's speech in creation and preaching. Trueman
writes, "The preached word is the Word of God, and therefore
stands in close analogy to God's speech in creation."[71] God hides
his presence in humble preachers; he fills them with the Spirit's power, apart from which they cannot accomplish anything.
Only a heart that has been changed through the ear, that is,
through the hearing of the word, welcomes the word and loves
it. The heart, not the hand, is indispensable to the reception
of the word first proclaimed by the mouth so that we can perceive it through the ear. The emphasis on hearing rather than
seeing God places us in a passive position to receive his word,
permitting it to accomplish its justifying work in us. Helmer
writes aptly, "The experience of justification is hidden to all
the senses except hearing. The human recipient of the word is
the hearer of the gospel. Hearing is privileged as the sense that
reliably perceives God's true word."[72] The ears are the instruments of God's justifying action. Whoever "hears" the gospel
and "believes in it," Peter teaches, is "an obedient child of God"
(1 Pet 1:14).[73] Faith comes not by seeing God—this would crush
us, for no mortal soul can survive seeing him; rather, faith is

produced by hearing God's word, which makes us his children, along with all his other blessings. The word preached in the power of Holy Spirit possesses a divine, efficacious power to create anew and make us a reborn child of God if we cling to it.[74] The word, when received, is implanted in our hearts, lives there, and generates life. Christ and his precious goods belong to us by a passive reception of faith. As Luther says, "If you believe, you shall have all things; if you do not believe, you shall lack all things."[75] To unbelief, Christ is offensive, even though Christ in himself is a consoling agent; consequently, all "precious" goods are lost. To faith, God is "precious" (1 Pet 2:7). As Bayer writes, "*Reality is constituted by one's assessment*": faith or unbelief.[76] With faith, the causal power of God, there is truth and clarity; apart from faith, everything is error and darkness. Faith possesses its creative power, enabling us to perceive that God is merciful to the humble. Unbelief also has its creative power, causing people to negate God and make him a liar, not worthy of trust. The unbeliever, says Bayer, "attributes truth to himself and lies and nothingness to God."[77]

In his *On the Councils and the Church* (1539), Luther makes use of Psalm 127:1 to speak of the three "orders" or "institutes" that are arranged in the medieval order of home, state, and church.[78] He writes:

> This Psalm 127[:1] says that there are only two temporal governments on earth, that of the city and that of the home, "Unless the Lord builds the house; unless the Lord watches over *the city*." The first government is that of the home, from which the people come; the second is that of the city, meaning the country, the people, princes and lords, which we call the secular government. These embrace everything—children, property, money, animals, etc. The home must produce, whereas the city must guard, protect, and defend. Then follows the third, God's own home and city, that is, the church, which must obtain people from the home and protection and defense from the city.[79]

The three orders are where "the works of God" are hidden.[80] None of them bears any soteriological power; they are the "masks"[81] through which God rules and mediates his power, and through which he provides for humankind and nature. They are also the concrete forms of our vocational obedience to God. They are the arenas where "faith is active in love," that is, where we express our God-given identity for the well-being of others. The vocational obedience in life's stations, in Cortez's phrase, "constitutes the particularities of our calling *coram mundo*, which we engage as an outworking of our universal calling *coram Deo*."[82]

The doctrine of three orders appears in Luther's sermons on the first epistle of Peter. This is borne out in his exposition of 1 Peter 5:7, which exhorts: "Cast all your anxieties on Him, for He cares for you." All offices and estates are the instrumental means of God's providential care in providing a peaceful and stable life on earth. The accent on these stations of life reflects Luther's high estimation of the creatureliness of this life.[83] "His Ockhamist instruction," Kolb writes, "prepared Luther to take the created order seriously and to perceive God's presence in it."[84] Luther rejects the so-called Platonic spiritualism that exalts the spiritual above the material; he affirms both, as they belong to the created order. Luther's doctrine of God is found in his exposition of the first commandment, where he writes that it is God's "most earnest purpose to be our God,"[85] and the first article of faith, where God is described as one who creates, gives, provides, and sustains all "out of pure, fatherly, and divine goodness and mercy, without any merit or worthiness of mine at all."[86] The temporal goods are God's gifts and cannot constitute our identity except by God, who alone is worthy of "fear, trust, and love above all things."[87] We incur divine displeasure if we put our trust in them rather than in God. As part of the explanation of the first commandment, Luther writes:

God will tolerate no presumption or trust in anything else; he makes no greater demand on us than a heartfelt trust in him for every good thing, so that we walk straight ahead on the right path, using all of God's gifts exactly as a shoemaker uses a needle, awl, and thread for his work and afterward puts them aside, or as a traveler makes use of an inn, food, and lodging, but only for his physical needs. Let each person do the same in his or her walk of life according to God's order, allowing none of these things to be a lord or an idol.[88]

Parsons rightly points out that "vocation is the sphere in which men and women partner with God in genuine co-operation. It is concretely in the realm of calling, or vocations, that Luther speaks of God working through a person to fulfill his will, even in the ordinary duties of life."[89] It is not that God needs us to work his purpose, something that God could achieve by himself. But instead, God "does us the honor of wanting to effect work with us and through us."[90] His inclusion of us in his work is an occasion for our performance of good works by obeying God's commandments; otherwise, "his commandments would be given in vain."[91] Both God and humans work together to bring about an action: we should labor, without which God "gives us nothing"; and God gives, not because of our labor but because "it is the divine blessing,"[92] Luther writes, as "we do no work from which we gain sustenance."[93] The work we perform, which is rightly ours, and the sustenance, which is solely God's—the two must be separated, as is heaven from earth.[94] The triumph of any order—ecclesial, political, and household—is to be attributed to the abundance of God's blessings hidden in it, not our labor. To transfer the victory of a community to human agency is to sin against the God of the first commandment; it, too, magnifies the self-curved nature and establishes the self as lord. While all earthly labors are instrumental causes, God is the efficient cause. What Luther teaches here is not monergism in which only God is active, doing all, and human beings are completely passive, doing nothing. "According to Luther," Gregersen writes, "human beings are not entirely passive when they are used by God as his instruments."[95] God acts impassively, not subject to human passion; we act causally, contingent on God's prior act. The more proximate we are to God, the more we are empowered to act, though the effectiveness remains God's. Saarinen captures Luther well: "An individual is doing his or her best, and God freely grants success or failure. Divine acceptance is not causally necessitated by the person's own efforts or merits but remains a free act of God. Thus we have a kind of covenant in which God remains totally free, but the individual is also granted the status of secondary co-worker."[96] What human labor produces, Saarinen further clarifies, are "fruits but not merits."[97]

Every estate of life is God's gift, not to be achieved by merit but only received with gratitude. We remain faithful to our callings and perform our vocations, not worrying about what might transpire as the outcome but trusting in God's faithfulness to accomplish his will. We must perform our callings in accordance with God's will, Luther stresses, so that our prayers may not be hindered, especially when praying the fifth petition of the Lord's Prayer: "Forgive us our trespasses."[98] Commenting on Song of Solomon 1:4, "Draw me after you," Luther emphasizes prayer as a weapon against Satan and all ills in all life's stations:

No manner of life is without its special burden. Marry a wife: immediately you will discover a flood of ills! You will find things which displease you in your wife and in your children, and the care of stomach will occupy you. Similarly those who are in government experience a host of evils, for Satan is nowhere inactive. Prayer, then, is all that remains; by prayer let us overcome various hazards and rocks on which we run aground.[99]

The cross reveals what kind of God he is in suffering for us so that we might become a certain kind of person empathetically suffering with others. The cross fosters our way of being in the world. Christ's passion becomes ours in a joyous exchange. Just as the cross is imposed upon Christ so that he must bear it himself, so, too, we are not relieved of the cross that we must bear ourselves. As Sasse claims, "To believe in the cross always means also to carry the cross."[100] To whatever vocations we are called, we are never free from the vocation of the cross, unless by infidelity and death. Believers submit to the God-imposed cross through which God mortifies the old Adam and its vices so that he might renew the new Adam. The annihilation of the sinful Adam does not necessarily occur in monasteries, in deserts, or in churches, or among the pious; they can happen in daily life, schools, offices, homes, politics, or whatever life's stations God places us.[101] Whoever gladly obeys God, Wingren writes, "for that reason, receives more crosses and suffering in his vocation than does a man who, before God, is cold though honest."[102]

St. Peter taught that the genuineness of faith undergoes suffering as through the fire of purification (cf. 1 Pet 1:9; 4:1–2). "For God allows us to be tested by such ills so that the glory of the Word may be demonstrated and the divine power magnified in our weakness. Otherwise there would be no way to demonstrate His glory and mercy."[103] Faith alone, not human works, perceives that the cross that comes upon believers does not stem from a vindictive, wrathful God but from a gracious, merciful God who has not forsaken those who suffer for Christ's sake. We "sanctify God as Lord" (1 Pet 3:15) by accepting the God-imposed cross paradoxically as the hidden, blessed work of God: as an alien work, as in law, it condemns all possibilities and human agency in salvation, leaving believers completely naked and inextricably helpless; as a proper work, as in gospel, the cross instills in them a trusting relationship with God and a rightful belonging to him.

Gabriel Biel, a scholastic theologian of Luther's era, believes that God will not withhold his grace to those who "do what is in them."[104] On the contrary, Luther asserts, "while a person is doing what is in him, he sins and seeks himself in everything."[105] Thesis 16 of his *Heidelberg Disputation* states, "The person who believes that he can obtain grace by doing what is in him adds sin to sin so that he becomes doubly guilty."[106] What should one do when one realizes that doing one's best only sins doubly? Luther specifies two options: "a theology of glory" opts for complete indifference since nothing we do could acquire grace but instead sins doubly, but "a theology of the cross" opts for complete trust in God because there is nothing to do except "fall down and pray for grace and place your hope in Christ in whom is our salvation, life, and resurrection."[107] A theologian of glory places their trust in "doing what is in [them]" and remains trapped in their eccentric self; a theologian of the cross relies on Christ alone and is freed from self-entrapment. The annihilation of self is the true condition of the possibility of God's work in their opposite; as 1 Peter 5:6 states: "Humble yourselves therefore under the mighty hand of God, that in due time He may exalt you." Humility is not created by human efforts; humility is created by God, who performs through the law an alien work of humbling us to prepare us for grace. The law exposes sin (Rom 3:20); the gospel disposes of it. "Through the knowledge of sin, however, comes humility, and through humility grace is acquired";[108] as Peter declares, "God gives grace to the humble" (1 Pet 5:5). The law humbles us, causing us to despair not of God but of our ability to save ourselves. God's alien work of crucifying the old Adam and his confidence in good works leads to his proper work of redeeming us, making us saints *ex nihilo*.[109] The paradoxical action of God inheres in Luther's doctrine of justification, in which God's dual, contradictory activities coincide to create something new. "Thus an action that is alien to God's nature results in a deed belonging to his very nature: he makes a person a sinner so that he may make him righteous."[110]

All human attempts at self-justification, either by reason, will, or meritorious works, cease, not so that we might culminate in the abyss of sheer despair where there is no respite but in the bosom of our heavenly Father, where there is nothing but sheer delight. This is indeed the gospel Peter proclaimed, before which there is nothing to do except respond with the sacrifice of praise (1 Pet 5:11). This book is written with a hope that God may grant us grace to understand, retain, and commend it so that others may join with all the saints, the dead and the living, and conclude as David did in Psalm 119:103: "How sweet are Your Words unto my taste! Yes, sweeter than honey to my mouth!"

CHAPTER 1

God's Word as Performative
Christian Obedience
and Holiness as Passive

In speaking of the word of God, Steinmetz discerns in Luther a distinction between the "Call-Word" and the "Deed-Word."[1] The former refers to the word used to name already existing things. For instance, Adam names the creatures but he did not create them. The latter "not only names but effects what it signifies."[2] Luther, says Forde, lays stress on "what the words do, not merely in what they mean."[3] When God speaks in Genesis 1:3, "Let there be light," these words, Luther writes, "are the words of God, not of Moses; this means that they are realities. For God calls into existence the things which do not exist (Rom 4:17). He does not speak grammatical words; he speaks true and existent realities. . . . Thus, sun, moon, heaven, earth, Peter, Paul, I, you, etc.—we are all words of God."[4] Hebraically, one of the meanings of the term "word" refers to not only that which is spoken, that is, the speech itself, but also to that to which the spoken word points, that is, the resultant reality. Pelikan writes, "The Word [is] the concrete action of God."[5] All creaturely things of this world, including the occurrences of human history, have their being in God's "Deed-Word." They are, Pelikan continues, "all words of God because, in the mystery of divine providence, each of them was a deed of God."[6] Pelikan's assessment is drawn from Luther's exposition of Psalm 2, where he writes, "In the case of God to speak is to do, and that the word is the deed."⁷ Luther elaborates, "When Scripture says that God is speaking, it understands a word of reality [*verbum reale*] or action, not just a sound, as our words are. For God does not have a mouth, a tongue, for he is Spirit. Therefore the mouth and tongue of God refer to, 'he spoke, and it happened.'"⁸ Luther's Reformation discovery of the effective character of God's word—in Bayer's words, "that the verbal sign (*signum*) is itself the reality (*res*)"—permeates his thinking.⁹ The sign does not have as its referent an absent object but the object as the present reality. Bayer observes that Luther contrasts the language of philosophy with the language of theology: "A sign in philosophy is the mark of a thing that is absent, but a sign in theology is the mark of a thing that is present."¹⁰ God's word, says Bayer, "actually constitutes reality" that has not existed beforehand.¹¹ The majestic word does not simply convey information but creates something out of nothing (*ex nihilo*) that no creature could do. It is the all-determining origin of all realities; it is performative of new occurrences that correspond to itself. Kolb and Arand recognize at least five different functions of the word of God: it "creates," it "establishes" the relation between God and his creatures, it "elicits faith," it "simultaneously reveals and hides God," and it "kills and makes alive."¹² All of these are represented in the first epistle of Peter. Commenting on 1 Peter 1:23, "You have been born anew, not of perishable seed but of imperishable, through the living and abiding word of God," Luther declares that the eternal word "is everything from which we live put together, food and nourishment."¹³ The word by which God accomplishes all things out of nothing governs and shapes the entirety of his theology.¹⁴

Rebirth: God's Word, Not Human Works

Peter writes, "You have been born anew, not of perishable seed but of imperishable, through the living and abiding word of God" (1 Pet 1:23). New birth is not a result of human works;

it is purely God's work. We cannot make anew actively; we must "grow or be born" passively.[15] Luther illustrates, "Just as a carpenter cannot make a tree, but the tree itself must grow out of the earth, and just as we all were not made children of Adam but were born as such and have inherited sin from our father and mother, so we cannot become children of God by means of works but must be born again."[16] The word, for Luther, is "the divine womb in which we are conceived, carried, born, reared, etc."[17] Birth, both old and new, requires a seed. The seed of which Peter speaks is "not flesh and blood" but the imperishable "eternal word" from which we are born anew. The seed, Luther avers, is "nothing but the gospel" by which new life comes.[18] Regeneration begins with the proclamation through which God deposits the seed in human hearts. Through the Holy Spirit, the seed takes root there. Then an entirely new person is born, with everything new, including "words," "thoughts," and "works."[19]

Physical birth differs from spiritual birth. In physical birth, when a seed is received, it is no longer seed; it is changed. In spiritual birth, the seed that is implanted in us is eternal; it does not undergo change. "But it changes me in such a way that I am changed into it and what evil there is in me because of my nature disappears completely. Therefore this is an extraordinary birth—a birth from an unusual seed."[20] We become God's children, for Luther, "in a purely passive, not in an active way"; that is, we simply "let ourselves be made and formed as a new creation through faith in the Word."[21] God's word creates faith by which it becomes a personal word, effecting in us new realities. As Bielfeldt contends, "Now the external Word becomes *my* word, for it is God's Word for me."[22] The word, applied to us, frees us from ourselves and everything that holds us in bondage so that we can become what we otherwise could not—namely, his beloved, just as the word says.

Peter further substantiates the enduring nature of the word of God from Isaiah 40:6–8, where the prophet says, "All flesh is like grass and all its glory like the flower of the grass. The grass withers, and the flowers fall, but the word of the Lord abides forever" (cf. 1 Pet 1:24–25). "All flesh is like grass" speaks of the inefficacy of "all the glory and pomp of flesh."[23] Flesh refers to the whole person, oriented away from God; it seeks to satisfy its own desires, not the things of God. All human works of righteousness, reason, and free will may seem like flowers to the world, but to God, they are perishable grass. The flowers of the flesh are blown away by the Spirit through the instrumentality of God's word. "The spirit blowing on the grass is nothing else than the Spirit convincing the world of sin, and thus through the ministry of the Word the Spirit condemns all verdure and flower of the grass."[24]

While all creaturely things die through the word, the word itself never dies, as it is "a divine and eternal power."[25] When the word penetrates our hearts and is grasped by faith, it cannot perish, nor does it allow us to perish. It creates and carries us if we take hold of it. Nothing can undo the word, not even the gates of hell; as Paul proclaims in Romans 1:16, "I am not ashamed of the Gospel; it is the power of God unto salvation to everyone who has faith." The word truly brings God and all his gifts to his reborn children. The word creates its own reality, just as it says. God creates by speaking creation into existence, and by the same word, he preserves all that exists. Both creation and recreation rest on the causative power of God's word, not human works. Just as God's word ("Let there be light!" [Gen 1:3]) brings creation into being, so also it brings about new birth ("Whoever believes is born of God" [1 John 5:1]). The word of promise effects rebirth, making a new creature out of an old creature and changing a sinner into a saint. As Kolb and Arand intimate:

> This word from God has immediate effect and validity. That word of promise is a creative Word, which establishes the new

identity that this child of God belongs to him and is no longer a sinner because God no longer regards him as a sinner. God's view of things, God's Word, determines reality. God stands by his Word, his Word of forgiveness. Through it he creates trust in the untrusting person.[26]

Law: The Creation of Hunger

Just as newborn babies yearn for physical milk, so we, too, strive for the word, which Peter describes as the "pure spiritual milk."[27] This milk we imbibe is unadulterated, unlike the milk we purchase from a store. The Word nourishes the soul, just as physical food feeds the body. The word of God by which we are born anew sustains us in our new life. Those who "have tasted the kindness of the Lord" (1 Pet 2:3) in his word will relish it; they will continue to feed on the life-giving word through which "they grow up to salvation" (1 Pet 2:2). The word is applicable to every need in life and death. Luther writes with excitement, "It is not enough to hear the Gospel once; one must study it constantly, in order that we may grow up. Then when faith is strong, one must provide for and feed everyone."[28] While unbelievers neither know God nor taste milk, believers have tasted the kindness of God in the word. Reflecting on Psalm 34:8; "Oh, taste and see that the Lord is sweet; blessed is the man who trusts in him," Luther provides the rationale for the sequence that "tasting" precedes "seeing": "this sweetness cannot be known unless one has experienced and felt it for himself; and no one can attain to such experience unless he trusts in God with his whole heart when he is in the depths and in sore straits."[29] No one can know this sweetness unless he has appropriated it for himself; yet this appropriation presupposes trust in God. "Such a person will experience the work of God within himself and will thus attain to His sensible sweetness and through it to all knowledge and understanding."[30] Hearts that have tasted the gospel will pine for more of it, and they will be filled "with good things," just as the word says. To taste God's goodness is to have one's heart touched by it so that it cannot do without it. "To have tasted," for Luther, is "to believe in my heart" that Christ is sweet to me, as honey is to my tongue.[31] It is to reap from the gospel the joyous exchange in which all our sins are Christ's, and his righteousness is ours.[32] Because we are God's and he is ours, we have everything he has.

The distinction between law and gospel inheres in Luther's exposition of the word of God. The paradox consists in that the word creates in us "hunger" for the goodness of God, as the law creates hunger for the gospel. Luther likens hunger to what "a good cook" does, "as the saying goes. It makes the food taste good, for the heart and the conscience can hear nothing more delightful."[33] As law, the word causes us to yearn for spiritual milk and find satisfaction in it. Only when sinners feel their sin and misery under the law do they long for the word; "this good," Luther stresses.[34] Only the hungry would be filled; as Mary says in her Magnificat, "He has filled the hungry with good things" (Luke 1:53).[35] Just as God creates the world *ex nihilo*, so, too, he does wonderful things in Mary despite her poverty and lowliness. The assertion that Mary "merited or earned the privilege of bearing God's Son through her great virtue," Kreitzer writes, does not find acceptance in Luther's theology.[36] Out of pure grace, God regards Mary as worthy of bearing the title "Mother of God."[37] In response, Mary accepts God's word, consenting in faith to be the agent of virgin birth. Kreitzer explains, "Mary's humility was not a virtue that some-how merited her position as Jesus's mother, but rather a belief in her own lowliness and unworthiness. Mary recognized that all the blessings given to her came from God's grace, and responded in the beautiful words of *The Magnificat*, 'My soul magnifies the Lord.'"[38] She forgets herself and ascribes all glory to God alone. Like Mary, whose heart is steadfast in God, we renounce our own efforts and abandon ourselves to God.[39] We trust in God's word, as Mary did, allowing it to work in us the "precious works" of God in their opposites: exalting the humble and filling the hungry.[40] Only when we are reduced to a state of poverty and lowliness through the law (God's alien work) can God perform his proper work of filling and exalting through the gospel. Callous hearts boast of their own holiness, do not feel their sin and sore condition, and therefore shun the good. Those who suffer the oppression of the guilty conscience and the fear of death in the last hour relish the word most.[41]

Proclamation of the Word: The Vehicle of God's Power

In *The German Mass*, Luther affirms that "preaching and teaching of God's word is the most important part of the divine service."[42] The means by which the word of God comes to us is the preacher, the vehicle of God's grace. Poetically, the breasts at which the babes suckle for milk refer to the instruments of the life-giving Word. Luther adduces this from his reading of Song of Solomon 4:5, where the groom speaks to the bride, "Your two breasts are like two fawns," and Song of Solomon 1:13, where the bride says to the groom, "My beloved is to me a bag of myrrh that lies between my breasts."[43] The two breasts are like twin fawns, pure and delicate. This analogy suggests that the word the preacher brings is a pure consolation to those who suffer assaults, just as milk from the mother's breasts is comfort to the baby.[44] The groom (Christ) must rest on the breasts (the preachers), the instruments through which the word proceeds.[45] God's immanence and intimacy with us are like a fragrance we perceive by smelling a bag of myrrh lying in our bosom. Luther captures the mystery of faith through his bridal Christology, of which he writes, "In short, his feeling for me is like that of a bridegroom for his bride."[46] We encounter God whose sweetness is conveyed through the proclamation of his Word.[47]

God invests his power in Moses in Exodus 4:12, "I will be with your mouth," just as he did with the psalmist in Psalm 81:10, "Open your mouth wide," to bring their proclamation to fruition.[48] Luther interprets these texts, saying, "'Preach boldly. Speak out, be hungry; I will fill you. I will be present there and say enough.'"[49] Luther's theology of preaching is drawn from his understanding of God's word as causative of a reality that corresponds to what it says. Just as the world was created by God's speech, so is the church birthed by God's speech through his appointed servants. "Preaching is God's own speech to people," Wilson writes, not "mere speech about God."[50] Luther's "picture of God," Wingren contends, "is not the far-off deistic God who is remote from the preached word and is only spoken about as we speak about someone who is absent."[51] God is "preached" not as one who is detached from his people but "as belonging to us."[52] Luther avers, "Those who preach the Gospel are not themselves directly the preachers, but Christ speaks and preaches through them."[53] Only faith perceives "the power of God hidden in [the] human activity" of preaching; the hearer "trusts wholly, not in the mask [preacher] of God but in the Word behind the mask."[54] Through preaching, we are allowed, in Trueman's words, "to participate by analogy, in the creative power of God."[55] God hides his presence in humble and insignificant preachers, God's masks through which he achieves his saving act; he fills them with the Spirit's power, apart from which their ministry bears no fruits. The God who speaks is the same one who acts efficaciously, drawing us into the orbit of his self-knowledge. Luther avers, "Therefore [the word] is surely a divine power. Indeed, it is God himself" who establishes through the preached Word the saving relationship between miserable sinners and the merciful God.[56] Preaching, says Trueman, "is a redescription of reality in light of God's revelation of Himself in Christ—which challenges the era to accept the preacher's account; which—if he is faithful to Scripture—is God's account rather than the account of the world."[57] Luther's understanding of the effective nature of God's "Deed-Word" ought to occupy the central place in the church's worship: "Spare everything except the Word."[58] Whoever hears the preacher hears "Christ himself in person" (cf. Luke 10:16).[59] Preaching is an occasion of, to borrow Headley's phrase, "the continuing presence of Christ in time";[60] it is where God meets us, Steinmetz writes, to effect "new possibilities where no possibilities existed before. The Word of God is a Word that enriches the poor, releases the captives, gives sight to the blind, and liberates the oppressed."[61]

Peter declares exuberantly, "That Word is the good news which was preached to you" (1 Pet 1:25). Though the "voice or speech" by which the word goes forth fades, Luther writes, "the meaning and the truth" proclaimed remains.[62] The voice that expresses the word comes from outside, remains external, and then disappears, but the word that enters the heart lives there and becomes active.[63] The word spoken and the reality that proceeds from it mutually coinhere. Luther identifies "the sound of a word" as "a reality with God."[64] The word that proceeds from the mouth of a humble preacher becomes the occasion of God's power by which the identity of being God's children is created. "To preach Christ" is, for Luther, to bring about a contemporaneity of his presence and his gifts; "to feed the soul, make it righteous, set it free, and save it, provided it believes the preaching. Faith alone is the saving and efficacious use of the Word of God, according to Romans 10:9."[65] Justifying righteousness, Chester writes, "is received by faith through the preaching of the biblical word, with those who believe drawn out of themselves and into total reliance on the promises of God. People do not encounter God by looking inward, but instead they encounter God as the convicting power of the word turns them outward toward Christ."[66] God's word is a creative power that brings about a new reality, that which has not

existed before. No works could create our righteous identity
except by the word, the seed, through which God "makes all
who cleave to it children of God, as John 1:12 says. It is on such
a precious blessing that our salvation rests."[67]

Luther makes a transition from God's acting to the response
of his human creatures. The word Peter preached, Luther
writes, is "before your eyes. . . . You need not search far. Do
no more than take hold of it when it is preached. For it is so
near that one can hear it, as Moses also says in Deut. 30:11–
14: 'For this commandment which I command you this day is
not too hard for you, neither is it far off. It is not in heaven;
neither is it beyond the sea. But the Word is very near to you;
it is in your mouth and in your heart.'"[68] By the phrase "the
commandment is not too hard for you," Moses did not, Luther
contends, teach that the fulfillment of it lies in human powers,
in which case God's grace would have been rendered superflu-
ous.[69] Moses intends to show that the commandment "is not
fulfilled by merely hearing and doing, but only if the Word is
in your mouth and heart."[70] Here Luther identifies two ways
in which the commandments can be fulfilled: either ears and
hands or mouth and heart. The first is by hearing and doing,
referring to people who claim that they could fulfill them if
they could hear them. This is a form of works-righteousness,
as they seek to justify themselves through their own strength.
However, Moses's prescription is contrary: "In your mouth, I
say, and in your heart [the commandment] must be if you want
to fulfill it, not in your ear or hand."[71] The sinful self is deeply
"curved in on itself."[72] It wills its own desire, has its own love
or its own favor; it pleases itself rather than pleasing God. "For
the heart contains what I wish, what I love, what I favor, what
pleases me."[73] The corrupted nature naturally repudiates the
law of God. Luther writes, "The law demands an inner nature
which loves it and has pleasure in it; thus it is satisfied and fulfilled if it is loved."[74] The heart that loves the law is a work of

grace; in Hamm's words, "The heart of a sinful person, which orbits around itself, is so transformed by the influx of grace that it now revolves around God, can love God and the neighbor wholly. . . . Without grace there would be no human ability to love, no fulfillment of God's commandments, and no ethically meritorious works."[75]

Luther accentuates the power of the spoken word. "Christ wrote nothing, but said all things; and the apostles wrote few things, but spoke a great deal. . . . For the ministry of the New Testament was not written upon dead tablets of stone, but it was to be in the sound of the living voice."[76] The fulfillment of the commandment begins with the mouth, followed by the heart. By this, Luther sees the importance of preaching as a vehicle of God's grace. The word must "first [be] preached by the mouth and then believed as a result of hearing."[77] The order of salvation proceeds from preaching (oral) first, hearing (aural) second, and believing (faith) third; faith comes by the hearing of the word preached—that is, through the "ears"[78] that faith has created. The fulfillment of the law occurs when it is received and "loved in the heart" (Ps 1:2).[79] Luther imagines God saying, "'You will not fulfill My commandment when you hear it, but only if you love it with your heart. This you will not do unless the Word has been preached with the mouth and believed in the heart. So My Commandment will become neither too difficult nor too distant.'"[80] The gospel itself is a living voice that continues to be heard by the preachers through whom God draws people to himself. Luther concurs with Paul, who quotes Moses's text as it appears in Romans 10:8, "The Word is near you, on your lips and in your heart," to stress that "the heart believes for righteousness through the Word of faith."[81] The linguistic sign and its resultant reality are one; what God speaks, that it is. In Hampson's words, "[God] not only pronounces us righteous but actually makes us righteous."[82] The preached word presents the gift of righteousness not as an absent object that lies beyond our grasp but as the present reality that lies within our grasp. Luther asserts, "The Word of God indeed proclaims things hidden and not manifest, and they are grasped only by faith."[83]

That word "is not in heaven; neither is it beyond the sea" (Deut 30:12–13). Paul does not quote this passage from Moses "word for word," Luther notes; thus Romans 10:6–8 reads, "Do not say in your heart: 'Who will ascend into heaven?' (that is, to bring Christ down) or 'Who will descend into the abyss?' (that is, to bring Christ up from the dead)."[84] Paul's slightly varied rendering of Moses's text, Luther argues, is an occasion for his repudiation of the theology of work-righteousness.[85] Whoever claims to fulfill God's commandment by works or human powers—that is, by "hand" rather than by "heart"— denies Christ's ascension into heaven and descent into hell. The work-righteous thus deny the second article of faith, that Christ "died for us and rose again that we might be justified by the Word of faith and fulfill the law."[86]

God's commandment is fulfilled when the word preached does not remain outside us but enters through the ears and into our hearts by the Holy Spirit and is loved through faith, not works.[87] Luther avers, "There is nothing in the heart unless it is written there by the Spirit of God."[88] For the law to be loved in the heart is beyond human powers unless by "the Spirit of Christ within them" (1 Pet 1:11). By ourselves, we are inept in perceiving the "grammar of divine agency,"[89] the language of Scripture. Luther stresses, "Yet if one of these is lacking, the Spirit without the language is better than the language without the Spirit."[90] Christ and the Spirit are intimately bound in Luther's soteriology. What Christ has acquired for us through his mediatorial activity does not profit us unless the Spirit teaches our hearts to receive and love it. Human powers cannot create trust in Christ, faith's object; faith's object discloses its own trustworthiness through the Holy Spirit, the effective agent, so that it is received in our hearts. Watson writes aptly, "When through the outward preaching of the Word and the inward witness of the Holy Spirit, faith is created, that which is promised in the Gospel becomes effective for the believer. Christ . . . enters by the Gospel through a man's ears into his heart and dwells there; nor does He come empty-handed, but brings with Him His life, Spirit, and all that He has and can."[91]

The Holy Spirit achieves what Maschke calls the "hermeneutic of contemporaneity"[92] of Christ's presence with the hearer to whom a gospel word is spoken. He elaborates, "Interpretation by itself is an exercise of the letter only. . . . Only when hermeneutics connects to homiletics and [the] active life of the Church does the Spirit come into his prominent role and Christ becomes really present."[93] The gospel is purest if Christ is the subject and substance of proclamation. Luther declares, "The milk is adulterated if anything but Christ is preached."[94] Against the word's adulteration via its admixture with human doctrines, the Holy Spirit ensures that it remains "true, pure, and unadulterated milk."[95] Preaching, if it is faithful to God's self-revelation in Christ, is efficacious; it bears its regenerative power not on account of the preacher but due to the inherent, performative authority of God's word that the Spirit vivifies in human hearts. The Holy Spirit's sole office is to create faith in Christ; the Spirit ensures that "we hear the voice of God, that is, that we believe."[96] Whoever "hears" the gospel and "believes in it" is given a righteous identity.[97] Kolb writes, "The direct address of the hearers with the intended impact of Christ's death and resurrection 'for them' made the sermon an instrument of God's bestowal of faith, and thus his act of re-creation and renewal."[98] The sermon is prolific in character, as it does things just as it says. It is God's "speech-act," the power of the word at work. In Silcock's formulation:

The sermon is God's dynamic word that he speaks into the human situation under the condition of sin. Because his word is Spirit-filled and Spirit-energized, it is a divine speech-act: it does what it says, and it says what it does. It is a word that goes to work, destroying strongholds (2 Cor. 10:4) and delivering captives, raising the dead, and giving a future to people without hope.[99]

Luther is thrilled at the word that does what it says. This in no way means he ignores the existential condition of his people to whom he ministers. The pure gospel is sweet, suckling milk to the new baby. The baby can only receive milk, "the softest food," not the solid kind. Christ to him is not "bitter," says Luther, "but sweet, fat grace."[100] However, we must also preach the cross as the vocation of the Christian, that he would suffer as Christ did. "That," says Luther, "is a strong potion and strong wine."[101] Here Luther's pastoral heart shines when he teaches us to observe the proper time when the sweet milk and strong wine are to be offered. He counsels against preaching strong doctrine when the Christian is too young and weak to bear it, but instead at a time when they are mature and can receive it.[102] For Luther, to preach a strong doctrine, like bearing the cross with Christ, to a newborn Christian, is like "boil[ing] a kid while it is still at her mother's milk," as taught in Deuteronomy 14:21, and in Exodus 23:19, "Do not cook a young goat at its mother's milk."[103] The meaning of these texts is, for Luther, that "civil mercy" is extended to a kid, even at the expense of justice.[104] This, Luther avers, is in line with the apostolic teaching in Romans 14:1, "Welcome the man who is weak in faith." A good teacher accommodates themself to the level of the students and bears their burdens, as a fulfillment of the "one law" that Paul taught in Galatians 6:3, "Bear one another's burdens."[105] We must refrain from loading strong doctrine upon those who have not attained maturity and certainty of faith, lest we destroy them as through unbearable, strong storms.

A newly married man must refrain from joining an army but remain with his wife at home during the first year, lest possible danger comes his way (Deut 24:5). Luther uses the above biblical texts to summarize the teaching of St. Peter: "Preach gently to the young and weak Christians. Let them enrich themselves and grow fat in the knowledge of Christ. Do not burden them with strong doctrine, for they are still too young. But later, when they grow strong, let them be slaughtered and sacrificed on the cross."[106]

Revelation and Concealment:
God as Preached and Not Preached

Luther relishes the paradoxical nature of the word in revealing and concealing. The word reveals God as he is toward us, that is, "in a more pleasing and friendly manner"[107] that "faith and confidence are able to exist."[108] At the same time, the word conceals from us God as he is in himself, that is, "in his might and wisdom (for then he proves terrifying)."[109] The distinction between God's hiddenness "in his majesty" and God's hiddenness in the crucified Christ remains part of the Reformer's doctrine of God throughout his career. It does not entail, for Luther, a bifurcation of God's being but one and the same God: "From an unrevealed God [he] will become a revealed God. Nevertheless [he] will remain the same God."[110] As Jüngel rightly points out, "Briefly, the differentiation between God and God can never be understood as a contradiction in God."[111] To borrow his phrase, "God corresponds to himself" precisely within the dialectic distinction between the hidden God and the revealed God.[112] The antithesis between them, Gerrish notes, bears an "appearance" of "a contradiction in God. . . . The problem is noetic, not ontic—in our understanding, not in God's being."[113] The differentiation between the hidden God and the revealed God, Bertram notes, is not to be confused with the distinction between

God's self-relatedness in his immanent life and God's external relation to the world in the economy of salvation. God is triune, eternally, and before his historical manifestation.[114] The distinction between the hidden God and the revealed God means the selfsame God assumes the contradiction of the "curse" of the hidden God and the "blessing" of the revealed God to conquer it "in himself." Drawing on Luther's exposition of Galatians 3:13, Bertram offers a Trinitarian solution to the noetic contradiction in God's being: "There the 'awesome conflict' (*mirabile duellum*) between the 'curse' and 'blessing,' in both instances God's own, becomes the 'joyfullest of conflicts' (*iucundissimum duellum*). There the 'bifurcation' [contradiction] becomes . . . 'the sheer immensity of what all the God of the gospel rescues us from, namely, God's own self, even though it took being triune to do that, because it took Christ.'"[115] The "most delightful comfort,"[116] says Luther, consists in the vicarious act God does for us in actuality: God assumes the antinomy of wrath and mercy in himself to conquer it for faith, thereby creating via the preached word a people of God's mercy, not his wrath.

Underlying the distinction between the hidden God and the revealed God is Luther's distinction between two types of theology: *theologia crucis* and *theologia gloriae,* as taught in thesis 20 of his *Heidelberg Disputation.*[117] A theology of glory tampers with the God hidden "in his own majesty," but a theology of the cross leads us away from it to the God revealed "in his Word." He writes, "God must therefore be left to himself in his own majesty, for in this regard we have nothing to do with him, nor has he willed that we should have anything to do with him. But we have something to do with him, insofar as he is clothed and set forth in his Word, though which he offers himself to us and which is the beauty and glory with which the Psalmist celebrates him as being clothed [the clothed God]."[118] The distinction between God in his majesty and God in his word, Forde admits, corresponds to the distinction between

"God-not-preached and God-preached."[119] God does not will that we should occupy ourselves with God's naked majesty, that is, "God-not-preached" but the incarnate God, namely, "God as he is preached."[120] We must be "guided by the word and not by that inscrutable will."[121] As Peter says, "That word is the good news which was preached to you" (1 Pet 1:25). God's naked majesty will surely annihilate us by its dazzling glory unless we cleave to "this God, clothed in such a kind appearance and, so to speak, in such a pleasant mask, that is to say, dressed in His promises—this God we can grasp and look at with joy and trust."[122] Salvation lies solely in Christ, in whom God has become, to use Mattes's phrase, "a graspable God,"[123] the God "with whom we have to do" (cf. Heb 4:13). "The terrifying aspect" of the hidden God that Luther sets "against the loving side of God in Christ," Leppin discerns: "cannot be rationalized."[124] The emancipation of the terror of God's hidden majesty, Gerrish explains, is a "practical" kind, necessitating clinging to God only as he wills to be located in his word.[125] Likewise, Forde echoes, "The only solution for God's absolute judgment is absolution, and that arrives only by giving the crucified Christ to sinners unconditionally."[126] The wrathful deity—"God-not-preached"—is beyond the gaze of mortal souls unless shielded by the merciful deity: "God-preached." Forde expands:

> There is nothing we can do about God in majesty, God in the abstract, God-not-preached. The only solution to the problem of God-not-preached is God-preached. The only answer to the question of what the hidden God is up to is the concrete, present-tense, here-and-now proclamation: God sent his word and healed them—for Luther, that means the living word, it means that God arranged not to send something so abstract even as "the revealed word," not even to send a book; but God arranged and authorized to send a preacher to say, "I declare to you . . ." in the name of God.[127]

Any attempt to know God by "the hybris of reason," to use
Weber's thoughts, "must then end in the hybris of despair."[128]
The absolution of the wrath of God's naked majesty occurs
by the proclaimed word, not by human works. Simultaneity
inheres in the distinction between the hidden and the revealed
God, and in the corresponding distinction between God's wrath
and his mercy. McGrath states, "Both the *Deus absconditus* and
Deus revelatus are to be found in precisely the same event of
revelation," and likewise both "God's wrath and his mercy are
revealed simultaneously."[129] Reason perceives God as wrathful; faith perceives God as merciful. Only faith, created by the
preached word, McGrath claims, can grasp "the real situation
[mercy] which underlies the apparent situation [wrath]."[130]

The Triune Life, Holiness, and the Baptismal Word

The Trinitarian structure and substance of the apostolic proclamation are apparent in 1 Peter 1:2: "chosen and destined by
God the Father and sanctified by the Spirit for obedience to
Jesus Christ and for sprinkling with His blood." All three persons work together as one God in achieving redemption for us.
First, Christians are "chosen and destined," not by themselves
but by God's will. Second, we become righteous and holy not by
virtue of piety but by the blood of Christ (Eph 4:24). The Father's
election and foreknowledge is founded solely on his Son; as
1 Peter 1:20 says, "He was destined before the foundation of
the world but was made manifest at the end of times." Third,
Christians are holy not by their own strength or works of merit
but by the sanctifying agency of the Holy Spirit. Pless writes
rightly, "Peter's language is echoed in Luther's Explanation of
the Third Article of the Creed in the *Small Catechism*,"[131] where
he holds that no one can create faith in God nor bring themselves to God unless by the Holy Spirit: "I believe that by my
own understanding or strength I cannot believe in Jesus Christ

my Lord or come to him, but instead the Holy Spirit has called me through the gospel, enlightened me with his gifts, made me holy and kept me in true faith."[132] This summary of the message of his *De servo arbitrio* for children expressed Luther's conviction that the human will is not free and thus is incapable of receiving the grace of God unless by the Holy Spirit. Harink explains, "The Holy Spirit creates and sustains the bond between the election and the holiness of the people of God by distinguishing the people of God from other peoples."[133] God has predestined us to be holy, setting us apart through the Holy Spirit to be the object of faith in Christ. Luther avers, "Nothing is holy but the holiness that God works in us."[134] Through the Holy Spirit, Harink notes, we are drawn into "God's triune life through the vicarious obedient and sacrificial death of Jesus Christ."[135] We encounter God, Wengert writes, "backward"[136]—that is, by "the reversed Trinity,"[137] moving from the third article through the second to the first. The movement by the Holy Spirit through the Son to the Father is a gift of grace, one that transforms life and makes us totally his. So "when we begin with the Holy Spirit," Wengert avows, "we actually begin at the end":[138] the end of the old Adam, of all human reasoning and good works, of the unmediated experience of God, and of the punitive voice of the law. It is when everything in us and in the world dies that God's justifying action *ex nihilo* becomes operative: making an unbeliever a believer, and making the ungodly, who in themselves are unworthy, the objects of God's attraction by which they are made attractive.

Both Paul and Peter hold that faith in Christ secures justification for us. Luther notes that Scripture identifies faith with obedience; here he has in mind Romans 1:5, "the obedience of faith," and Romans 16:19, "Your obedience is made known to all."[139] Peter expresses it, Luther perceives, slightly differently from St. Paul, saying that we are set apart by the Holy Spirit "for obedience to Jesus Christ and for sprinkling with His blood."[140] Luther contends, "For faith makes us obedient and subject to Christ and His Word. Therefore, to be submissive to the Word of God and Christ and to be sprinkled with His blood is the same as believing."[141] Believing and obeying the word of God and the sprinkling of Christ's blood are essential to becoming "sincerely holy in the spirit before God."[142] By the expression "sprinkling," Peter alludes to Moses's sprinkling of the tabernacle he built and the people in it (Exod 24:6). But such sprinkling applies to only the external purging with the blood of goats and lacks efficacy (Heb 9:13–14). The only sprinkling that is efficacious is the blood that Christ shed for sinners; to deny this is to bring dishonor and shame to the name of Christ. Luther specifies how to preach aright: "To sprinkle means to preach that Christ shed His blood, intercedes for us before His Father, and says: 'Dear Father, here Thou seest My blood, which I shed for this sinner.' If you believe this, you are sprinkled."[143] Luther declares, "Therefore only this is the Gospel" that Peter was commanded by Christ to proclaim.[144]

Peter quotes Leviticus 19:2 in 1 Peter 3:15–16, saying, "But as He who called you is holy, be holy yourselves in all your conduct, since it is written: 'You shall be holy, for I am holy.'" The predicate "holy" is reserved for God alone; it is exclusively his. We become holy not by turning inward for resources but by turning outward, allowing God alone to "reign, live, and work in us," says Luther.[145] Harink writes aptly:

> The holiness of God's people is rooted first of all in God's very being, then in God's action of calling and setting apart a people for himself, and finally in God's people reflecting God's character and action in its life before God and among the nations. God's people must *become holy* because they are first *made holy* by God who himself is *holy*. Becoming holy is a matter of being transformed by, conformed to, and sharing in the prior action and character of God, and that in turn is a matter of obedience and the right orientation of desire.[146]

The obedience or faith of which St. Peter speaks has as its object God's word, not human efforts. "You must be holy because you have the Word of God, because heaven is yours, and because you have become pious and holy through Christ."[147] Obedience includes hearing and believing: "He who hears the Gospel and God's Word and believes in it is an obedient child of God."[148] Holiness is a predicate of faith; as Luther confesses, "Therefore we are all holy if we walk in faith."[149] We are wholly holy according to faith, not according to flesh, which remains with us. No saints are exempted from feeling the flesh and struggling over it. In Scripture, Luther recognizes, the saints refer to their own righteousness in calling God for help; David did this in Psalm 86:2: "Keep my life, for I am good." It is not an assertion of the merits of achievements in which one boasts; rather, it is God's attestation of true faith expressed in good works. Luther uses this verse to oppose the enthusiasts who attribute their holiness to a "special revelation" apart from the external word.[150] Such claim to holiness is a sign of a lack of faith and the true knowledge of Christ.[151] We are holy by faith, through which we "feel" the revelation of Christ in us.[152] Whoever is seized by such revelation and feels it, says Luther, is truly "a Christian," and he is given a participation in all God's benefits. In Luther's own words, "He enters with the Lord Christ into a sharing of all His goods. Now since Christ is holy, he, too, must be holy, or he must deny that Christ is holy."[153] Our holiness is not intrinsic but extrinsic; it is not actively manufactured by human efforts but passively received by faith. As taught in his Galatians commentary, Luther teaches two kinds of "holiness":[154] "passive holiness" is God's gift, which we receive, not achieve; "active holiness" is the practical outworking of the gospel in the performance of holy deeds for neighbors. Kleinig writes:

> Our passive holiness is alien to us, part of the receptive life of faith, something received from God the Father and available

to us only in Christ; it is an extrinsic heavenly saintliness that is always received and yet never possessed. It is communicated by the spoken word of God. God gives it to those who keep on receiving it from him. . . . By sharing in Christ's holiness, we who are holy by faith in him do holy work; we are holy in what we do and how we live. His holiness covers us and pervades our whole physical existence.[155]

We are holy not by a holiness we obtain from pious acts but from Christ's holiness, which is conveyed to us through the baptismal word. Luther writes, "You and I are holy; the church, the city, and the people are holy—not on the basis of their own holiness, but on the basis of a holiness not their own, not by an active holiness, but by a passive holiness. They are holy because they possess something that is divine and holy, namely, the calling of the ministry, the Gospel, Baptism, etc., on the basis of which they are holy."[156] Expanding this, Luther quotes Galatians 3:27—"If you have been baptized, you have put on the holy garment, which is Christ"—to speak of baptism as a created means in which God's word appears.[157] Baptism is no "small and empty sign"; it is "a very powerful and effective thing."[158] Baptism effects "a change of clothing,"[159] from the garment of Adam and its sins we acquire from old birth to the garment of Christ and his righteousness we acquire from new birth. This change occurs not by the performance of law but by rebirth through baptism. We put on Christ, whose righteousness and salvation are ours, and thus are placed outside the law and its jurisdiction.[160] Baptism kills the old Adam and buries it and all his vices with Christ; it raises up the new Adam, with Christ and all his virtues. The garment of the slavery of sin in Adam is replaced by the garment of freedom of righteousness in Christ, if only we believe this. As Tranvik opines, "Baptism doesn't simply point to a Christ abstract and remote. Rather, it is an astonishing *rupture* in our life whereby Christ himself in word and water drowns us and raises us up. This event forms the entire horizon of the Christian life. It does not need to be supplemented by good works."[161] Baptism clothes us with "the holy garment, which is Christ."[162] Luther elaborates:

> In baptism, then, it is not the garment of the righteousness of the law or of our own works that is given; but Christ becomes our garment. But He is not the Law, not a lawyer, not a work; He is the divine and inestimable gift that the Father has given to us to be our Justifier, Lifegiver, and Redeemer. To put on Christ according to the Gospel, therefore, is to put on, not the Law or works but an inestimable gift, namely, forgiveness of sins, righteousness, peace, comfort, joy in the Holy Spirit, salvation, life, and Christ himself.[163]

In stressing the creative power of faith, Luther quotes Mark 16:16: "He who believes and is baptized will be saved; but he who does not believe is already condemned."[164] Faith, he writes, "trusts this Word of God" we hear in baptism and renders effectual in us God's promise of grace hidden in it.[165] The justifying word attached to baptism creates its corresponding reality, that the ungodly, in Luther's own words, "may be righteous and heirs" of eternal life.[166] We are holy not in ourselves but only in Christ, whom faith grasps. Peter describes what the holy living to which we are called looks like. We are to "gird up [our] minds" (1 Pet 1:13), meaning that once we have grasped true faith, "that one is justified by faith alone," we must cling to it and let nothing tear us away from it.[167] To gird our mind, Luther notes, is to fasten our mind to that which is true, as St. Paul expresses himself in Romans 3:28 ("We hold that").[168] The girding of the mind is of a "spiritual" kind. Physical holiness can be attained through "the girding of loins" (Isa 11:5); but spiritual holiness is possible through "the girdle of faith," which makes us "a bride of Christ."[169] Where faith is loosened by false doctrine, idolatry and adultery are inevitable. While in Galatians 5:22–23, Paul speaks of "the fruit of the Holy Spirit," here Peter speaks of the fruits of faith, that we should "purify our souls by obedience to the truth" (1 Pet 1:22) through the Spirit. Faith brings our body into conformity to the Spirit; faith "gives room to the Spirit" through whom it overcomes the residual sin in us, even after baptism.[170] Faith has "begun" its work of mortification of the body and "continues" to subdue the flesh and its evil lusts until we die.[171] True faith must guard against any claim to holiness through works; it must tame the flesh, lest it be turned into an occasion for carnal liberty. The remedy for innate evil is not by external means, such as fasting and doing good works—both of which St. Bernard, Luther observes, had rigorously practiced, but without finding relief for his guilty conscience. Luther is so thrilled by the performative authority of God's word that he exhorts us to persevere in it, laying hold of it and enjoying it, as one would enjoy "a wine" that flourishes the souls.[172] Commenting on Zechariah 9:17, he notes that wine differs in kind and produces different results. Some incite evil lusts within; others gain vitality from it. "This wine, the Gospel, subdues lust and makes chaste hearts."[173] The means of acquiring holiness, for Peter, is "obedience to the truth in the Spirit," namely, the gospel or the word itself. Luther has Peter say: "'When one takes hold of the truth with the heart and is obedient to it in the Spirit, this is the right help and the most powerful remedy. Otherwise you will find no remedy that could quell all evil thoughts in this way.'"[174] The word itself possesses such grace that the more we progress in it, the more it tastes sweeter than honey. Evil inclination is evacuated from the heart that is seized by the expulsive power of the word. Dieter writes, "The renewal process does not grasp a person in its entirety before death. Hence the law's demand for complete fulfillment is not completed in this life, and the human remains a sinner before God's law."[175] As law, the word performs an alien work of judging evil thoughts in order that, as gospel, it might perform a proper work of removing them to create a chaste heart.

The power to change from the old to the new and the secret to victory in new life lie not in "doing what lies within"[176] but solely in trusting in the word that, Luther insists, "is everything," and apart from which nothing exists, consists, or persists. "Everything" hinges upon the causative nature of God's word. Of this, Ebeling summarizes:

> That is, it is the word through which he creates and brings about my acceptance of him as God, my honoring of him as God, my faith in him, my readiness to receive him, my trust in him and my self-abandonment to him, so that I am set free from myself and from all the powers to which I sold myself. God's word in this strict sense can only be the word of faith, that is, the word which makes a total demand upon man that he should receive what is given him and accept the gift of grace. For in the sight of God, man is not one who acts, for he can become righteous in his sight through faith alone.[177]

Hence, Christians can do nothing except be passive and permit God's word to effect in them his saving purpose, and in response offer a sacrifice of praise to God: "To Him be the dominion forever and ever. Amen" (1 Pet 5:11).[178]

CHAPTER 2

Christ, the Chief Cornerstone
Justifying Faith and Works of Love

"Scripture," Luther avers, "insists on going to the truth of the matter and praises the Lord Christ as our Mediator through whom we must come to the Father. O what an inestimable blessing has been given to us through Christ! It enables us to step before the Father and to demand the inheritance of which St. Peter" proclaims (1 Pet 1:4).[1] We preach Christ, "the clothed God,"[2] that very God who "called us out of darkness into his marvelous light" (1 Pet 2:9). Whoever bypasses the "clothed God," or the preached word (cf. 1 Pet 1:25), in Luther's estimation, "does not deserve to be called a theologian."[3] The gospel, "the genuinely evangelical words"[4] that we proclaim, and not good works that we boast, delivers us from all contraries of life: sin, wrath, death, and hell.

> Thus when I hear that Jesus Christ died, took away my sin, gained heaven for me, and gave me all that He has, I am hearing the gospel. No one can invalidate this truth. The depths of hell can do nothing against it; and even if I am already in the jaws of the devil, I must come out and remain where the Word remains, if I can take hold of it. Therefore, St. Peter says with good reason that you need not look for anything else than what we have preached.[5]

St. Peter was acquainted with the Scripture from which he derives a true knowledge of who Christ is and what he has done for us. He recalls Isaiah 28:14–16, where the prophet proclaimed, "Therefore hear the Word of God, you scoffers . . . you have said: 'We have made a covenant with death, and with Sheol we have an agreement . . . We have made lies our refuge . . .' Therefore thus says the Lord God: 'Behold, I am laying in Zion for a foundation a Stone . . . a precious Cornerstone, of a sure foundation, etc.'"[6] Luther observes that, with Peter, Paul also quotes this verse in Romans 9:33, affirming that Christ is "a precious Cornerstone" upon which our faith is founded.[7] So Peter exhorts in 1 Peter 2:4, "Come to Him, to that Living Stone, rejected by men but in God's sight chosen and precious." This is a direct quotation from Psalm 118:22–23, Luther's "beloved psalm" that had "proved a friend and helped [him] out of many great troubles."[8] In his preface to Psalm 118, Luther laments, "Sad to say, there are few, even among those who should do better, who honestly say even once in their lifetime to Scripture or to one of the psalms: 'You are my beloved book; you must be my very psalm.'"[9] For him, the words of Scripture, including his favorite psalm, are not "mere literature" for theological discussion; they are "words of life, intended not for speculation and fantasy but for life and action."[10] This psalm, like all others, possesses the power of contemporaneity. Luther writes, "The Word of God, because it is eternal, should apply to all men of all times. For although in the course of time customs, people, places, and usages may vary, godliness and ungodliness remain the same through all the ages."[11]

A Christological Reading of Psalm 118

Christ is hidden in the Psalter, and the Holy Spirit draws him out and makes him present to us. Luther writes, "Therefore let us permit the Holy Spirit to speak, as He does in the Scriptures."[12] He provides a Christological reading of Psalm 118 where he interprets the word "rejected" to mean the suffering,

death, and humiliation of the cross, and the phrase "the chief
Cornerstone" as referring to the resurrection, ascension, and
reign of Christ.[13] The psalmist illustrates this by the parable of
a building with two different builders. When a stone is unfit
and useless for a building, it must be discarded. An effective
builder knows how to use the stone in such a way that it fits into
the wall without endangering the building's structural integrity. The way of Christ is opposed to the way of the world. Not
knowing how to use Christ's way, the world condemned and
rejected him. But "God, the real Builder, chose him and made
him the cornerstone of the foundation on which the whole
Christian church, made up of Jews and Gentiles, stands."[14] To
the unbelieving world, Christ is the rejected; to the righteous
ones, the rejected Christ is priceless and noble. The wisest, holiest, and most learned go their own way, find this stone offensive, and thus repudiate it vehemently. Poor, miserable sinners,
the outcast, and the unlearned receive Christ gladly and have
him as the foundation stone. The latter are "the most necessary,
most useful and best people on earth," who feed on the word
of God and live in congruence with God's will.[15] However, the
former builders treat the word of God and those who preach it
with disdain, for they do not meet their building regulations.
As builders, they do it "*ex officio*, for they must see to it that
their building has no crack, rent or disfiguration."[16] These two
buildings are opposed to each other, just as faith and work are.

The rejected building possesses a "mighty Builder, who on
one Stone" bears two strong and everlasting walls. The predicate, "the Chief Cornerstone," is given not without purpose,
Luther notes, for the Holy Spirit uses it to declare that Christ
is the Savior of both Jews and Gentiles.[17] Christ is the cornerstone, in which the two walls, Jews and Gentles, converge. They
are made one building, as said in 1 Peter 2:10: "Once you were
no people, but now you are God's people; once you had not
received mercy, but now you have received mercy." The "you"

refers to the Gentiles, who are incorporated into the people
of God as are the Jews, and this is a fulfillment of what was
already prophesized in Hosea 2:23: "Those who were not My
people I will call My people" (cf. Rom 9:25). Jews and Gentiles
are made one people without distinction through one faith and
are bestowed a common inheritance, not out of any prior worth
in themselves but purely out of God's mercy. Luther writes,
"We must both confess that we have nothing of ourselves but
are all sinners, that we must expect piety and heaven from
Him alone."[18] The builders who build on their own works are
reduced to naught before this mighty Builder, who is the Lord
himself.[19] The paradoxical action of God lies in that God elects
those whom the world rejects. Luther quotes St. Paul, who
writes in 1 Corinthians 1:27, "God chose what is foolish in the
world to shame the wise." Of this, Luther writes, "This is a particularly great work in which He makes the rejected Stone the
selected Cornerstone."[20] God's work contradicts human work
and cannot be perceived unless the Holy Spirit teaches us. That
God works contrary to our work must continue to amaze us, as
the psalmist declares, "It is marvelous in our eyes" (Ps 118:23).
Only through the eyes of faith can one understand the truth,
that the rejected is the selected stone, and that he is powerful
enough to conquer all contraries of life—sin, death, and hell—
if only we believe.[21]

Theologia Crucis vs. *Theologia Gloria*: Christ, Fully God and Fully Man

Peter is well-grounded in Scripture, as all preachers ought to
be. In 1 Peter 2:6, Peter quotes verbatim Isaiah 28:16 ("Behold,
I am laying in Zion a Stone, a Cornerstone chosen and precious"), which testifies of Christ. Luther sees plainly in this
verse the sum of the orthodox faith, that Jesus is fully God and
fully man but one person. It teaches that Christ is "a precious

Cornerstone, of a sure foundation" (Isa 28:16) of faith. The stone of which Peter speaks is not "a physical stone" but "a spiritual" kind on which faith is built. As taught in the first commandment, God forbids us to put our trust in anything but him alone, lest we commit idolatry. Thus, the stone, the "sure foundation" on which faith rests, must surely be God himself. More than that, he must also be man, says Luther,

> because He must be part of the building, and not only a part but also the Head. Now when one constructs a building, one stone must be like the other, so that every stone has the character, nature, and form of the other. Therefore, since we are built on Christ, He must be like us and of the very same nature as the other stones that rest on Him, namely, a true man as we all are.[22]

The building is faith; Christ is this stone, in whom we trust. Luther stresses, "Since we have been laid on the Stone who is the Chief Priest before God, we also have everything He has."[23] No building can stand on unstable stones. The prophet Isaiah calls Christ a stone "of a sure foundation." Thus, our building, that is, our faith, is immovably certain. Christ has been bestowed on us, serving us with all that he has; conversely, we rest on him, believing that all he has achieved works for us. The stone is given to us as pure gift and does not demand anything in return. "This Stone," says Luther, does not "take anything from us."[24] As sheer gift, it is unilateral, apart from human merits. For Luther, justification cannot be reciprocal in which God receives something from us even as we receive something from him. We can only come as poor beggars, with no capacity of reciprocal benefit for God except to cling to God for the fulfillment of our needs. We do not give him anything but "receive benefit from him alone. For we do not bear Him, but He bears us. Sin, death, hell, and everything we have lie on Him."[25] The passive reception of Christ, whom God has made the foundation, shields us from "sin, death, and hell," enemies Christ's descent into our flesh has conquered. Luther elaborates on the soteriological purpose of God's becoming one of us:

> Behold, Christ died for you! He took sin, death, and hell upon Himself and submitted Himself. But nothing can subdue Him, for He was too strong; He rose from the dead, was completely victorious, and subjected everything to Himself. And He did all this in order that you might be free from it and lord over it. If you believe this, you have it. For we are not able to do all this with our own power. Consequently, Christ had to do it. Otherwise there would have been no need for Him to come down from heaven.[26]

Underlying these two builders is Luther's distinction between two types of theology: the *theologia crucis* and the *theologia gloriae*, as taught in thesis 20 of his *Heidelberg Disputation*.[27] A theologian of the cross must occupy himself with this cornerstone, Christ, whom the world rejected but God elected to be the foundation. Otherwise, one may fantasize a god according to their image or rely on other humanly devised means. A theologian of glory has as its foundation "free will, human works and piety," the exact opposite of a theologian of the cross for whom Christ, his grace, and his righteousness are the foundation. "God decrees,"[28] says Luther, that righteousness is to be obtained not through works but rather through faith. The cross repudiates any acquisition of righteousness through law and a person's own piety but instead leads to Christ, the only righteousness. Preachers of the law and works "agree with Christ as winter and summer agree," and so they, Luther avers, "must reject this Stone."[29] Luther puts it differently: "Christ comes because they should reject their works. But this they cannot endure, and they reject Him."[30] Both free will and human works are crucified as foundations for faith. The fallen will wills only its fallenness; it cannot turn toward

God unless by God's grace. As thesis 14 of his *Heidelberg Disputation* teaches, "free will, after the fall, has power to do good only in a passive capacity, and it can always do evil in an active capacity"; and human works cannot acquire justification before God, as thesis 25 of the same teaches "He is not righteous who does much, but he who, without work, believes much in Christ."[31] Human performance is no preparation for grace; on the contrary, despair of our own ability is a condition of possibility for receiving grace.[32] God performs an alien work of condemning all merits of works, reducing everything to nothing, in order that he might accomplish his proper work of conferring his righteousness *ex nihilo*. True builders "sanctify Christ as Lord" (1 Pet 3:14) by submitting to the paradoxical action of God, in which they relinquish all foundation stones but Christ, the cornerstone, in whom we have everything. The rejected stone becomes our cornerstone not by human performance and self-chosen piety but only through the annihilation of them at the foot of the cross. To preach Christ, for Luther, is to extol "this Stone [as] a foundation in order that you may despair of yourself and lose heart, regard your own works and piety as something altogether damnable, rely solely on Him, and believe that Christ's righteousness is your righteousness."[33] We rely on no other stone but Christ alone, just as natural stones rely on their foundation stone. Grace is hidden in the rejected stone whom God has made our cornerstone. Luther elaborates:

> Now this stone does not serve itself, but it lets itself be trampled on and buried in the ground, so that one does not see it. The other stones rest on it and are visible. Therefore He has been given to us in order that we should take from Him, rely on Him, and believe that all He has is ours, that all He can do has been done for our benefit, so that I can say: "This is my own possession and treasure with which my conscience can comfort itself."[34]

From Isaiah 8:13–15—"Let Him [the Lord of hosts] be your fear, and let Him be your dread. And He will become a sanctuary, and a stone of offense, and a rock of stumbling to both houses of Israel"—Peter adduces that Christ alone, and not works of the law, is our sanctuary and the holiness upon which our faith is founded. "You need no other holiness," says Luther, "except that you believe."[35] Those who grant the power of saving to the law both misuse the law and oppose Christ—and then stumble and fall. Their buildings do not fit Christ's, as their thoughts and ways contradict his. All human achievements, riches, and power collide with the stone and are crushed by it. They fall through their own fault, not through any fault of Christ, who remains "a Stone that will make men stumble, a Rock that will make them fall . . . because they disobey the Word, as they were destined to do" (1 Pet 2:8). Luther further clarifies, "The Word of God is a stumbling block, not indeed by its own fault but by the fault of the depraved flesh which loves darkness rather than God's light (cf. John 3:19), and so that which is given as a cure becomes a poison for the flesh. Life becomes death, salvation becomes destruction, because men attack, blaspheme, reject, and persecute it."[36] Peter was aware of Jesus's teaching in Matthew 21:44, "And he who falls on this Stone will be broken to pieces; but when It falls on anyone, It will crush him." Luther stresses, "This Stone is no *joke*.[37] It has been laid, and It will remain in position. He who wants to collide with It and scoff at It will have to cave in."[38] The stone exposes the inefficacy of the law, the futility of our righteousness, and the barrenness of our piety as the foundation. Consequently, all God's "precious goods" are lost because Christ, "the choice and the precious Stone," is rejected.[39]

Faith in Christ preserves us from shame and damnation, the opposite of justification. Luther quotes the prophet Isaiah, who proclaimed, "And he who believes in Him shall not be put to shame" (Isa 28:16; 1 Pet 2:6). The Holy Spirit uses these words to highlight two things: the predicament of the unbelieving world, that it falls under God's judgments and must suffer shame, and by contrast, that believers are saved and spared this shame purely by God's power.[40] The prophet's words are so efficacious, says Luther, that they annihilate everything as a foundation for faith; the power of free will, all human performance, and human doctrines will "fall as dry leaves drop from a tree. For it is ordained that what does not rest on this Stone is already lost."[41] There is no residual desire for God and no remnant goodness in us that could form the basis of our saving relationship with God. God laid this stone as a firm foundation through which he performs two contradictory but glorious activities: his alien work of condemning our own righteousness, in order that he might do his proper work of covering us with Christ's righteousness.[42] Luther teaches the proper function of the law in thesis 23 of his *Heidelberg Disputation*: "The law brings the wrath of God, kills, reviles, accuses, judges, and condemns everything that is not in Christ."[43] The law itself does not make a sinner a saint, a reality only the gospel creates. Ebeling holds, "What the law says, and the events it recounts, are mere words and signs. But the words and events of the gospel are reality, the very substance of what they describe."[44] Luther proves himself a true theologian, as he willingly places himself under the burden of the law in order that he might come under the blessing of the gospel. Yeago captures the paradox in Luther: "The work of the law is precisely to insist that the self-giving of God in the flesh and blood of Jesus of Nazareth is our good, and nothing else."[45] The law crushes a sinner so that Christ alone is the foundation. It causes Luther to die to himself, not relying on his own righteousness but to live, to borrow Hampson's phrase, "*extra se* (outside himself) by an alien righteousness" of Christ.[46] Luther declares:

I despair of myself and remember that my righteousness and my truth must collapse and that I depend on the eternal existence of His righteousness, His life, His truth and all His goods. That is the foundation on which I stand. . . . Only he who relies on it will not be put to shame; he will remain, and no power can harm him.[47]

The Simultaneity of Saint and Sinner: "A Battle and a Camp"

Each person comprises a dialectic between two parts: "the inner being, which is faith, and the outer being, which is the flesh."[48] To faith, believers are wholly pure inwardly. This happens when the word of God penetrates the heart and lives there. Consequently, it removes all vices to make a chaste heart. The justifying "Word of God finds no uncleanness in him."[49] But as far as we are still in the flesh, evil inclinations of the old Adam abide. This is so because faith has not had "full power over the flesh."[50] The "coincidental opposites"[51] of sin and righteousness characterize justified existence. Luther teaches this in his exposition of the parable of the Samaritan in Luke 10:34–35. A man went down from Jerusalem to Jericho, fell into the hands of murderers, and was left half-dead. The Samaritan bound up his wounds and left him attended. This man is in the process of being healed, though he has not yet reached perfection. Luther describes, "Only one thing is lacking: he is not completely well. Life is there, but he does not yet have perfect health but is still in the care of the physicians. He must continue to be cared for."[52] Likewise, the Lord Christ and eternal life are certainly our possessions. But we cannot enjoy them fully because residual sin clings to the old Adam while we still live as aliens and exiles on earth.

Luther augments this teaching by another parable recorded in Matthew 13:33: "The kingdom of heaven is like leaven which a woman took and hid in three measures of meal, till it was all leavened." In preparing the dough from flour, all the leaven must penetrate it. But the leaven has not yet thoroughly soaked into the dough. The flour must be worked until it is leavened thoroughly. Likewise, through faith we have in the word of God everything that is Christ's, but the word has not yet fully done Christ's regenerative work in us; it continues to work in us renewal.[53] Quoting John 13:10, Luther avers that Jesus teaches we are completely clean, except our feet still require washing.[54] With this, Luther affirms the simultaneity of our status as both saint and sinner. They are opposites "in one person" in whom "two natures are opposed to each other, the old and the new man."[55] Concerning the extrinsic nature of justification, Cummings elucidates, "Man as he is in himself (*intrinsice*) is a sinner. But God chooses to see man as different from how he is in himself, and thus *extrinsice* man can also be righteous. From this point of view there is no contradiction, only a change of point of view."[56] Viewed through law, we are sinners; viewed through the gospel, we are saints. The language of grace is necessarily contrary to human logic. "While counter-logical," Cummings writes, "grace is not illogical or arbitrary."[57] Christ is completely ours through faith, and this frees us from any anxiety concerning our justified status before God. "The monster of uncertainty," for Luther, is conquered not by looking within for sign of transformation, or at the quality of self-performance; it is conquered by looking "at God himself as he promises, and at Christ himself, the mediator."[58] "In faith," says Hamm, "[the believer] is taken outside himself, away from the necessity of providing to God in works, and instead is taken into the righteousness of Christ."[59] Faith directs the sinner's attention away from themself to Christ, the only basis of justification. It, Hamm writes, "puts sinners in a cognitive and affective relationship to Christ's righteousness that is brought existentially near through the word of judgment and salvation."[60] Christ's presence in faith does not effect an intrinsic change to our humanity; it effects a change of a person's position before God in which Christian righteousness is added to the sinful person. Justification thus makes something new, constituting the sinful creature as righteous, though he remains what he always was— namely, sinful.

Since faith makes us holy and certain of salvation, Peter advises us to proceed to deal with the evil within us; as 1 Peter 2:11 reads, "Beloved, I beseech you as aliens and exiles to abstain from the passions of the flesh that wage war against your soul." Peter conceives of the Christian life as "nothing but a battle and a camp."[61] We are to conduct ourselves "as obedient children." Therefore, "do not conform to the passions of your former ignorance" (1 Pet 1:14). The true Christian bemoans that as God's child, they are never beyond ease or peace, as she still constantly faces the assaults of the devil and sin. "As long as flesh and blood remain, so long sin also remains. Consequently, constant warfare is necessary. He who does not experience this dare not boast of being a Christian."[62] Luther has Peter say, "Be armed in such a way that you guard against sins which still cling to you, and that you constantly fight against them. For our worst enemies are in our bosom and in our flesh and blood. They wake, sleep, and live with us like an evil guest whom we have invited to our house and cannot get rid of."[63] The old nature and the renewed nature are opposed to each other, and while believers "feel" the desires of the flesh, they are not to "yield" to them,[64] for the flesh no longer reigns; the Spirit dominates the flesh and is lord over it. Luther affirms, "The spirit must busy itself daily to tame the flesh and to bring it into subjection, must wrestle with it incessantly, and must take care that it does not repel faith."[65] We conquer evil lusts by resisting them constantly with the word of God. We must despair of our own powers and rely on our Lord God. As Scripture teaches, Luther notes, our Lord is "the Lord of hosts" (Ps 24:10); he is also "the Lord mighty in battle" (Ps 24:8).[66] Paradoxically, Luther adds, "God shows

His might by letting His people wage war constantly and by letting them take the lead where the trumpets always sound."[67] Even when we are baptized, we still must be vigilant, for the battle with residual sins abides. Christians exercise their baptismal identity through a repeated repudiation through the law of the old identity with all its vices and a daily rising through the gospel of the new identity with its righteousness and holiness.[68] Participation in everyday events is where the internal battle between the old Adam, with its self-interest, and the new Adam, with its care for others, is most acute. In life's vocation, we wage against the devil and sin, like a soldier drawing his sword in battle with his enemies. We enter confession not flippantly by slackening our reins but reverently by taking the lead, drawing on the word of absolution as the remedy for our sins.[69]

Joy, the Effect of Faith: Hearing vs. Seeing God

"The gospel with its 'for you,'" Wengert writes, "creates faith in God. That is its point, its goal."[70] The justifying action of sinners occurs, Hamm notes, "in faith and faith-filled hearing of the word,"[71] totally independent of any pious emotions we feel within. Yet the heart that grasps the word through hearing rejoices in being addressed by that word. Justifying faith reaches beyond the cognitive into the affective, touching the heart with emotions such as joy or peace.[72] Using the rose as a symbol of faith-generated joy, Luther instructs:

> Such a heart is to be in the midst of a white rose, to symbolize that faith gives joy, comfort, and peace; in a word it places the believer into a white joyful rose. For [this faith] does not give peace or joy as the world gives and, therefore, the rose is to be white and not red, for white is the color of the spirits and of all the angels. Such a rose is to be in a sky-blue field, [symbolizing] that such joy in the Spirit and in faith is the beginning of the future heavenly joy.[73]

Joy is a distinct experience of the heart that has tasted the good news of freedom Christ offers. Commenting on 1 Peter 2:3, "For you have tasted the kindness of the Lord," Luther exults, "If this [justifying word] goes to the heart, then one relishes it. For how could I not derive joy and delight from it? Surely I rejoice heartily if a good friend gives me 100 guldens. But he whose heart is not touched by this cannot rejoice over it."[74] Luther's doctrine of faith is not framed within the frigid language of the courtroom but within the passionate language of a wedding, a happy occasion in which Christ (the groom) fills the bride's (the sinner) heart with overflowing joy by absolving all her sins in exchange for his righteousness. Luther exults, "Is that not a *happy wedding feast*, when the rich, noble, and good bridegroom, takes the poor, despised, bad little harlot in marriage, sets her free from all evil and graces her with all good things?"[75] He continues:

> What man is there whose heart, upon hearing these things, will not *rejoice to its depth*, and when receiving such comfort will not grow tender so that he will love Christ as he never could by means of any laws or works? Who would have the power to harm or frighten such a heart? If the knowledge of sin or the fear of death should break in upon it, it is ready to hope in the Lord. It does not grow afraid when it hears tidings of evil. It is not distributed when it sees its enemies. This is so because it believes that the righteousness of Christ is its own and that its sin is not its own, but Christ's, and that all sin is swallowed up by the righteousness of Christ.[76]

The jubilant feeling of being received into God's favor also finds succinct expression in Mary, "who boasts, with heart leaping for joy and praising God, that He regarded her despite her low estate and nothingness."[77] God's work in Mary is his work done in the depths of lowliness and poverty, the opposite of human work that is done in the heights of glory and power.[78]

Mary, a person of lowliness and nothingness, for Luther, is an instance of God's contrary work:

> Out of that which is nothing, worthless, despised, wretched, and dead, He makes that which is something, precious, honorable, blessed, and living. On the other hand, whatever is something, precious, honorable, blessed, and living, He makes to be nothing, worthless, despised, wretched, and dying. In this manner no creature can work; no creature can produce out of nothing.[79]

Mary permits God's will to be done in her, and from this she receives consolation and gladness and places her trust in him. Her faith arises not from anything she brings but from "the work God had done with her."[80] She was so enraptured by God's grace that all that is within her is set in motion, inclining her to confess, "My soul magnifies him" (Luke 1:46). Joy is not self-generated; it is derived from the knowledge of the salutary contrary work of God, that God alone looks at the unpleasant places, the miserable and sore condition from which all eyes would avert, and makes something out of nothing.[81] Luther quotes Daniel 3:55, "God beholdest the depths," to speak of God's way "of seeing that looks into the depths with their need and misery"; not to leave them there without reprieve but to "bring help to many, perform manifold works, show Himself a true Creator, and thereby make Himself known and worthy of love and praise."[82] The proud repudiate God's "seeing, working, and helping," and thus strip themselves of all "pleasure, joy, and salvation."[83] God's "seeing, work, help, method, counsel, and will" are gathered up in Christ, who was sent by the Father into the depths of all miseries in order to do his work there—namely, to deliver us from them. Faith in Christ vivifies the affective character of the justified existence, marked by reciprocal joy, praise, and "true love for His bare goodness."[84] Helmer writes aptly, "The affect that characterizes justification is joy, and the emotion is expressed in physical postures of dancing and leaping 'for joy.'"[85] In Luther's words:

> And this is the source of men's love and praise of God. For no one can praise God without first loving Him. No one can love Him unless He makes Himself known in him in the most lovable and intimate fashion. And He can make Himself known only through those works of His which He reveals in us, and which we feel and experience, namely, that He is a God who looks into the depths and helps only the poor, despised, afflicted, miserable, forsaken, and those who are nothing, there a hearty love for Him is born. The heart overflows with gladness and goes leaping and dancing for the magnificent pleasure it has found in God. There the Holy Spirit is present and has taught us in a moment such exceeding great knowledge and gladness through this experience.[86]

The creation of a joyful heart occurs, most significantly, through hearing, not seeing. Luther writes, "What man is there whose *heart*, upon *hearing* these things [the riches of God's grace], will not *rejoice to its depth*?"[87] There lies an intrinsic linkage between "ear" and "heart" in Luther's doctrine of faith. The phrase "be opened" in the story of healing of the deaf in Mark 7:34, Luther writes, "is nothing else than to cause one to hear, just as earth is opened and dug out. . . . But this opening means to cause one to be obedient and to believe. For faith is obedience, as in Rom. 1:5 states: 'To bring about obedience to the faith.'"[88] The phrase "Thou hast opened My ears" could assume an active sense, that God has "made me obedient" to him, which for Luther is "a bit forced." He prefers a passive sense, referring to the sinner's passive reception of God's salvific work in him. That is, God has "brought it about that people were made to believe"[89] in him. Faith is passive in two senses:[90] first, it is because of its receptive character, that it only receives God's forgiveness and does not cause it; second, it is because the receptive action itself is generated not by human will or reason but by the Holy Spirit—it is a gifted reception. Braaten clarifies, "Faith is subjectively the result of the creative impact upon the sinner of God's acceptance."[91] The passive character of faith consists in that faith does not possess anything of its own except it grasp God's "speech-act" that first grasps us. As Bayer notes, "theologically, the capacity to hear receptively"[92] flows from a prior, gratuitous action of God.

In his exposition of 1 Peter 1:25, Luther considers the "ears" as an indispensable vehicle of fulfilling the word of God in "hearts." There he quotes Deuteronomy 30:14: "In your mouth, I say, and in your heart it must be if you want to fulfill it, not in your ear or hand."[93] The heart is changed through the hearing of the word, the aural aspect of proclamation. The Holy Spirit's sole aim, Luther avers, is to make sure "that we hear the voice of God, that is, that we believe."[94] Whoever "hears" the gospel and "believes in it" will be saved.[95] The "ears" are the instruments of God's justifying action. Luther intimates:

> For if you ask a Christian what the work is by which he becomes worthy of the name, "Christian," he will be able to give absolutely no other answer than that it is the hearing of the Word of God, that is, faith. Therefore the ears alone are the organs of a Christian, for he is justified and declared to be a Christian, not because of the works of any member but because of faith.[96]

The emphasis on hearing rather than seeing God is where faith is created; as Luther states, "Do not attempt to see Christ with your eyes but put your eyes in your ears."[97] The accent on hearing, Jenson notes, highlights a fundamental distinction between the God of Israel and the idols; the former can be "heard" ("ears") and the latter can be "seen" ("eyes"). He writes:

> I have flaps on my eyes but none on my ears and can aim my eyes but not my ears. Sight, stretching across space, is a controlled and controlling relation to external reality; hearing,

stretching across time, is uncontrollable. I see what I choose
to look at; I must hear what is contingently addressed to me. I
hear the Lord when he speaks; I see the non-gods who negoti-
ate in the space I make by looking for them.[98]

That God can be heard discloses the character of God as an
active agent of speech. "It was," Pelikan holds, "in the very
nature of God to want to speak and to be able to speak, and
therefore by definition God was never speech-less."[99] On the
other hand, it locates us in a position of, as Laffin puts it, "passive receptivity before divine address."[100] The preached word,
Luther writes, is "before your eyes. . . . You need not search far.
Do no more than take hold of it when it is preached. For it is
so near that one can hear it."[101] Commenting on hearing God's
voice in 2 Peter 1:18, "we heard this voice borne from heaven for
we were with Him on the holy mountain," Luther teaches, "All
of this [the gospel and its privileges] we now believe. We grasp
it only with our ears and have it in the Word of God."[102]

Reason leads us away from God into works that condemn us.
Faith leads us to God, who saves us. Of the instrumental causal-
ity of faith, Luther writes, "God our Father has made all things
depend on faith so that whoever has faith will have everything,
and whoever does not have faith will have nothing."[103] Hamm
is particularly helpful for his theological precision on faith as
the instrument by which we receive, not produce, God's righteousness. He writes, "Faith does not justify through its active
ability to love or through its sparks of feeling but rather only
through its passive receiving" of justifying righteousness "from
outside in." Hamm elaborates:

> Faith is the way of pure receiving, of the sinner's conscience
> being given the gift of Jesus Christ's righteousness. This is
> bestowed upon believers when they trust the gospel: they
> know themselves to be nothing, but they trust everything to
> saving acts of God. The point of this "evangelical" faith lies in

its "only": you need "only" to believe, for "when you believe you have"; you need not and dare not reflect on the ability to love, your repentance, or your works of obedience to God, because these are all irrelevant for your salvation.[104]

The faith by which we acquire the heavenly inheritance comes not from ourselves but from God, "who creates it in us because Christ has merited this with His blood—Christ, to whom He has given the glory and whom He has placed at His right hand to create faith in us through the power of God."[105] A treasure of great benefits is offered in the word; it is received by faith, whose virtue lies in its ministerial function. So 1 Peter 1:9 states, "As an outcome of your faith you obtain the salvation of your souls." Luther observes in the economy of salvation a logical sequence: "Faith follows from the Word, the new birth follows from faith, and from this birth we enter into the hope of looking forward to the blessing with certainty."[106] We obtain all of this—"the new birth, the filial relationship, and the inheritance"—through faith, not through works.[107] "To believe," for Luther, is "the greatest work" we cannot perform unless "the Spirit of God" works it in us (cf. Eph 1:17–19).[108] For God to create faith in us is "as great a work" as for him to create the universe again.[109] Therefore, "faith is a power of God. When God works faith, man must be born again and became a new creature. Then good works must follow from faith as a matter of course."[110] Luther provides the meaning of Peter's teaching that "we are guarded through faith for salvation by the power of God" (1 Pet 1:5): "The faith which works in us the power of God—which dwells in us and with which we are filled—is such a tender and precious thing" that it enables us to perceive all that pertains to salvation and preserves us from being deceived by falsehood or error.[111] The graver assaults that confront the people living as exiles, for Luther, may not be physical but spiritual, depriving them of the proper perception of the truth of Christ. Faith in the God who has chosen them enables believers to assert, "'This doctrine is right. That one is false. This life is right. That one is not. This work is good and well done. That one is evil.' What such a person concludes is right and true; for he cannot be misled but is preserved and protected, and he remains a judge of all doctrine."[112]

Apart from Spirit-created faith, all works we do are vitiated and are of no real service to God. "Faith, the trust of the heart,"[113] indeed constitutes reality; as Luther avers, "As you believe, so it will happen to you, because this faith is not taken from human judgement but drawn from the Word of God."[114] Faith determines the shape of one's relation to God—but so, too, does unbelief. Reality constituted by faith is opposed to that constituted by unbelief. To unbelief, God and the abundance of his blessings are of no saving efficacy; to faith, God and all his goods are precious. As Peter says, "To you therefore who believe, He is precious" (1 Pet 2:7). Faith and its object are intrinsically linked; one cannot do without the other. Objectively, faith's object, Christ or the gospel, is given, not merited; subjectively, it is fulfilled through faith, the receptive action. The same sentiment appears in Luther's doctrine of the Lord's Supper, where he holds tightly the connection between faith and promise: without faith, the promise is of no use to us; without the promise, faith is empty of content.[115] Dieter captures Luther well: "Faith cannot create the object of belief; the object must be given to it. Faith must also have a subjective side. If something is given to me and I do not accept it, the object remains outside of me."[116]

"The Best of All Ways of Life": Faith and Love

The people of faith love the cross, their "sure foundation." As stones, they hear the gospel and cleave to this cornerstone so that their confidence is only on Christ. Luther writes, "Then I must also be prepared to retain the form of this Stone; for if I am placed on Him through faith, I and everyone with me must do the kind of works He did and lead the kind of life he led."[117] Through faith, we are alike and are all equal before God; we are constituted as one spiritual building, fitted on each other and united through love, rid of the vices mentioned in 1 Peter 2:1. Only through faith in Christ are our works and our lives made holy. The work we perform and the life we exemplify correspond to the way and the work of Christ, as stones would fit the cornerstone, on whom we are placed; they are, Luther avers, "a fruit of faith and a work of love."[118] Here is an instance of faith forming love rather than love forming faith, and of faith operating through love rather than faith justifying through love. It concurs with what Luther had already taught in his Galatians commentary, that for Paul, "works are done on the basis of faith through love, not that a man is justified through love."[119] "We become like him," says Luther, "in such a way that the building fits together; for the other stones must all be adjusted and arranged according to this Stone. This is love, a fruit of faith."[120]

In justification, "God does not need works."[121] But a justifying faith truly works and produces works. Just as a good tree produces good fruits, so, too, a righteous person produces righteous deeds. Luther teaches, "Actually [works] come forth from you because you have already been made a Christian."[122] Since the identity of a Christian is created by faith alone, a true Christian can exemplify his new existence that is in conformity to it. Faith, that which generates our new being, inevitably forms our doing. In his Galatians commentary, Luther avers that faith of a "true and living" kind "arouses and motivates good works through love."[123] Likewise, in his exposition of the first epistle of Peter, true faith is not "an indolent and sleepy faith" but "a living and active thing" that expels all false devotions and doctrines. The freedom faith acquires for us is twofold: negatively, it liberates us from the evil "passions of the former ignorance" (1 Pet 1:14); positively, it frees us to live for others, serving and helping our neighbor. The form that true freedom assumes is servanthood; as 1 Peter 2:16 says, "Live as free men, yet without using your freedom as a pretext for evil; but live as servants of God." Justifying faith does not encourage self-indulgence or unbridled passion; rather, it safeguards Christian liberty against its licentious abuse.[124] In the intrinsic connection between faith and work, the former is the presupposition of the latter, and is succinctly stated as follows:

> For here nothing else is necessary than faith, that I give God His due honor and regard Him as my God, who is just, truthful, and merciful. Such faith liberates us from sin and all evil. Now when I have given God this honor, then whatever life I live, I live for my neighbor, to serve and help him. The greatest work that comes from faith is this, that I confess Christ with my mouth and, if it has to be, bear testimony with my blood and risk my life. Yet God does not need the work; but I should do it to prove and confess my faith, in order that others, too, may be brought to faith. Then other works will follow. They must all tend to serve my neighbor. All this God must bring about in us. Therefore we should not make up our minds to begin to lead a carnal life and to do what we please.[125]

In his Galatians lectures of 1535, Luther discerns that Paul exhorts the Galatians to persevere in "the perfect doctrine of faith and love."[126] Likewise, for St. Peter, "the best of all ways of life" consists of "nothing else than faith and love."[127] St. Peter expresses emphatically the importance of "the external manifestation" of an efficacious faith.[128] Faith and love are united in such a way that "where there is no faith, there can be no good works either; and, on the other hand, that there is no faith where there are no good works."[129] Luther extols the unconditional character of faith, apart from any human cause or contribution, that it "does not permit itself to be bound to any work"; he, too, stresses the prolific nature of faith, that it does not "refuse any work" and will fructify in due course (cf. Ps 1:3, "it yields its fruits in its season");[130] as Jeremiah 5:3 states, "O Lord, Thy eyes have regard for faith." Faith trusts God, believing that all works performed in faith count before God; as Wannenwetsch writes, "Faith as the hidden agent of the works makes them perfect, i.e. whole, undivided (Greek *teleios*), even though it may be just a small and unspectacular gesture."[131] For Luther, the efficacy of faith permeates all works without distinction, causing them to be equally well done before God. "For the works are acceptable not for their own sake but because of faith, which is always the same and lives and works in each and every work without distinction, however numerous and varied these works always are, just as all the members of the body live, work, and take their name from the head, and without the head no member can live, work, or have a name."[132] Faith, not "the distinction in works," is the impetus behind our deeds.[133] Since faith has abolished "all distinction between works," that all works are equally valid, we do all works, great or small, willingly and gladly, and without any thought of reward.[134] Whenever we distinguish between works, evaluating which work is more pleasing to God, we lapse into doubt or despair, wondering if they are ever well done before God.[135]

The change from hatred to love is God's action and is made possible by rebirth through the word with faith. Peter speaks of the purpose for which we are saved: "for a sincere love of the brethren, love one another earnestly from the heart" (1 Pet 1: 22). He reiterates the theme of love in 1 Peter 3:8: "Have sympathy, love of the brethren, a tender heart, and a friendly mind." This verse, Luther writes, comprises the "truly precious, golden works, gems and pearls that please God."[136] Luther unites faith to love, asserting that whoever boasts of the gospel and its consequent liberty must "first" serve their neighbors.[137] Bayer explains, "The salvific faith which relies on the Word of God of the only Mediator produces the love which fulfils all the commandments. Determined by faith, love is free and above worldly things."[138] Just as the causal agency of faith inheres wholly in all works without distinction, so, too, the precious blood of Christ is shed wholly for all Christians without distinction. Christ spent no less on a lesser saint than he did on a greater one. We do not differ in the precious treasure with which we are redeemed except in understanding and faith. Some may have a better grasp of it; some possess a milder faith than others.[139] In Christ, Christians possess everything he has and thus become "his brother."[140] With these possessions, they now serve their neighbors as Christ did, "a work of love" that is pleasing to God.[141]

There are two kinds of love: a specific kind of love—namely, brotherly love—and love in general.[142] Brotherhood means all Christians are God's people without distinction and have equal access to all inheritances in Christ. "Therefore just as we have the grace of Christ and all spiritual blessings in common," Luther teaches, "so we should also have body and life, property and honor in common, so that one serves the others with all things."[143]

By contrast, love in general is greater than brotherly love, as it reaches our enemies, those who possess nothing that appeals to or attracts us. Both faith and love are efficacious in their negations: "For just as faith is active where it sees nothing, so love should also not see anything and do its work chiefly where nothing lovable but only aversion and hostility is seen."[144] Faith is operative, despite contrary evidence and experience; likewise, love is effective where it meets with its opposite, the unlovable. Human love has no regard for sinners, the despised, and the unlovable; it is selfish and self-seeking. As in Aristotle's ethics, says Luther, "the object of love is its cause."[145] It loves only what could benefit itself, not what could benefit others. "In all things, it seeks those things which are its own and receives rather than gives something good."[146] On the contrary, God's love gives rather than receives; in Luther's words, it "turns in the direction where it does not find good which it may enjoy, but where it may confer good upon the bad and the needy."[147] We are to love those who in themselves are deprived of good and are unworthy to be loved, just as God loved us, who in ourselves are empty of any virtue that might cause God to love us.[148] For Paul, as for Peter, love consists, Luther writes, "not in receiving but in performing; for it is obliged to overlook many things and to bear with them."[149] This is contrary to Aristotle, who holds, in Luther's words, "that all power of the soul is passive and material and active only in receiving something."[150] "The love of the cross"[151] supplies the very attitude, action, and motivation of love.[152] True love is performed independently of the recipient's attitude (gratitude or ingratitude), irrespective of the person (friends or foes), and without a consideration of its outcome (praise or blame).[153] Steinmetz asserts, "[True love] does not attempt to place other people under obligation to itself or engage in any kind of subtle spiritual blackmail. It considers no good work wasted, even when it is despised by the recipient."[154] True love emanates from true faith; it gives all only to benefit others, without any thought of reward.

Of 1 Peter 4:8—"Above all, hold your unfailing love for one another, since love covers a multitude of sins"—Luther teaches that the human covering of sin by love is no basis of justification before God; it is not to be confused with the divine covering of sin by faith. He maintains that "only faith shall cover your sin before God. But my love covers my neighbor's sin, and just as God covers my sin with His love if I believe, so I must also cover my neighbor's sin."[155] Works of love do not free us from sin before God; only faith does. If human loving could overcome sin and merit divine favor, that would have undermined grace. Though faith precedes love, they are not separated. Commenting on Galatians 5:6, "Faith is working through love," Luther teaches that for St. Paul, the faith that justifies is "effective and active" through love, its "tool."[156] The same sentiment occurs in St. Peter, who teaches that those whom faith justifies are also inspired to works: "Maintain good conduct among the Gentiles, so that in case they speak against you as wrongdoers, they may see your good deeds and glorify God on the day of visitation" (1 Pet 2:12). True faith enlivens the affective character of believers, causing them to move outside themselves and live toward one another. "Abstract faith"—faith alone, apart from works—justifies, and the "incarnate faith"—faith with works—is part of justified existence;[157] in Hamm's formulation: "Love no longer forms faith; faith itself has become the form of a life guided by love."[158] A faith without love is nothing, Luther avers, "but a counterfeit faith, just as a face seen in a mirror is not a real face, but merely the reflection of a face [I Cor 13:12]."[159]

The faith that acquires for us the "great distinction"[160] to be God's beloved is not an indolent but an active kind, accompanied by love. Love is no merit for faith but a fruit of it. We do not give God anything by love but receive everything from him by faith. The inestimable riches we receive from Christ by faith we now share with others by love. Faith has liberated Luther from self-curvedness for uncoercive deeds of love; he thus declares, "I will therefore give myself as a Christ to my neighbor, just as Christ offered himself to me."[161] Faith does its alien work, causing him to forget himself and "see" beyond himself into what is "necessary, profitable, and salutary" to others, freely and joyfully serving them with the abundant goods he receives from Christ.[162] Luther sums up: "Thus, it is faith that saves us. But it is love that prompts us to give ourselves to our neighbor. . . . That is, faith receives from God; love gives to the neighbors."[163] In declaring this, Luther asserts that Peter's first letter is "a truly golden epistle."[164]

God's Judgment and Fear: Living Aright

Antipathy to good works is not part of the Reformer's doctrine of faith. First Peter 1:17—"And if you invoke as Father

Him who judges each one impartially according to his deeds, conduct yourselves with fear throughout the time of your exile"—affords Luther to teach two things: God's fearful judgment on all without distinction, and a righteous identity that expresses itself in reverence of God.[165] The old creature in us must undergo its crucifixion and come under God's judgment. "And whoever would live without this crucifying and this fear and the judgment of God, does not live aright."[166] Luther uses this text to place his congregants under the law in which they hear God's word of judgment against moral laxity or ethical passivity. The judgment of God differs from that of the world. The world does not execute judgment fairly and has regard for persons who are learned, wise, and powerful. But God judges the deeds, irrespective of the person. Both the son of King Pharoah and the son of a common person, whom Luther cites as examples, share the same fate before God; both are slain by the word.[167] The person is "immaterial" to God; and no one, both the pious and the wicked, can escape God's judgment for their evil deeds.[168] Unlike the world's standards, God's judgment is an undifferentiated kind; he is no less indulgent with God's children than with others.[169] Faith distinguishes us as children of God, bestowed with the privilege of invoking God as our Father. By faith, we acquire an imperishable inheritance that is now hidden, which awaits its full revelation at the end. Despite this hiddenness, we possess all his blessings and can address God as Father with confidence. Even so, he remains a judge who executes his impartial judgment. It is folly to assume that because we receive "the great distinction" to be God's children, God will spare us on that basis.[170] As 1 Peter 4:17 says, "For the time has come for judgment to begin with the household of God; and if it begins with us, what will be the end of those who do not obey the Gospel of God?" St. Peter, Luther contends, learned from Jeremiah 25:29 that God's "dearly beloved children who believed" in God are "the first to be subjected to suffering and to be led into the glowing fire," and from Jeremiah 49:12, where God speaks a word of judgment—in Luther's rendering, "'I smite My dear ones to show you what I will do to My enemies.'"[171] If God inflicts such a stern judgment on the pious, how much more severe will his punishment on the wicked be? The time has come for God's wrath to be poured out, beginning with the righteous. "When the Gospel is preached, God begins to punish sin [as in law], in order that He may kill and make alive [as in promise]."[172] People feel the negative effect of the law before they reap from the gospel the fruit of consolation. Just as the word of mercy does what it says, so does the word of wrath. Luther writes, "Consider what kind of words these are. The greater God's saints are, the more terribly He lets them be knocked about and perish. What, then, will happen to the others?"[173] When the word of wrath comes, it kills; the result is deadly, with no hope of recovery; it terrifies the saints through the law, which condemns them unless they cleave to the word of mercy that consoles them. "The godless feel this word of anger, both in this life through various afflictions and in the future life, if they do not turn and come to repentance."[174]

God imposes judgment upon the faithful according to "the works[, which] are fruits and signs of faith."[175] "As you live, so you will fare. God will judge you according to this," that is, according to the fruits with which you prove your faith.[176] He chastises his own, primarily with "a mother's rod," in order that he might impel them to live in reverential "fear" while on earth.[177] This fear, for Luther, is "fear mingled with love."[178] Fear with love draws us closer to the one we honor rather than causing us to flee from him. On the contrary, for Luther, "fear without love" is abject terror, for instance, fear of falling in the hands of a ruthless executioner whom we spurn.[179] "Fear without love," Luther writes, "is a fear mixed with hatred and hostility."[180] God does not will that he be revered with servile fear, as a slave cowers in fear before a tyrant, but with filial fear, as a pious son fears his beloved father.[181] We do not revere the Father for fear of pain and judgment, as do non-Christians and the devil.[182] We fear him like a devoted child fears that they may dishonor her father. With this kind of fear, we do not indulge in sins, and we serve others willingly, even as pilgrims here on earth.[183]

All earthly goods are God's gifts; they are entrusted to us, not primarily for self-enjoyment but for the benefit of others. Temporal goods are to be used only for bodily existence and must not be allowed to define our identity; only by Christ, who is "worth more than all that," should do this.[184] Our identity is so bound up with the God of the first commandment that God imposes judgment upon those who have as their lords creaturely things, such as human achievement, power, pedigree, or prestige. As holy people, we live in reverential fear as pilgrims on a journey to heaven, where our Father and his blessings reside. Since we are no longer citizens in the world, we must act like "aliens and exiles," abstaining "from the passions of the flesh" (1 Pet 2:11) and staying as guests overnight in an inn where nothing there belongs to us, and from where we must depart for the "lasting city" that awaits us (Heb 13:14).[185]

CHAPTER 3

Christ as Gift and Example
Expiatory and Exemplary Suffering

Based on 1 Peter 2:21, 3:17, and 4:1, Luther holds that Scripture presents the life of Christ, particularly his passion, in two ways:[1] first, "as a gift" that saves us, and second, as "an example" that summons us to follow him. Christ's expiatory suffering on the cross achieved redemption, which we grasp by faith, not by works. First Peter 3:18, "Christ also died for sins once for all," is "the chief article and the best part of the Gospel," says Luther.[2] Once Christ is received passively as a gift, that he made full satisfaction for all sins, he ought to be received actively as an example, that "you should follow in His steps" (1 Pet 2:21). The distinction between Christ as gift and Christ as example corresponds to faith and love; these two dimensions sum up the totality of the Christian life. Luther states, "Although we are righteous through faith and have the Lord Christ as our own, we are nonetheless also obliged to perform good works and to serve our neighbor."[3] The example Peter prescribed was none other than the suffering of Christ. The cross constitutes the form of the Christian life. Luther writes, "We should imitate Him in our whole life and in all our suffering."[4] No matter where we are in life, we suffer according to his example—not because of any of our vices but simply because we obey his word, as Christ did. Suffering that is pleasing to God is an innocent kind, as Christ suffered innocently, for he is without sin (1 Pet 2:22).

Those who shun the cross, Luther writes, do not really know God "hidden in his suffering."[5] "It is only through suffering and the cross," Forde says, "that sinners can see and come to know God."[6] However, "there is no true knowledge of Jesus Christ where human beings refuse the cross in their own lives," Lienhard affirms; that is, there is no true knowledge without "conformity to the suffering humanity of Jesus Christ. Knowledge of God and of salvation in Jesus Christ and new life are thus inseparable. For the reformer, an orthodoxy which is not also an orthopraxis would be inconceivable."[7] The suffering of Christ and of the Christian are distinguished but are inseparably one; the latter has its basis in the former. As gospel, Christ the sacrament has completed all that is needed for us to enter God's favor and has banished every impediment to the enjoyment of all blessings reserved for us in heaven. As law, Christ the example becomes "a mirror" that acquaints us with the knowledge of our deficiencies that we might cling to God for aid.[8] The law does not supplement the gospel; likewise, Christ as example does not complete some lack in Christ as gift. Christ as example emanates from Christ as gift, just as works of love do from the "faith alone"[9] that justifies. Our old Adam must continually die under the cross so that Christ's exemplary suffering is not lacking in us and becomes a visible part of our own being, as it did with Christ. Luther declares, "He who is a Christian must also bear a cross."[10]

Scripture and the Gospel: The Written and the Living Voice

Scripture informs us that God keeps his promise not because of the quality of our pious works but out of sheer grace. It leads us away from our works to faith in God. Luther cites Romans 1:2, where Paul teaches that God promised the gospel "beforehand through His prophets in the Holy Scriptures." We learn from the Old Testament the promise concerning Christ, as Christ himself testifies in John 5:39—"You search the Scriptures . . . and it is they that bear witness to Me"—and similarly in John 5:46: "If you believe in Moses, you would believe Me; for he wrote of me."[11] Insofar as the law and the prophets bear witness to Christ, they are, Luther opines, "also gospel,"[12] for what was proclaimed and written beforehand in the Old Testament corresponds to what was preached or written later in the New Testament. "Luther assigns a primary place to the Old Testament as Scripture," Pelikan notes, "preferring the term 'proclamation' to the New Testament."[13] Both were written "on paper word for word," but "the Gospel, or the New Testament, should really not be written but should be expressed with the living voice which resounds and is heard through the world."[14] The apostles call the Old Testament scripture that foreshadows Christ. But "the Gospel is a living sermon of the Christ who has come."[15] Both the Old and New Testament bear the same gospel content: Jesus Christ. As Genesis 22:18 teaches, "In our Seed shall all the nations of the earth be blessed." In Adam, all are cursed and cannot escape condemnation; in Christ, all are blessed and receive salvation. This is why Peter stresses "grace is coming to you" (1 Pet 1:13), which simply means "Jesus Christ is revealed to you." In Luther's words:

> For God will listen to no one who does not bring Christ, His dear Son, with him. God has regard for Him alone, and for His sake He also has regard for those who cling to Him. He wants us to acknowledge that we are reconciled to the Father through the blood of the Son and for this reason need not be afraid to come before Him. For the Lord Christ came, assumed flesh and blood, and attached Himself to us for the purpose of acquiring such grace for us before the Father.[16]

St. Peter teaches, "The prophets who prophesized of the grace that was to be yours searched and inquired about this salvation" (1 Pet 1:10). The prophets delivered "the good news to you through the Holy Spirit sent from heaven"; they served us with "things into which angels long to look" (1 Pet 1:11). Like the prophets, the apostles were Spirit-filled vessels who were commissioned by Christ to preach the true gospel so that we may learn what true faith is and benefit from it. Luther sums up the substance of the gospel: "For since He gave us Christ, His only Son, the highest Good, He, through Him, also gives us all His good things, riches, and treasures, from which the angels in heaven derive all pleasure and joy."[17] The gospel brings to us the "imperishable, undefiled, and unfading" inheritance of God (1 Pet 1:4) that we could not grasp by the physical eyes but only by the eyes of faith. Luther writes, "St Peter orders us to close our eyes and see what the Gospel is. This will give us joy and delight."[18] Elsewhere, he reiterates: "In faith one must close the eyes to everything but God's Word";[19] as 1 Peter 1:8 reads: "Without having seen Him, you love Him; though you do not now see Him, you believe in Him and rejoice with unutterable and exalted joy." On earth, the joy of salvation we feel is real but is imperfect, unlike the perfect joy of angels. We grasp some of it here, but in heaven, this joy is of such magnitude that no human heart can contain its full revelation. These things—blessedness, righteousness, and the heavenly blessings—in which angels find delight are proclaimed and "kept in heaven for you, ready to be revealed on the Last Day" (1 Pet 1:4–5). Luther writes, "It is still hidden, still covered, locked and sealed up. Yet in a short time it will be revealed and exposed to our view."[20] These words St. Peter preached are not "unnecessary words" but creative words through which "everything is alive."[21] Henceforth, we should hold on to them with full confidence, says Luther, "so that [ours] is a genuine faith and not a colored or fictitious delusion and dream."[22]

Christ as Gift: The Cross as the Locus of Redemption

Luther draws from 1 Peter 1:18–19—"You know that you were ransomed from the futile ways inherited from your fathers, not with perishable things such as silver or gold, but with the precious blood of Christ"—to speak of the cross as the locus of redemption. Peter impels us to live in fear of God through a meditation on how much our redemption cost. Christ's sacrificial death has reconciled us to God and brought about, to borrow Forde's phrase, "a reversal of direction":[23] "from devil to God, death to life, sin to righteousness, and keeps us there."[24] The cross has transposed us from being citizens of this world to those of heaven, the subjects of the devil to those of God. This change in position was obtained not through magnificent miracles but through the foolishness and weakness of the cross (1 Cor 1:25). God does not meet us in his majesty, might, and glory, which would have terrified us, but in his humility, his weakness, and the shame of the cross, where he presents himself as a merciful God.[25] The means of redemption is not by "perishable things such as gold or silver" but by "the precious blood of Christ" (1 Pet 1:18). It cost the death of God's son, his blood, "the noble, precious treasure," to redeem us, something no human mind can comprehend and no human power could achieve.[26] Along with medieval thinking, Luther writes, "Just one drop of this innocent blood would have been more than enough for the sin of the whole world. Yet the Father wanted to pour out His grace on us so abundantly and to spend so much that He let His Son Christ shed all the blood and gave us the entire treasure."[27] Therefore we must not treat God's grace with contempt but rather be so moved by it that we conduct ourselves in fear, lest we trample underfoot this inestimable treasure by which we are redeemed. Everything that is not sprinkled by the blood is of the flesh, and therefore is evil and condemned. All other means of acquiring grace without Christ lead us into blindness and wickedness, the opposite of justification. Luther concedes no greater sin than the attempt to become pious by works and worship God by reason. Such an attempt profanes Christ's innocent blood and provokes God's wrath.[28]

When speaking of being ransomed by "the precious blood of Christ," Luther cites Isaiah 53:7, "Like a Lamb that is led to the slaughter," and the figure of the paschal lamb in Exodus 12. The Lamb is Christ, who is without blemish, and whose blood was shed for the remission of our sin. The grace that is obtained through the blood was not merited but was eternally "destined" for us. God has promised us grace and revealed in history what he had decreed from eternity before the creation of the world. Luther declares, "We did not merit this and never asked God that the precious blood of Christ be shed for us. Therefore we have nothing to boast of. The glory belongs to God alone. God promises us this without any merit on our part."[29] As 1 Peter 1:20 says, "He was destined before the foundation of the world but was made manifest at the end of the times." Christ was already promised in the prophets but hidden there. Now, however, he was preached openly and heard everywhere "at the end of the times" (1 Pet 1:20). "The end of the times" stretches from "the period from Christ's ascension to the Last Day."[30] It is equivalent to "the last hour," as Christ calls it.[31] What is in view is not the imminent return of Christ after his ascension but that the proclamation of the gospel of Christ is "the last one."[32] There has been progressive revelation; one follows the other. The old patriarchs certainly knew God, but the revelation was often veiled and not as clear as that which came later through Moses and the prophets (cf. Exod 6:3). The clarity of revelation shines in the Christ who has manifested himself to us "for the last time."[33] "Therefore," Luther admits, "this is the last one."[34] The gospel was "most perfectly" revealed in Christ, with no more following.[35]

Peter's epistle, like Paul's, covers the entire soteriological descent (incarnation, suffering, burial, resurrection) and ascent (ascension) for us in which we participate by the Holy Spirit. The person of Christ and the work of Christ correspond to each other. Christ and his saving activities mutually coinhere. Nagel contends, "Who he is [person] and what he does [work] are all together in his being born, living, doing, suffering, dying, rising and saving."[36] These verbs sum up the entire story of salvation, but in "a differentiated unity." The Incarnation, Calvary, Easter, and Ascension are of one piece. In Nagel's formulation: "No one of these may be played off against the other. His achieving salvation for man is whole and complete."[37] The redemptive work of Christ establishes for believers "a covenant with God and a sure promise."[38] "The children of wrath" (Eph 2:3) cannot approach God "on their own initiative" or "without employing means."[39] We have no access to God because of Adam's sin. The inaccessibility of God is abolished by the mediation of Christ. This was taught in Romans 5:2, "through [Christ] we have obtained access to God in faith." Luther stresses, "Therefore we must bring Christ, come with Him, pay God with Him, and carry out all our dealings with God through Him."[40] Christ has acquired "for us" all his benefits, not for God and himself, as they have no need of this—as Peter declares, "for your sake. Through Him you have confidence in God, who raised Him from the dead and gave Him glory, so that your faith and hope are in God" (1 Pet 1:21). Through Christ, the one Mediator, who intercedes for us, we ascend to the Father and possess all his blessings. We acquire "the friendship of God,"[41] says Luther, not through the premise of Gabriel Biel, "accomplishing that which is in one," but through "prevenient grace."[42] Out of pure mercy, God called Abraham "My Friend" (Isa 41:8)—"the loftiest and most agreeable consolation."[43] People cannot naturally befriend or love God above all else unless first transformed by grace. Thesis 21 of Luther's *Disputation against Scholastic Theology* (1517) states, "No act is done according to nature that is not an act of concupiscence against God."[44] Zechariah 1:3, "Return to me, . . . and I will return to you," disproves free will, viewing humanity's turning to God as the cause of God's turning toward humanity. "Return to me" is the language of the law that demands that we turn to God, which we cannot do by ourselves. Luther avers, "The law merely gives a command, but nothing is accomplished; something is accomplished, however, through the gospel, when the Spirit is added."[45] In Christ, believers do not feel the condemnation of the law, nor do they feel the dread of the wrath of God. God is not opposed to believers: "No longer does God drive and smite us. No, He deals with us in the friendliest manner possible and renews us."[46] These enemies—"Law, sin, wrath, and death"—no longer abide, and in their stead are these inheritances: "righteousness, joy, life, and a filial confidence in the Father, who is now placated, gracious, and reconciled."[47] These heavenly blessings of God are predicated upon "a completely new birth and a new existence" issued by the regenerative power of God's word.[48] All of this is not due to works but solely because of God's "sheer mercy."[49] Therefore, we can speak boldly of God as our Father and boast proudly of our "great distinction" as children of God.[50]

Faith does not possess any intrinsic worth except for the object it clings to. Luther writes, "Thus we have faith in God and through that faith also a hope. Faith alone has to save us. But there must be a faith in God. For if God does not help, you have no help at all."[51] The "living hope" (1 Pet 1:3) into which we have been reborn is wrought by faith's object, Christ, and what he has come to do for our sake. Faith lays hold of Christ's efficacious activities in his death, resurrection, and ascension, through which "we have obtained access to God" (Rom 5:2). Luther avers, "We owe all this to Christ's resurrection from the dead, to His ascension into heaven, and to the fact that He sits at the right hand of God. For He ascended into heaven to bestow His Spirit on us, to give us a new birth, and to give us the courage to come to the Father."[52] To preach aright is not to preach about our works but to preach "only"[53] the resurrection of Christ (which of course includes his death as well); otherwise, he is no apostle. This is something lacking in the Epistle of James, and Luther thus rejects its apostolicity. Luther writes, "[This epistle] does not once mention the Passion, the resurrection, or the Spirit of Christ. . . . Whatever does not teach Christ is not yet apostolic, even though St. Peter or St. Paul does the teaching. Again, whatever preaches Christ would be apostolic, even if Judas, Annas, Pilate, and Herod were doing it."[54] "The greatest power of faith" is bound up with the resurrection of Christ, which Luther regards as the "chief article" of faith.[55] Resurrection renders effectual the cross, that Christ buried our sins for which he died but bestows his righteousness on us by his resurrection. "Just as Christ by his death takes our unrighteousness upon himself," Zachman intimates, "so by his rising he bestows his righteousness upon us."[56] The two events—cross and resurrection—comprise a single meaning: a celebration of victory over the contraries of sin, death, and the devil. Commenting on Romans 4:25, "He died for our sins and rose for our justification," Luther writes, "[Christ's] victory is a victory over law, sin, our flesh, the world, the devil, death, hell, and all evils; and this victory of his he has given to us."[57] Without it, all hope vanishes; all that Christ did and suffered would be of no benefit to us (1 Cor 15:17).

Christ's ascension (1 Pet 3:22) is not only his coronation, that he is lord over all creatures and all powers, but also ours, that we become lords over them as well. All this is written for our comfort so we know that all powers and authorities in heaven and on earth, even death and the devil, are reduced to naught. They are under our dominion, just as they are under Christ's. "They must serve and aid us, just as everything must serve the Lord Jesus Christ and lie at His feet."[58] Christ's ascension does not mean he resides at the Father's right hand, Luther writes, "with nothing to do and . . . enjoying himself."[59] His ascension at God's right hand does not mean inactivity or impassivity but his continual intercession for us before the Father. We enter the heavenly sanctuary, not relying on our own strength but on Jesus Christ and all that he has acquired for us. Webster puts it aptly: "And his priestly work is not fragile, vulnerable, a hesitant attempt to persuade God to forgive. It's utterly authoritative, utterly effective, utterly reliable, because it's the intercession of the Son of God himself, whose saving work is finished; whose sacrifice for us has been offered and accepted; and who is now empowered to act as the advocate for sinners."[60] The ascended Christ continues to serve as our vicarious representative through whom we can freely approach God's throne and boldly possess all the inheritance of God. Such inestimable treasure is made known to our hearts by the Holy Spirit whom Christ sends, causing us to ascend through Christ's mediation to God and say, "'Behold, I come before you and pray, not in reliance on my petition, but my Lord Christ represents me and is my Intercessor.'"[61] These are "words of fire," if we believe it, declares Luther; "otherwise everything is cold and does not go to the heart."[62]

Impassive "Existing for Himself"; Immanent "Belonging to Us"

The endearing character of God is disclosed; as Luther avers, "The Lord Christ should not be isolated as existing for himself but should be preached as belonging to us."[63] We are to occupy ourselves, not with the hidden God in his majesty but with the revealed God "preached as belonging to us." We are to hold fast to the word St. Peter proclaimed; in Kolb's words, "This hidden God comes out of hiding as the God Revealed so that he can continue the conversation he began at creation, but he approached humankind in the strangest of places—in crib and cross and crypt. As a baby, a criminal, a corpse, God seeks to engage sinners in a tête-à-tête once again, Luther read in Scripture."[64] Faith grasps God not as he exists in himself, which is terrifying, but as he exists for us, which is precious. For God does not exist for himself, dwelling in his self-contained and transcendent aloofness; he exists for us, giving himself and all his precious belongings to us. The same accent occurs in Luther's *Meditation on Christ's Passion* (1519), where he asks, "Of what help is it to you that God is God, if he is not God to you?"[65] Likewise, of what benefit is it to us if he is "precious and good in himself,"[66] an assertion that does not help us, unless he is "precious to us"? His preciousness lies in the free bestowal of his boundless goodness without remainder, "like a precious gem which does not keep its power to itself but breaks forth and radiates all its power so that I have everything it is."[67] His belonging to us as our heavenly Father, whom we invoke through Christ, is the basis of our belonging to him who grants us "the great distinction" of being his beloved.[68] In his sermon on John 6:57, Luther uses the analogy of cake to speak of the union of divinity and humanity in Christ.[69] Here in his sermon on 1 Peter 2:12, the same analogy is used to speak of the believers' relation to Christ. Believers are, he writes, "one with Christ and wholly one cake"[70] so that what is Christ's is ours. God must be "preached as belonging to us" in Christ, through whom we may belong to him; Christ descends to our flesh and we ascend to the Father through him—"in his skin," Luther writes, "and on his back."[71] Neither human preparations nor penitential piety produces the justified self; only Christ and God's eternal goods (righteousness, life, and heaven) can do this. The new identity participates in Christ's righteousness, life, and heaven, and overrides sin, death, and hell, which are of the old identity. The new identity thus is a gift of grace, not a human achievement; it is wrought by Christ's redemption. That "I may belong to him" is the teleological principle of God's justifying action, the point of the second article of faith in the Creed. Luther writes:

> Christ has redeemed me, a lost and condemned human being. He has purchased and freed me from all sins, from death, and

from the power of the devil, not with gold or silver but with his holy, precious blood and with his innocent suffering and death. He has done all this in order that *I may belong to him*, live under him in his kingdom, and serve him in eternal righteousness, innocence, and blessedness, just as he is risen from the dead and lives eternally.[72]

Not until God is ours through Christ could we ever "be his."[73] The mediation of Christ is the initiatory basis of God's belonging to us and our responsive belonging to him. God's "downward movement" to us in grace is the cause of our "upward movement" to him by faith.[74] As Hamm elaborates, "A person does not ascend to God on high on the rungs of his powers of knowledge and love but is snatched out of misery by God's word. All our life, this upward movement of faith remains connected to the downward movement of Christ to us in his word."[75] God seizes us in Christ, through whom we seize him in return. Luther exults in the simple expression "he who believes," conceding to faith the instrumental efficacy to make a person, who in himself is unworthy, a worthy recipient of forgiveness. Unbelievers experience the contrary of grace, that Christ is no consolation to them but rather is damnation. Therefore, to unbelief, Christ is offensive, even though Christ in himself is a consoling agent. However, to faith, God is "precious"; as Peter says, "To you therefore who believe, He is precious" (1 Pet 2:7).

God wills to be divinely good and belong to people and is in no way determined by the attitude of those on whom he gladly bestows his goodness. Luther avers, "Therefore He proves that he is good by nature, and that His goodness does not stand or fall by the vice or virtue of another, as human goodness" is often conditioned by the responses of another.[76] It is God's glory to gladly waste his precious goods on the thankless, without demanding anything from them in return. As part of the explanation of the first commandment ("I am the Lord your

God"), Luther declares, "It is God's most earnest purpose to be our God."[77] In other words, "God's most earnest purpose" is to belong to us and share with us all his abundance, regardless of how we feel toward him. Steinmetz warns against confusing "the ancient Greek understanding of love as *eros*, which desires an object because that object has value in itself, with the biblical understanding of love as *agape*, which confers value on the otherwise valueless objects of its affections."[78] While human goodness is dependent on the virtue of another, God's goodness is irrespective of any external factors. Human belonging is often conditioned by the good it might gain from others. Such perspective fosters self-preoccupation, an instantiation of sin. Divine belonging is unconditional; in Luther's words, it "turns in the direction where it does not find good which it may enjoy, but where it may confer good upon the bad and needy."[79] The unconditional, and prior, love of God is ardently expressed in the language of betrothal, in which "the groom gives his bride not gift, but himself, the deepest love of his heart and all his property. He goes ahead of his bride; he seeks her out."[80] Paulson eloquently explains that the gift that God gives is "no less than his own self." He expands:

> God does not operate simply as a great "Cause" with many little effects. The post office also gives, but what it gives is this or that letter or package, not itself. What God gives is not merely various gifts, as if these expressed some affection, or stood as signs of his care as in a birthday card. God gives not just "things," or "effects," but his own self. . . . When God gives, he gives sacramentally, not figuratively; he does not give signs of his affection, he gives—Him.[81]

The uncaused character of God's belonging to us flows from the being of God, says Luther, "who is precious and good in himself."[82] The highest manifestation of God's belonging to us is the gift of himself; it is the apostolic proclamation of God's self-sacrifice in his Son, a priestly act that appeases God's wrath and effects our reconciliation to God. Christ's once-for-all sacrifice shields us from the dread of God's wrath and covers us with the consolation of God's mercy. Luther exclaims, "Oh what an inestimable blessing has been given to us through Christ! It enables us to step before the Father and to demand the inheritance."[83] The significance of the person of Christ is hidden in the atoning act Christ came to do. Hearts that grasp the "for us" aspects of Christ's person rejoice; otherwise, Christ and his goods do not benefit us, even though he remains precious in himself.

Victory over Hell and the Devil's Power: Preaching to the Spirits in Prison

Luther regards 1 Peter 3:18, which speaks of Christ's preaching to "the spirits in prison"—namely, the unbelieving souls from the time of Noah's ark—as a "strange" and "obscure" text. Peter's words might be construed as supporting a postmortem encounter with Jesus Christ, a view at least Luther seems to be leaving behind at this point.[84] Luther suggests the contrary view, that after Christ's ascension, "he came in the spirit and preached, yet in such a way that His preaching was not physical," for the resurrected Christ no longer acts according to the natural senses of the body. The text, says Luther, did not indicate a physical descent to the souls to whom he preached when he died. He finds support of this in the phrase in 1 Peter 3:20, "in which," which accentuates the "new existence" Christ assumed via resurrection and ascension. Luther expands, "He entered into a spiritual existence and life such as He now has in heaven. Then He went and preached. Now He did not descend again into hell after He had assumed such a new existence. Therefore one must understand these words to mean that He did this after His resurrection."[85] So the preaching of which

Peter spoke is "spiritual," one that corresponds to the new life Christ now lives.[86] The preaching communicates "inwardly in the heart and in the soul, so that it is not necessary for Him to go with the body and preach orally."[87]

The meaning of phrase "to the spirits in prison, who formerly did not believe" is linked to the concept of time. Time understood by us is not applicable to a being like God, says Luther, "for before God everything takes place in one moment."[88] For God, "a thousand years are as one day," as St. Peter teaches in 2 Peter 3:8 (cf. Ps 90:4). Luther elaborates, "In the existence in which Christ is, those who lived in the past and those who are living today are alike before Him. For His rule extends over both the dead and the living. And in that life the beginning, the middle, and the end of the world are all in one lump."[89] Yet this is not so in creaturely existence, where time is calculated linearly. Such measurement of time is restricted or distorted; it cannot capture the whole picture of a thing under scrutiny. Suppose we are analyzing a piece of wood, Luther illustrates. We cannot grasp the full measure of it unless it lies within the reach of our vision, or our vision is "crosswise," viewing it from the top.[90] The "lengthwise"[91] vision cannot encompass this life, as this unfolds sequentially until the Last Day. Before God's crosswise vision, everybody is alike, irrespective of whether it is the first human being to be born or the last one. For God sees everything at once, like a human eye that can see two separate objects at once. Preaching was addressed not to "all spirits," Peter stresses, but to "those who formerly did not believe." This is to be understood figuratively, according to what is called "synecdoche, *ex parte totum* ['the whole from a part']," in which a part represents the whole.[92] Preaching applies not to those who formerly disobeyed but to those who are like them, to those who are similarly disobedient. Luther concludes, "Thus one must look from this life into that life."[93] Despite the obscurity, Luther acknowledges, it is safer not to affirm Christ's physical descent into hell, where he preached to dead souls, but to emphasize that Christ's presence is spiritually felt through the preached word. His ascension is not to be taken as inactivity or aloofness from us. Instead, "Christ ascended into heaven and preached to the spirits, that is, to human souls, and among them there were unbelievers in the days of Noah."[94] Christ's spiritual preaching occurs through the physical office that he administers. Christ invested his power in the apostles so that they could preach the gospel orally and physically to the spirits who are held bound to the devil's prison. God hides in the preacher, the created form that the word assumes, and through which his presence is mediated.

Of 1 Peter 4:6, "For this is why the Gospel was preached even to the dead, that though judged in the flesh like men, they might live in the spirit like God," Luther acknowledges this is "another strange text." Yet "flesh" refers to the "whole" person as they live their natural life; "spirit" means the "whole" person as they live their spiritual life.[95] The word "dead" speaks not of the dead but of the living—that is, of the unbelievers, Peter qualifies, who are "judged in the flesh" but made "alive according to the spirit."[96] Luther provides his own interpretation of the strange phrase "preaching to the dead," saying that the gospel message "was unconcealed neither from the living nor from the dead, neither from the angels nor from the devils, and that it was not preached secretly in the corner but was proclaimed so publicly that all creatures, if they had ears to hear, could have heard it, as Christ commanded in Mark 16:16: 'Go into the world and preach the Gospel to the whole creation!'"[97] The gospel proclaimed through its minister reaches those who are "judged in the flesh like men" but "live in the spirit like God" (1 Pet 4:6).

Luther's 1533 sermon on the article "Jesus's Descent into Hell" lays stress on the victory Christ has won "for us." Luther affirms with the Creed that "Christ, God and man in one person, descended into hell" to combat the devil, something the world cannot do.[98] Luther writes, "Hell has been torn apart through Christ and the devil's realm and power has been entirely destroyed. For this purpose He died, was buried, and descended, so that they would no longer harm or conquer us, as He Himself says in Mathew 16:18."[99] The creedal article on Christ's ascension cannot be grasped by reason but by faith; likewise, faith, not reason, grasps this article on his descent. Luther advises against speculating "further how it happened or how it is possible" and instead laying hold of the word, which delivers "its true essence," that is, Christ's triumph over all destructive powers of hell and the devil.[100] The *Formula of Concord* exhorts us, like Luther, to "only hold to the Word" from which we derive comfort that neither hell nor the devil can sever us from faith in Christ.[101] As part of the explanation of the second article of faith in his Creed, Luther sums up the whole narrative of redemption Christ has accomplished: his cross, burial, resurrection, ascension, and ultimate triumph over the devil and his forces.

> Christ suffered, died, and was buried so that he might make satisfaction for me and pay what I owed, not with silver and gold but with his own precious blood. . . . Afterward he rose again from the dead, swallowed up and devoured death, and finally ascended into heaven and assumed dominion at the right hand of the Father. The devil and all his powers must be subject to him and lie beneath his feet until finally, at the Last Day, he will completely divide and separate us from the wicked world, the devil, death, etc.[102]

Likewise, in his exposition of 1 Peter 3:20–23, Luther includes as the substances of faith Christ's death, his descent into hell, his resurrection from the dead, and his ascension to God's right hand, where he reigns over all powers and we reign with him.[103] The benefits Christ has accomplished are conveyed through baptism, "a covenant of a good conscience with God" (1 Pet

3:21). By way of analogy, baptism "corresponds" to the ark; it saves us, just as the ark saved Noah. Just as "water . . . drowned everything that had life," so, too, Luther explains, "baptism drowns everything that is carnal and natural; it makes spiritual men."[104] Not by our works but by faith in God's promise attached to baptism, as to Noah's ark, are we saved.

Christ as Our Example: The Vocation of the Cross

In his *Meditation on Christ's Passion*, Luther teaches that whoever is seized by the knowledge of God's "friendly heart" that the cross mirrors must adopt Christ's passion as "the pattern" for his whole life.[105] Of this, Lienhard writes, "Christ can only be an example for human beings on the condition that he is, also and above all, sacramental, i.e., that his death is to be realized in me and I am to die with him before I can imitate him."[106] The distinction between Christ as sacrament and Christ as model corresponds to the distinction between the passive righteousness we receive and the active righteousness we perform. Just as we passively receive his righteousness by faith before we actively perform works by love, so, too, do we passively receive Christ as gift by faith before actively following Christ as example by love. Christ's exemplary suffering exists not as a meritorious action imposed upon the believer but as the distinctive mark of his "cruciform" existence. As Forde writes, "God makes himself 'vulnerable' in Jesus, so we ought to too. Misery loves company."[107]

Christ's death is not for himself but for us, that he might become our redeemer. But Peter also speaks of another aspect, "that he might offer us to God" (1 Pet 3:18), so we might bear the cross in following Christ as our example. Christ and his followers are one; by the very act of his self-sacrifice, says Luther, Christ takes us with him and offers us to God.

[Thus] it is necessary for all those who believe in Him to suffer too and to be put to death according to the flesh, as happened in His case. In this way He presented us to God as living in the spirit yet dying in the flesh, as St. Peter says later (cf. 1 Pet. 4:6). On the other hand, we are one sacrifice with Him. As he dies, so we, too, die according to the flesh; as He lives in the spirit, so we, too, live in the spirit.[108]

Just as Christ suffers in his whole person, so also do his followers. However, Luther draws a sharp distinction between Christ's passion and the Christian's bodily suffering. Rittgers writes aptly:

Christ bears the believer's suffering, but the believer does not bear Christ's physical tribulations. The Christian can suffer in the body for Christ but not with Christ, because the Savior's suffering is viewed as unique and as belonging to him alone. Christ suffers in and with the Christian, but the Christian does not suffer in and with (and certainly not for) Christ; the divine-human relationship of suffering is seen as unidirectional.[109]

The cross the Father imposed upon his Son is exclusively the Son's, which secures heaven for us. To meditate on Christ's passion aright, for Luther, is not to be aroused with "sympathy for Christ but terror at one's own sins," which occasions Christ's redemptive suffering.[110] In his sermon on John 19:16–17, Luther makes it clear that the cross Jesus bore was his own, just as Paul's cross was his own, as he said in 2 Corinthians 12:7, "A stake was given me in the flesh, a messenger of Satan to beat me with his fists, to keep me from being too elated." The word "stake" means "cross"[111] that he alone had to carry. Some of the fathers[112] suggest that Christ became so exhausted under the burden of the cross that he could not continue his cross-bearing, which is why Simon of Cyrene took over and completed it for Christ. As an example, Luther cites Ludolph of

Saxony, who wrote, "We should bear the Lord's cross and help Him to carry it: namely, in our hearts, through memory and compassion; with our mouths, through frequent and devout thanksgiving; in our bodies, through flagellation and mortification, so that we may give thanks to our Savior with heart, mouth, and works."[113] With Augustine, Luther avows that Simon did not help Jesus and complete what is lacking in his cross-bearing but rather they "laid the cross on Simon, to carry it after Jesus" (Luke 23:36).[114]

Just as Christ was not exempted from his cross, so was Simon not so exempted. In his exposition of 1 Peter 4:13, "But rejoice insofar as you share Christ's sufferings," Luther avers that St. Peter disavowed that we should "feel Christ's sufferings in order to share them through faith."[115] Rather, the apostle said that Christ suffered, and we, too, suffer and undergo a "glowing fire"[116] because of "communion with God. For if we want to live with Him, we must also die with Him. If I want to sit with Him in His kingdom, I must also suffer with Him, as St. Paul often says (Rom. 6:5; 2 Tim. 1:11)."[117] The "only reason" for our cross-bearing, Luther counsels, is for us to "steadfastly adhere to Christ and God's Word."[118] The cross his disciples endure is theirs, not a means of meriting grace but a means of conformity to the image of Christ. Deficiency lies not in Christ as sacrament, which for Luther is thoroughly perfect and completely efficacious. What is deficient is the imitation of Christ as model, the other aspect of the pair; in Rittgers's words, "There is much left for Christians to suffer as they seek to become more perfect imitators of Christ and as they seek to put to death the old Adam who resides within them."[119] Rittgers's rendering fleshes out the meaning of Colossians 1:24: "Now I rejoice in my sufferings for your sake and in my flesh I complete what is lacking in Christ's sufferings [Christ as model] for the sake of his body, that is, the church." Christ's exemplary suffering is laid on all believers, that they are not exempted from suffering and the crucifixion of the flesh. Just as all blessings of Christ—"faith, the name, the Word, the work of Christ"—are accrued to us by virtue of faith in Christ, so, too, Christ's exemplary sufferings are ours by faith, as we bear our cross for his sake.[120] According to Christ as example, Luther reasons, "Christ's sufferings are fulfilled in the Christians every day until the end of time."[121] The suffering God makes "precious"[122] flows from faith in Christ as sacrament, which makes us worthy of cross-bearing. Luther declares, "I must believe in His cross; but I must bear my own cross. I must put His suffering into my heart. Then I have the true treasure. St. Peter's bones are sacred. But what does that help you? You and your own bones must become sacred. And this happens when you suffer for Christ."[123] Believers must first be equipped with Christ's benefits and acted upon by Christ before they can really assume the cross for Christ's sake; in Rittgers's formulation, "Christians must first receive Christ's passion as a means of grace before they can regard it as a model to imitate. Christians cannot suffer with Christ before they have embraced the full benefits of Christ's suffering for them; they cannot act like Christ until Christ has acted upon (and in) them."[124] Furthermore, God greatly rewards suffering that does not stem from evils and vices we commit but simply because we "want to have none but Christ, and no other God."[125] Luther quotes here Matthew 5:11–12: "Blessed are you when men revile you and utter all kinds of evil against you on my account. Rejoice and be glad, for your reward is great in heaven."[126] In cross-bearing for Christ's sake, Christians derive comfort from the knowledge that our sufferings are "in common with Christ and that He regards all our sufferings as His own."[127] Christ binds himself to the sufferers, assuring them that he knows their pain firsthand, and that joy follows pain.[128] Righteous sufferers are never out of God's protection and comfort.[129] We rejoice in physical suffering in light of the future, eternal joy awaiting us. We will be exalted as "lords" over all enemies, just as Christ is, "when His glory is revealed" (1 Pet 4:13) on the Last Day.[130] "The Spirit of glory and of God" will glorify us, just as he glorified Christ (1 Pet 4:14).[131]

A Christian's life has two facets viewed from different perspectives: "A Christian lives not in himself, but in Christ and in his neighbour. . . . He lives in Christ through faith, in his neighbour through love."[132] The former defines our righteous identity, a gift of the "faith alone" that justifies; the latter describes our righteous deeds, the fruits of the "faith alone" that justifies.[133] Kolb and Arand express it in this way: "The passive righteousness of faith provides the core identity of a person; the active righteousness of love flows from that core identity into the world."[134] The gift of "the passive righteousness of faith" must be exercised in "the active righteousness of love," or else we indulge in sin. The distinction between Christ's passive righteousness and our active righteousness corresponds to that between Christ's "alien righteousness" and our "proper righteousness."[135] Both correspond to the pair of Christ as sacrament and Christ as example, the former grounding the latter. As 1 Peter 2:21 bears out, "our proper righteousness," which we work with Christ's "first and alien righteousness," says Luther, "follows the example of Christ," the other aspect of the pair. Luther expands:

> This proper righteousness goes on to complete the first for it ever strives to do away with the old Adam and to destroy the body of sin. Therefore it hates itself and loves its neighbor; it does not seek its own good, but that of another, and in this its whole way of living consists. For in that it hates itself and does not seek its own, it crucifies the flesh. Because it seeks the good of another, it works love. Thus in each sphere it does God's will, living soberly with self, justly with neighbor, devoutly toward God.[136]

The phrase "this proper righteousness goes on to complete the first" does not mean that Christ's alien righteousness is incomplete and needs our proper righteousness to complete it. Christ's alien righteousness is, Luther writes, "an infinite righteousness" that "swallows up all sins in a moment" so that sin no longer rests on Christ. Consequently, whoever is united to Christ has "the same righteousness as he" so that sin no longer remains in them. "This righteousness is primary; it is the basis, the cause, the source of all our own righteousness"; it is "given in place of the original righteousness lost in Adam."[137] To "complete the first" thus means to exercise our works or the exemplary actions of imitating Christ, therefore completing what is lacking in the Christian life, not what is lacking in Christ's alien righteousness. Just as the pair of Christ as sacrament and Christ as example belong together, so do the pair of Christ's alien righteousness and our proper righteousness. Just as law and gospel must be preached, so, too, must Christ as gift and Christ as example be preached. In his Galatians commentary, Luther speaks of the "proper time" in which preaching Christ as gift and Christ as example should be done, to reap its proper fruit.[138] Christ as gift must be proclaimed so that the troubled conscience finds healing in the gospel. However, Christ as example must be held up so that haughty hearts may be brought to repentance through the law. This, too, prevents the abuse of freedom we obtain through Christ.

The theology of the cross should not be converted into a discursive discipline that often leaves our hearts unmoved. It "can never be a brilliant statement about life's brokenness," Hall notes, "because it participates in what it seeks to describe. Apart from participation, it is empty chatter."[139] The cross is not a theory but an event, a causative kind, in which we feel the power of and are moved by the apostolic language of self-sacrifice to participate in his cause. The more the pious recognize Christ as the Savior who blesses them with his precious goods, the more they are impelled to love their neighbors with the same favor with which they are blessed. The cross enables us to participate in the prophetic pattern of cross-bearing and subsequent glory; as Luther stresses, "Those who thus make Christ's life and name a part of their own lives are true Christians."[140] Despite being completely pure and without sin, nonetheless Christ subjected himself to the verdict of God's judgment and died the death of God-forsakenness under the law to blot out our sins and bestow on us his righteousness. Christ did all this "for us," before which we could do nothing except be caught in awe and moved to action: "Ah, should I then not also suffer something because it pleases Him? Now he who contemplates this would surely have to be a stone if it did not move him. For if the master takes the lead and steps into the mire, it stands to reason that the servant will follow."[141] We meditate on the cross, not so that we can shun it but to suffer it. The suffering of Christ becomes the image of those who belong to Christ because "Christ's passion must be met not with words or forms but with life and truth."[142] The proper meditation on Christ's sufferings is not an abstract intellectual exercise, completely devoid of any emotional engagement with Christ's passion; rather it arouses in us a feeling of the effect of our sins on Christ, as he suffered God's wrath for us. Luther cites Bernard of Clairvaux as one who felt the negative but salutary effect of the law the cross has on him: "St. Bernard was so terrified by this that he declared, 'I regarded myself secure; I was not aware of the eternal sentence that had been passed on me in heaven until I saw that God's only Son had compassion upon me and offered to bear this sentence for me.'"[143] Tomlin writes, "The process [of meditation] is to lead not to mystical union with Christ, but to a proper imitation in the sense of the shared experience of *Anfechtung*."[144] Such assessment finds approval in Luther, who writes, "For since the Lord steps to the front in the fray, how much more should His servants rejoice to step forward."[145] Pondering this emboldens us to "prevail and to arm ourselves in our thoughts, in order that we might go through with joy" (1 Pet 4:1). The shape and reality of a life lived by a "truly Christ-formed"[146] person is marked by suffering rather than glory, weakness rather than power, external contradiction rather than internal satisfaction. Yet he suffers, not as a supplementation of what is lacking in Christ's redemption but as an implementation of Christ as our example, which is lacking in the Christian life. As Luther affirms, "For when we have put on Christ, the garment of our righteousness and salvation, then we also put on Christ, the garment of imitation."[147]

Christ as gift and Christ as example are one. The latter emanates from the former, just as works of love flow from an effective faith. This is intrinsically linked to what Luther teaches in thesis 27 of his *Heidelberg Disputation*: "Actually one should call the work of God an acting work and our work an accomplished work, and thus an accomplished work pleasing to God by the grace of the acting work."[148] Jesus Christ is an active agent, that is, to use Forde's phrase, "the operative power" behind all virtues.[149] Believers are passive recipients, who work nothing but simply allow God's work to be done in them. The "Christ who lives in us" has satisfied all the demands of God and so arouses us to works "through that living faith in his work." We live by "his action" in us and are "moved" to works.[150] "Deeds of mercy are aroused by the works through which he has saved us."[151] The language here is not of the law, which demands us to work, but of the gospel, which draws us to works, as a bride is drawn to her groom. "It is," Luther describes, "exceedingly attractive."[152] Commenting on Song of Solomon 1:4, "Draw me after you, let us make haste," Luther stresses the prior action of God as the dynamism and sustenance of all human actions. Unless the Spirit draws us, Luther explains, we will not be "glad to perform" our vocations; unless the Spirit inspires, "no one will accomplish anything, no matter how great his zeal and care."[153] Just as faith in Christ is "the impulse" of the works of love,[154] so, too, Christ as sacrament is "a stimulant" to our imitation of Christ as example. We are so acted upon by the operating power of Christ's saving work that we cannot remain idle but are motivated to be "imitators of God"; in Luther's own words:

> Since Christ lives in us through faith, so He arouses us to do good works through the living faith in His work, for the works which He does are the fulfilment of the commands of God given us through faith. If we look at them we are moved to imitate them. For this reason the Apostle says, "Therefore be imitators of God, as beloved children" (Eph. 5:1). Thus deeds of mercy are aroused by the works through which He has saved us, as St. Gregory says: "Every act of Christ is instruction for us, a stimulant." If his action is in us it lives through faith, for it is exceedingly attractive according to this verse, "Draw me after you, let us make haste" (Song of Sol. 1:4) toward the fragrance "of your anointing oils" (Song of Sol. 1:3), that is, "your works."[155]

Everything that is creaturely and worldly in us must die so that we live and act not out of our own natural ability but out of the causative power of God's love revealed in the cross. As Luther teaches in thesis 28 of his *Heidelberg Disputation*, "The love of God does not find, but creates, that which is pleasing to it."[156] God's love "creates" not only a saint out of a sinner but also forms in us a cross-shaped love,[157] characterized by giving and bestowing good upon the unlovable and unworthy, the complete opposite of a love "which seeks that which is pleasing to it."[158] These self-giving actions flow forth passively from Christ as "the accomplished work"; they are contingent upon "the grace of the acting work" of Christ. The exemplary works we do are secondary and pleasing to God because of the priority and primacy of Christ's expiatory work.

CHAPTER 4

The Word of Bestowal in Marriage
True Adornment and Household Holiness

The affirmation of creaturely things looms large when Luther attaches holiness to household order and its obligations. Price captures this well: "This spiritual connection to the earthly is most clearly seen in the roles of household management and parenthood in the *oeconomia*."[1] The word "oeconomia," used by Aristotle, Luther notes, refers to the "household economy," which encompasses the nuclear family and those who live in it, as well as their economic activities.[2] Like the other orders, marriage is viewed as a vocation, not to be entered flippantly but solemnly as an obedience befitting God's command. Luther uses 1 Peter 3:1–7 to instruct what constitutes true adornment as husbands and wives practice the cross-shaped vocation according to God's order.[3] Peter cites Sarah as the model to whom all women could aspire for godliness. To borrow Bayer's phrase, "the word of bestowal"[4] in marriage is an effective inducement for a couple to persevere in loving and serving despite the miseries that confront them. "The blessings of a promise, faith, and of a gift," Luther augments, are "more than mere wishes; they are indicatives and performatives; they actually bestow and bring about what the words say."[5] Sarah's barrenness is an instance of God's justifying work on account of the effectual nature of God's promise. Just as our identity is both saint and sinner at once, so also our condition in the household is marked by the "coincidental opposites" of "inner, spiritual delight" and "outward bitterness."[6] Marriage is a place where the tension between flesh and spirit, two irreconcilable opposites, is acute and abides until it lays hold of the promise that inheres in God's word. The old creature must suffer crucifixion through the word in order that the newness of life and power might reign in a home. The "truly Christ-formed"[7] person despairs of themselves and all inner resources; they do not look to rely on anything within or on any other creaturely means but "always has his face directed straight toward God and confidently awaits His coming and His help, no matter how it may be delayed."[8] Faith clings to the annihilating power of the Spirit's "outcry"[9] by which the "loud outcry"[10] of despair is replaced by hope, and fear by joy. And we will exult, as does Luther, that "this person is truly born anew in God."[11]

True Adornments: External vs. Internal

True adornment consists not in external decorations but in "the hidden person of the heart," where an unfading beauty of "a gentle and quiet spirit" dwells rather than the fleeting beauty of "outward adorning with braiding of hair, decoration of gold, and wearing of robes" (1 Pet 3:3–4). As examples of holy women, Luther cites Esther and Judith, who were outwardly adorned with precious ornaments (Esth 2:12, 17; Jth 10:3–4). However, Scripture also indicates that they did not choose adornment; they were forced to do so (Esth 14:16).[12] Neither is external adornment commanded nor forbidden. Luther cautions against pursuing it, lest women become obsessed with its endless acquisition; as Luther notes, "This is the way they are by nature."[13] Women should avoid external adornment except when it pleases the husband or other legitimate reasons require it. Should she wear ornaments to please her husband, her adornment is proper and is done "in the spirit."[14] Where "faith and spirit" are present, says Luther, wives will be inclined to adorn "the hidden person" with God's blessings. They pay no regard to external bearing, and confess, as Queen Esther did in Esther 14:16, "Thou knowest my necessity—that I abhor the sign of my proud position, which is upon my head on the days when I appear in public. I abhor it like a menstruous rag, and I do not wear it on the days when I am at leisure."[15] A godly woman adorns her faith with Christ's possessions; she is crucified to worldly adornments and recognition. For what appears magnificent before the world, such as silver and gold, is stench to her before God. Luther defines what true adornment is: "But that woman who is attired well and gloriously before God who goes her way in a gentle and quiet spirit."[16] Through faith, she, like all Christians, is adorned with Christ's possessions in extravagance. "This is a great and precious treasure and an adornment such as no one can praise sufficiently. God Himself regards it highly."[17] Instead of feeding their hearts with creaturely, fleeting adornments, women should occupy themselves with "the hidden treasure and precious ornament imperishably" in their hearts.[18] The soul that is decorated with an infinite treasure hidden in Christ is glorious before God and no longer in want.[19]

Luther instructs wives to cultivate "reverent and chaste behavior" (1 Pet 3:2) by which unbelieving husbands are persuaded of the Christian estate and won to Christ. Through the virtues of Augustine's mother Monica, Luther notes, her heathen husband and her wayward son were converted to Christ.[20] Obedience is external and does not produce Christian righteousness. Even so, wives must submit to their husbands because it is a holy order, sanctified by God in Genesis 3:16: "Your desire shall be for your husband and he shall rule over you." The Christian wife should consider God's ordained order, irrespective of the kind of husband she has. She should reckon with God's will that she be placed in the state of matrimony, and that her submission to her husband is a God-pleasing work;

"a high and noble treasure" she has.[21] She must be induced by such great treasure that she considers no greater joy than to obey her husband. "If she renders such obedience," Luther exults, "then all her works are golden."[22] Where God's word is attached, that work is "most beautiful and holy," even if it appears "disgraceful and shameful" before others, "for there is no greater and better adornment than the Word of God."[23] God takes with utter seriousness this command that he permitted husbands to annul the vows of their wives for their lack of obedience to God's design (Num 30:8). This is done for the sake of peace and harmony in the household.[24]

Sarah, Holy Matriarch: Honor Each Other as God's Vessels

To inspire women to lead a life of purity and reverence, Peter hails Sarah as an example of a saintly woman. Wives ought to submit to their husbands, "as Sarah obeyed Abraham, calling him *Lord*," a phrase that also occurs in Ephesians 5:22.[25] Luther shows regard for women and encourages them to stand firm as did Sarah, whom he singles out in his *Small Catechism*, Wengert observes, as a matriarch to emulate.[26] Sarah dignifies Abraham and calls him "Lord, not man or husband" (1 Pet 3:6).[27] Peter wanted these words to be "a mirror" through which all godly women learn to "hope in God" (1 Pet 3:5) and "respect" their husbands, Sarah's two distinctive characteristics.[28] Though Moses did not explicitly mention hope, Luther intimates, hope loomed high in Sarah's entire lot, considering the complex entailments of Abraham's calling.[29] In obedience to God's call, he left his native land and wandered about in the land of Canaan like a beggar. He was always on the move, with no fixed dwelling place. Confronted by perils, burdens, and inconveniences, Sarah followed her husband and respected him as lord. The honor she has for her husband includes not only allegiance to him and its implications but also praise for the virtue of her continence and chastity.[30] Hidden in Sarah's laugh at the word of promise for her son, says Luther, is "proof of her extraordinary continence and chastity."[31] The genuine chastity of the barren Sarah is a noble work she does to her husband. Her chastity appears inglorious before the world, Luther contends, because it is "concealed under a common cover" of a married woman.[32] And yet such a noble act puts to shame those "celibates who burn and are polluted day and night."[33] Kolb observes, "Sarah served as a model of Christian contentment and patience as she bore the burden of childlessness (Gen. 16)."[34]

Sarah epitomizes the story of a saint, whose holiness is reflected at home, her life's station where she demonstrated her vocational obedience according to God's design. Genesis 18:9 states that "she is in the tent," meaning she engages herself with nothing but her household demands, for that is "her position in life."[35] While Abraham is elevated as "a rule of faith and of good works," Sarah is esteemed as the luminary of "the highest virtues of a saintly and praiseworthy housewife."[36] Outwardly, the domestic works appear unholy before the world, but in God's sight, they are "holier" than all the pious duties of the monastic life.[37] Her place is naturally at home, where she looks after her own affairs and properly administers the household duties. Like "a tortoise," Luther describes, she "remains in her little shell," where she fulfills her role as a saintly housewife.[38] She faithfully conducted the obligations proper to her sex and fulfilled the tasks that required her attention. In praising Sarah as the model for emulation, Luther takes liberty to speak of the opposite with which he describes the female sex. He quotes Proverbs 7:11, which speaks of "the wicked women [who] have 'feet that do not tarry.' This is due to their curiosity to see and hear things which nevertheless do not concern them at all. Therefore levity in morals as well as garrulousness and curiosity are censured in

this sex."[39] Instead of being inquisitive about the kind of guests
she had, Sarah received them hospitably. She did not succumb
to curiosity, a habit that leads many women to sin. Her heart
rejoices, knowing that she is where God has placed her, and
has done right. The timidity of women, Luther observes, leads
to the practice of witchcraft and superstition, but the courage
of Sarah leads her to have God as Lord and submit to his bidding, despite appearances to the contrary.[40] She has no cause
for fear, as God sanctions her domesticity; as 1 Peter 3:6 says,
"And you are now her children if you do right and let nothing
terrify you."

Luther's discussion of a married life is traditional, nuanced
by patriarchal assumptions. Even so, Parsons notes, Luther
seeks "to soften any implicit harshness by an emphasis on mutu-
ality and love" as a fulfillment of the vocation.[41] The example of
Abraham and Sarah is set before us so that we know how to live
together amicably as spouses. Luther repudiates all capricious
activities in family life, prevalent in his times, as in ours: "Husbands generally are lions in their homes and are harsh toward
wives and domestics. Similarly, the wives generally domineer
everywhere and regard their husbands as servants. But it is
foolish for a husband to want to display his manly courage and
heroic valor by ruling his wife. On the other hand, it is unbearable if wives want to dominate."[42] Where there is "mutual love,
mutual play and friendliness" among spouses, marriage will be
extolled "everywhere by all," something Luther admits is rare
because of the perpetual assault of the devil.[43] Where there is
regard for God's work and will, peace and love abound in matrimony. Husbands must be patient and act thoughtfully, even
when wives fail to meet their expectations. "At times you must
be lenient, slacken the reins, give in, and also accord your wife
the honor that is her due."[44] The woman is God's vessel that
God uses to conceive, bear, nourish, and take care of their children. Wives live according to the commands or rules of their

husbands. Husbands must refrain from being "harsh with them,"[45] instead being tender with them and honoring them as God's "weaker vessels" (1 Pet 3:7). They are not to appraise their wives according to their faint nature but according to baptism. Husbands and wives share the same faith and are "co-heirs of the grace of life." Inwardly, husbands and wives are alike in status before God; they possess a common calling to faith and an identical inheritance of life in Christ. Outwardly, they differ in function, as the husband rules while the wife submits to him.[46] No harsh acts or blows other than God's word should make them submissive. Luther insists, "If you beat one devil out of her, you will beat two into her, as the saying goes."[47] Wives are timid in spirit; husbands ought to treat them in a such way that they can bear it. Husbands must proceed with care, as they would with a tool, without doing damage to it—for instance, we would not hack a good knife into a brick.[48] God does not prescribe a specific rule but leaves it to the husband to relate to his wife "considerably according to each wife's nature."[49] Husbands must not exercise their authorities arbitrarily; as God's vessels, they are to help and strengthen their wives, not do harm to them. The honor husbands give to wives does not necessarily mean providing creaturely things for them, nor does it refer to conjugal obligation.[50] Whoever enters marital union with sexual pleasure as its purpose, Luther warns, will end in "nothing but heartache."[51] Seeking pleasure through another person is a form of self-obsession (*incurvatus in se*), a consequence of human sinfulness and fallenness.[52] It is, says Hinlicky, "concupiscence or distorted libido."[53] Luther describes vividly how Abraham treated Sarah with utmost respect: "[Abraham] did not give an order and did not say: 'You must obey me; I compel you; I demand from you.' No, he said: 'I beg you,' and he does not consider action obedience; he considers it a favor, as though by a superior person, in accordance with Peter's precept (1 Pet. 3:7): 'Bestow honor on the female sex.'"[54] This is done so that "their prayers will not be hindered" (1 Pet 3:7). Where prayer is hindered, all forms of rascality and various assaults of the devil dominate a household. To honor each other is to treat each other as "God's work or vessel" through which God provides for marriage.[55] Luther, for one, humbly honors his dear wife Katharina: "I am an inferior lord, she is my superior; I am Aaron, she is my Moses."[56]

The Fifth Petition: God's Alien Work

In this fallen world, where we anticipate defeats and retreats in marriage, we are to exercise the fifth petition of the Lord's Prayer ("Father, forgive us our trespasses as we forgive"), allowing it to impel us to seek God's forgiving grace by which the voice of a guilty conscience subsides and the tempting of the old flesh to harbor bitterness or avenge diminishes. To pray this petition, Luther intimates, is to enter a battlefield where husbands and wives work together in their fight against the devil that they may abound in good works in the homes.[57] Commenting on Song of Solomon 1:4, "Draw me after you," Luther emphasizes prayer as a weapon against Satan and every ill in each of life's stations, including in the family: "No manner of life is without its special burden. Marry a wife: immediately you will discover a flood of ills! You will find things which displease you in your wife and in your children, and the care of the stomach will occupy you."[58] By prayer we overcome various hazards and inconveniences in a household. We make constant use of this petition because we need God's forgiveness and are never beyond the need for comfort and assurance of God's grace. We prostrate ourselves before God, asking him not to look at our sins, which deserve his judgment, but to look away from them and cover them with grace as he promises. This petition, Marty stresses, "is a prayer attached to promise [that God forgives] more than to threat [that we forgive]."[59]

Luther teaches us to pray aright, just as he teaches us to live aright. An effective prayer must allow God's counsel and works to reign above ours. His counsel is opposite to ours. We keep everything that is in us and rely on it as the foundation of faith, but God strips everything that is in us so that he might fill us with his abundance as the basis of faith. As Luther avers, "It is the nature of God first to destroy and tear down whatever is in us before He gives us His good things."[60] The paradoxical action of God is borne out in 1 Samuel 2:6: "The Lord brings down to hell and raises up." Just as God acts in full unity with himself within the distinction between law and gospel, so, too, he works as one God within the distinction between God's command that we forgive and his promise that he forgives. Just as the gospel is hidden in the law, so God's forgiveness is hidden in its opposite, that is, as McNair rightly perceives, "under the command" that we first forgive others.[61] The threat of judgment under the law, that we should forgive, is not the final word; it is causative, as it causes the assaulted to receive God's forgiveness hidden in it. By ourselves, we are incapable of receiving God's gift unless God renders us capable of it. Prayer is vitiated unless we renounce our own counsels and works. As law, this petition performs an alien work of crushing the old creature so that he relinquishes, Marty writes, "his rights to play God, to be judge, to establish the stands of his own integrity."[62] Not until "we are made purely passive before God,"[63] stripped by the law of the natural ability to govern our family, do we benefit from God's blessed work. God grants us what we wish, but often contrary to our expectations; as Luther says, "He gives to us in a such a way that He contravenes all of our conceptions, that is, our ideas, so that He may seem to us to be more offended after our prayers and to do less after we have asked than he did before."[64] Harmony and peace are the fruits of God's excellent counsel; they belong to a household that willingly submits to God's alien work, through which all human counsels come to an end.

Living in one accord with each other, Luther claims, is "the truly precious good works" we should aspire to do.[65] Failure to do so deprives us of a joyful conscience, without which we cannot approach God boldly. In the Large Catechism, Luther writes, "For where the heart is not right with God and cannot generate such confidence, it will never dare to pray. But such a confident and joyful heart can never come except when one knows that his or her sins are forgiven."[66] God has attached the promise of his forgiveness to this petition by which we can approach God with confidence, praying, "'Dear Father, I come to you and pray that you forgive me for this reason: not because I can make satisfaction or deserve anything by my works, but because you have promised and have set this seal on it, making it as certain as if I had received an absolution pronounced by you yourself."[67] This petition acquaints us with true knowledge of our unrighteousness, which arouses God's wrath so that we hide in God's mercy as the remedy. We pray this petition improperly if we imagine our forgiving causes God to turn to us with acceptance and grace; in so doing, we relegate God's agency to a secondary place, making it causally dependent upon human agency. God gives us nothing but forgiveness and grace, without any prior condition; as Luther says, "Not that you are forgiven on account of your forgiveness, but freely, without our forgiveness, your sins are forgiven. He, however, enjoins it upon you as a sign, that you may be assured that, if you forgive, you too will be forgiven."[68] Repentance is no cause of God's grace; rather, it is an occasion for its reception. We ask God to forgive us "as we forgive our debtors," Marty stresses, "for one reason: unless we forgive others we cannot experience new life; we will not know what forgiveness is, will have no criterion for measuring the gift of God."[69]

Those who find it hard to forgive are not without hope. The paradox here consists in that precisely by the confession of our inability to forgive through the law, we are made ready to receive God's forgiveness. Such a perspective inheres in Luther's exposition of the third article of faith, where the Holy Spirit is exalted as the effective agent, causing us to lay hold of Christ and come to God, which we by ourselves could not accomplish. With God's help, "suspicion and hatred" can be replaced by "utmost love and good will."[70] Where God's counsel abides, "love will remain, and harmony will not be disturbed . . . and love is readiest to forgive."[71] A Christ-formed mind sees God's word as precious treasure, apart from which forgiveness is "a rare gift."[72]

"The Word of Bestowal": Inherently Performative

Marriage was marred by sin, yet Luther avers that there is "nothing more beautiful than this union of hearts between spouses."[73] Luther's positive appropriation of a married life as God's gift is drawn from God's word: "For there is no jewelry more precious than God's Word; through it you come to regard your spouse as a gift of God and, as long as you do that, you will have no regrets."[74] That marriage is a gift, Bayer argues, is an implication of Luther's doctrine of the Lord's Supper as a gift.[75] Both are based on the word of God addressing us from outside. Yet they are not identical. The words of institution—"Take and eat! This is my body. Take and drink, this is a new covenant in my blood"—make the Lord's Supper a sacrament. Bayer says that "the word of bestowal" in marriage God spoke in Genesis 2:22—"The man shall be yours; the woman shall be yours"— bears "a similar performative role as gift."[76] But marriage bears no sacramental status, as it has no power to bestow forgiveness. Luther writes, "Nowhere do we read that the man who marries a wife receives any grace of God. There is not even a divinely instituted sign in marriage, nor do we read anywhere that a marriage was instituted to be a sign of anything."[77] However, God's word spoken in marriage, Bayer writes, "has its own objectivity and durability. It can be grasped when it steps in and grasps hold of us, setting us straight, supporting and strengthening us, taking away our illusions and letting us see ourselves and others from a new perspective."[78] We draw strength from the sacraments, the created forms in which the word of God comes; so we draw strength and assurance from "the word of bestowal" attached to marriage. Married people dwell "in the midst of demons"[79] and cannot withstand them by their own strength. Luther describes marriage as "a real monastery, full of trials."[80] Trials of all sorts are burdensome unless we grasp God's promise that unites us as one flesh and sustains troubled relationships. The power to tend and guard marital union lies in the objectivity of God's word that performs what it says rather than in the subjectivity of human beings. Luther exults, "This word is sure to make a bitter wormwood into a honey in your mouth and turn sorrow into joy."[81] Where the word, the only treasure that adorns a marriage, is disdained, there is chaos and aversion. "Nothing but awful threats" fill the home of Sodom, a place where the angels of God would not go and were not welcomed with hospitality. By contrast, "nothing but grace and life" fill the household of Abraham, a place the angels of God inhabit and where they befriend Sarah, even when she disbelieved God's promise.[82] Abraham's home is where God's word reigns, and consequently, says Luther, it "is nothing else than the kingdom of the forgiveness of sins and of grace, yes, a very heaven" where God's presence is felt.[83] In Tomlin's estimation: "The household was seen like a small church. The family was not a sideline, an irrelevance to serious Christian existence that was primarily lived in the monastery, convent or church, but the primary vocation in which to live the Christian life."[84]

"The word of bestowal" in marriage is no empty solicitude but inherently effective, causing a couple to see each other as God's gift. Commenting on Genesis 22:17, "I will bless you," Luther speaks of "a two-fold blessing: the blessing in words and the blessing in actuality." God's blessing is not "in words" but "in actuality." It is no mere "verbal blessing," a sort of recognition we offer without effect. God's blessing is, Luther avers, "truly divine, for when God blesses, the result is the thing itself," just as creation occurs as it were by God's "deed-word."[85] The blessing we receive in marriage is an effective kind, as it originates from God, who never lies; he effects what he says. Luther declares, "He is One who blesses with effect and does all things through what He says, because His Word is the thing itself."[86] The prolific nature of God's blessing causes Luther to remain in wedlock and break through mundane and tedious tasks at home; he exults:

> What does it matter? Is it not better that I please God in this manner? Does not God hear me when I call upon him? Does he not deliver me and bless me in various ways through my life's companion, the upright wife whom I have joined to myself?[87]

The self-emptying love in household order is not self-generated but created by the word, that life-changing power that underlies all our acts. Both spouses must undergo crucifixion through the law and come under God's fearful judgment, without which they will "not live aright."[88] Only a "truly Christ-formed" person, whose old Adam and its vices have been crushed by the law, will exhibit a kenotic life, characterized by self-giving love rather than self-seeking obsession. "Natural love, eros, seeks its own happiness in another," Hinlicky writes, and it "becomes concupiscence."[89] Through the eyes of faith, inconveniences and heartaches in marriage, Luther teaches, can be hallowed as "a wonderfully blessed cross" imposed by God as an alien work of sanctification, conforming us to his image. "Now, if one of the parties were endowed with Christian fortitude and could endure the other's ill behavior, that would doubtless be a wonderfully blessed cross and a right way to heaven."[90] Neither idealism nor perfectionism but the cruciform vocation is basic to the household existence. "In the present sinful place in which the dethroned powers of evil are not yet completely annihilated," Lazareth intimates, "true self-giving love is destined always to be crucified. The imperfect love of the Christian shares the tragic triumph of the perfect love of God in Christ. It is put to death, as was Jesus."[91] The cross is not self-chosen but is a sign of obedience to "the word of bestowal" in marriage. Nestingen captures Luther's thought well:

> When the word is near, the cross is always close at hand; you don't find it, the cross finds you. So the cross characterizes all vocations, but becomes particularly evident in families. To be someone's son or daughter is to be on the receiving end of their gifts and limits, their strivings and fears, faith and unbelief. Even—perhaps it would be better to say, especially— in the healthiest families, self-loss is an inevitable aspect of the relationships. Putting sinners together multiplies the risk exponentially.[92]

No matter how much joy and delight one can find in the estate of the household, no one can escape the pain and demand of being placed under such an order. The household order, as in other orders, is marked by the "coincidental opposites" of despair and hope, misery and delight. "Hope and despair," Luther writes, "these two things, direct opposites by nature, must be in us,"[93] just as in justification both saint and sinner are in us at the same time.[94] Paradoxically, God works within the dialectical tension between the two creatures in one person: he kills despair in the old to kindle hope in the new. God works "strangely" with his own, that is, through these opposites, despair and hope—just as he does through the opposites of law and gospel—to create a people who "must hope in despair, . . . for fear is nothing else than the beginning of hope and hope is the beginning of recovery."[95]

"Outward bitterness and drudgery" is universal to both believers and unbelievers, but "inner, spiritual delight" is particular to the believers.[96] Because of unbelief, we suffer "inward" bitterness; not only that, we suffer "both inward and outward bitterness" that becomes so unbearable that, Luther writes, "thence arises of necessity the loud outcry."[97] "The loud outcry" of "inconveniences, vexations and various crosses" in marriage will be vanquished by the word on which our confidence rests. We are placed before God as the passive recipients of God's word—to borrow Bayer's phrase, God's "speech acts"[98]—by which we are kept strong and safe in God's hands, even as we struggle through strife and sorrow. Delight and joy in marriage arise from a "firm faith that this estate together with all its works, however insignificant, is pleasing and precious in his sight."[99] To confirm the truth taught by Solomon—"unless the Lord keeps the house, household management there is a lost cause" (Ps 127:1)—God allows misfortunes and trials to emerge, Luther opines, "as an assault on unbelief, to bring to shame the arrogance of reason with all works and cleverness, and to constrain" faith in God.[100] In those situations, where perpetual complaints occur, God may delay in granting help, causing us to fear that he might have forsaken us, although the truth lies in the opposite, that God intends to create in us, through delay, a greater desire for his "more perfect grace."[101] Faith grasps God's proper work of exalting that which lies hidden in its opposite, that is, his alien work of humbling. As Kolb writes aptly, "For precisely in the trials of family life God hides himself and through them brings blessings"—as was illustrated in the narrative of Abraham and Sarah, who experienced God's delay in blessing them with their son.[102]

Reason and Faith: No Distinction in Works

As taught in his *Estate of Marriage*, Luther counsels that subjective feelings and personal desire must not be allowed to reign above God's word, lest we fail "to recognize [God's] works and persist in making evil that which is good, and regarding as bitter that which is pleasant."[103] Just as flesh is opposed to spirit, so reason is opposed to faith. Reason shows no regard for God's word and therefore disdains familial duties; faith has regard for God's word and therefore finds delight in them.[104] Both husbands and wives play their part in vocational obedience to the estate of marriage. Luther explains how a Christian husband ought to respond to household duties via the contrast of reason and faith:

> Our natural reason . . . takes a look at married life, . . . turns up her nose and says, "Alas, must I rock the baby, wash diapers, make its bed, smell its stench, stay up nights with it, take care of it when it cries, heal its rashes and sores, and on top of that care for my wife, provide for her, labor at my trade, take care of this and take care of that, do this and do that, endure this and endure that, and whatever else of bitterness and drudgery married life involves?" . . .
>
> Christian faith . . . opens its eyes, looks upon all these insignificant, distasteful and despised duties in the Spirit, and is aware that they are all adorned with divine approval as with the costliest gold and jewels. It says, "O God, because I am certain that thou hast created me as a man and hast from my body begotten this child, I also know for a certainty that it meets with thy perfect pleasure. I confess to thee that I am not worthy to rock the little babe or wash its diapers, or to be entrusted with the care of the child and its mother."[105]

In like manner, wives should look at household demands through the eyes of faith: "A wife too should regard her duties in the same light, as she suckles the child, rocks and bathes it, and cares for it in other ways; and as she busies herself with other duties and renders help and obedience to her husband. These are truly golden and noble works."[106] She should find joy in them and let God's will be done in her. Her holiness in household affairs surpasses all self-chosen acts of worship simply because she is in a "God-pleasing station," just as Sarah was.[107]

All works done in faith are equally holy before God. Luther avers, "In this [justifying] faith all works become equal, and one work is like the other; all distinctions between works fall away, whether they be great, small, short, long, many, or few."[108] Luther applies the effectual nature of faith to marital love. Since "all distinctions between works" collapse through faith,[109] a married couple loves and serves each other without differentiation in works, as all works are equally blessed of God. Faith, not different kinds of works, impels the couple to love. Whoever "lives in this faith," Luther contends, has no need of any external guidance on good works but naturally fulfills them as the occasion demands; likewise, a married couple who "thoroughly believes in their love" has no need of instruction in how to relate to each other but gives to each other spontaneously.[110] Luther writes, "Confidence alone teaches them all this, and even more than is necessary. For such a man there is no distinction in works. He does the great and the important as gladly as the small and the unimportant and vice versa. Moreover, he does them all in a glad, peaceful, and confident heart, and is an absolutely willing companion to the woman."[111] Those who live from Christ will live not in themselves but outside themselves, in Christ from whom they derive the power to act righteously toward their spouse with whom they live.

The Household's Cry of Desperation and the Holy Spirit's Cry of Consolation

The household is a battlefield in which the old and new Adams collide most fiercely, as each competes for its kingdom, the power to reign. When the old Adam reigns, the voice of despair dominates and finds no healing. But when the new Adam reigns, the voice of despair dissipates, and hope arises. When one's marriage is beset with crises of unbelief and fractures, a true theologian—or in Luther's own phrase, a "truly Christ-formed" family—discerns in that context that God is proclaimed still as belonging to us, even as we belong to him. It can perceive the true character of God hidden in the vicissitudes of life. When God seems to be against us, the truth is hidden in its opposite, abiding hope, as the Holy Spirit comforts the despairing "with sighs too deep for words" (Rom 8:26). To faith, "the loud outcry" of bitterness and desperation is not the cry of sheer despair; it can be vanquished by the Spirit's "outcry" of comfort and assurance. This is succinctly taught in his sermon on Galatians 4:6, where Luther expands:

> Your sins will also cry out; that is, they will produce great despair in your conscience. But Christ's Spirit will and must cry down that outcry, that is, causing your confidence to be stronger than your despair, as St. John says: "By this we know that we are of the truth and can calm our hearts before Him: If our heart condemns us, God is greater than the heart, and He knows everything. Beloved, if our heart does not condemn us, we have confidence before God, and whatever we ask, we shall receive from Him" (I Jn. 3:19–22). Thus this calling out and outcry of the Spirit is nothing else than a powerful, strong, unwavering confidence from our whole heart toward God, as our dear Father, from us, His dear children.[112]

In cross-bearing, we succumb neither to the prompting of the old flesh nor to the wiles of the devil. For hidden in the old Adam's cry of desperation expressed by a spouse, "What a drudgery married life is!," is the Holy Spirit's cry of consolation, "What a God-pleasing station you are in!," by which a spouse is assured of God's favor despite appearances to the contrary. The Spirit's cry drowns out the cry of the old Adam so that its selfish desires and subjective feelings no longer reign; it gains power over uneasy hearts and establishes them in the suffering love of the cross, by which we oppose the assaults of the devil.

Sarah's Laughter: Justification under Its Opposites

St. Peter did not make use of the entire account of Genesis 18. His exposition centers on Sarah as a model for women to emulate in wedlock. What is crucial for Luther is the power of God's word to create anew. Just as the word makes holy the works of a saintly housewife, so, too, it creates life out of the barren Sarah. What is humanly impossible is made possible with God. Sarah's laugh at the word of promise is an occasion for Luther to teach the doctrine of justification under its opposites: "the righteousness of faith set against the presumption and righteousness of works."[113] When a word of promise was given to Abraham, Sarah was absent and did not hear it. She showed no regard to her husband's words. Then God appeared to her "in the tent," gently reproved her, and reiterated to her his promise that was previously delivered to Abraham alone. Luther writes, "He stood turned away; that is, He had turned His back, to indicate that Sarah did not believe until she was reproached."[114] Here the paradox between God's actions in law and gospel comes into play. God repeated his own word to Sarah first to expose her unbelief for which she was reproached so that he could inflame her heart toward God, says Luther, "by a new light."[115] The barren Sarah had not totally abandoned hope for a child; nor had she resigned herself to her fate in utter despair. Her barren condition and Abraham's old age gave rise to her laughter, a deficiency of faith. "For this reason the Lord puts up with her weakness and is not offended by her laughter, which has its origin in her thinking about something that is impossible."[116] The faith of Sarah, "this saintly and chaste matron," abides and can be rekindled by the Holy Spirit; as Luther writes, "The Holy Spirit brings up these matters in order to strengthen" her faith, which was weakened by the old Adam.[117] God did not impose judgment upon Sarah for her unbelief;[118] instead, God entreated her with grace through the appearance of three distinguished persons. Here Luther sees evidence of the orthodox doctrine of the Trinity, drawn from the fact that Moses spoke of three as one.[119] The paradox consists in that her unbelief makes her the object of God's justifying grace. Underlying Sarah's response are the "coincidental opposites" of sin and righteousness; her unbelief is due to the old flesh that remains with her, though she is completely righteous before God. The holiest mistress is still tainted with residual sin, which requires perpetual cleansing by the word. The righteous saint still, says Luther, "is hampered by the thoughts of the flesh" and knows where to find relief from its assaults—that is, not by turning inward, where there are no aids, but by clinging to the word that arouses faith.[120] Consequently, doubt concerning the prophecy about the promise of a son dissipates. Her thoughts are held captive to the word, and they terminate upon hearing it. The word kills her laughter via the law but kindles faith in her via the gospel.

Later, Genesis 18:15 reads: "But Sarah denied, saying: I did not laugh. For she was afraid. He said: No, but you did laugh." Here Luther highlights the propensity of the corrupted nature to sin, as her unbelief was accompanied by lying. As Mattox notes, Luther, with Chrysostom, concedes Sarah's later denial is a lie.[121] She lied to hide from the divine visitors, who knew her innermost thoughts. She "adds a little sin,"[122] Luther asserts, by denying that she laughed, though she had laughed. "But this sin is pardonable," Luther claims, "because she fears God, obeys the prophets, and is subject to her husband. It is fear of Abraham, her master, that causes her to be thoroughly frightened and to deny that she has laughed."[123] She repented of her laughter at the words of God's prophets. "She is sorry because of fear, and in this fear she commits another sin."[124] The prophet opposes her with "a few words: 'No, but you did laugh,'" meaning she first sinned by laughing, followed by lying.[125] Yet Luther relegates her sin, reproved by the law, to "a little sin"; as he writes, "this is a cheerful and very friendly reproof," which incites Sarah to consider the unbelievable word by which her heart is imbued with faith and hope.[126]

Abraham's old age and Sarah's barrenness do not present any impediment to God's power to create new realities out of the humanly impossible. "The promise which they [Abraham and Sarah] apprehended through faith revives their dead flesh, as it were. Consequently, you must maintain that Isaac was born not so much from the flesh as because of the promise."[127] Through the creative power of God's word, Sarah was transformed from infertility to fecundity. Thus Genesis 18:14 reads: "Is anything too hard for the Lord? At the appointed time I will return to you, in the spring, and Sarah shall have a son." Sarah's womb is "closed" (Gen 20:18), and she is "altogether dead," meaning she is deprived of the power of fertility;[128] in Luther's own words: "Therefore, it is necessary for Sarah to hear a word by which she, as though brought back to life, may rise again to the hope of fruitfulness; for the word is truly a voice that raises from death. But it is death for Sarah to think that she is a corpse. This thought is corrected by the Word, and the corpse, as though recalled from death, begins to live again."[129] Only the word can create *ex nihilo* and bring life out of death, blessedness out of barrenness; as Bielfeldt opines, "Luther's theological language has objective reference. Theological statements assert the way in which things can stand between God and His creature."[130] The way things are is the fruit of God's creative word. God's word acts efficaciously, that Sarah will bear a child, just as it says. Sarah's hindrances— her barrenness and old age—are overcome not by active righteous deeds but simply by trusting in God's promise. Luther describes the existential condition of Sarah: "When she sees that her hope is futile, she submits everything to God. Yet she does not despair."[131] The despair the law creates is not sheer despair, which, for Luther, is the work of "a devil or a robber"; rather, it is, as Althaus writes, "a salutary despair, that is, [a Christian] does not despair of God's mercy but of himself and of his own capability so that he expects everything from Christ."[132] Sarah remains a passive agent who works nothing, while God is an active agent to whom she submits everything for the fulfillment of her desire for a son. Only the futility of hope prepares her for its fulfillment.

CHAPTER 5

The Word and the Spiritual Kingdom
Priestly Ministry and the Cross-shaped Life

For Luther, there are seven marks of the church: the preached word, baptism, the Lord's Supper, the power of the keys, the ministerial office, public worship, and the possession of the cross.[1] The ministry "to preach, to baptize, to absolve, and to administer the sacraments" is entrusted, and the congregations must comply with "this arrangement or agree to it. Whenever you see this done, be assured that God's people, the holy Christian people, are present."[2] All these things receive their meaning and substance from the primacy of the word. Luther breaks with the medieval concept of the hierarchy of estates in which the spiritual is elevated above the temporal. First Peter 2:9 teaches that all Christians are priests on account of Christ's priesthood. For Luther, "Christian priesthood is," Jorgenson writes, "a derived reality in which all share by being in Christ."[3] Christians are fully endowed with "the authority, the command, and the obligation" to perform three things that Christ did: to teach the word, to intercede for the congregation, and to offer spiritual sacrifices to God.[4] These three are the forms of our priesthood that we receive from Christ, the Chief Priest. Believers have no reason to live on earth apart from being the instruments through which God brings others to faith. "Thus you should also teach other people how they, too, come into such light. For you must bend every effort to realize what God has done for you. Then let it be your chief work to proclaim this publicly and to call everyone into the light into which you have been called."[5]

Luther attaches great value to the spiritual kingdom, considering it as "an exceedingly great blessing and much too precious" in God's sight that we must "resist it" when it deviates from "its proper function," namely, leading the people "in faith to God."[6] We do not resist secular power,[7] Luther insists, "for to suffer wrong [under it] destroys no man's soul," and thus "is but a very small matter" in God's sight.[8] But we must resist spiritual power, he writes, for "to do wrong [through the neglect of feeding the sheep, the sole purpose for which the spiritual kingdom is instituted] destroys the soul."[9] Thus St. Peter, Luther argues, devotes significant space in his first letter (1 Pet 5:1–14), offering instruction to those who govern in the spiritual realm on how to perform office or work according to God's will.

The official ministry of the word and the external manifestation of true faith in the holy cross are essential to the being—and not just the well-being—of the church. Where the word is, there is suffering as its proper outcome; where true faith is, the holy cross is presupposed, not as meritorious of justification but as an outflow of the justified status of God's children. In his *On the Councils and Church*, Luther holds that suffering is a mark of a true church.[10] This is a derivative of Luther's theology of the cross in which just as God's identity is known in its opposites, that is, in the weakness, suffering, and lowliness of the cross, so, too, the church's identity is recognized by weaknesses, suffering, and persecution. Because Christ is the shape and substance of our faith and life, the pattern of the cross is constitutive of the church's way of being in the world. Luther avers, "Wherever Christ is, Judas, Pilate, Herod, Caiaphas, and Annas will inevitably be also, so also his cross. If not, he is not the true Christ."[11] The word "cruciform"[12] is a predicate of both God-in-relation to us, as manifested in the suffering of the cross of Christ, and "Christian-in-relation"[13] to people, as believers concretize their faith in works of suffering service; the latter receives its validity and meaning from the former. The cross crucifies our old flesh so that we act in congruence with God's will, not in conformity to the world (Rom 12:2). As 1 Peter 4:1–2 teaches, "Whoever has suffered in the flesh has ceased from sin, so as to live for the rest of the time in the flesh no longer by passions but the will of God." The cross is God's alien work to purge the old Adam in order that the purity of the heart and quality of faith shine like gold as his proper work. Sanctification consists of two things: it kills the old creature in us and it renews the new creature in us in such a way that all our confidence is not in anything worldly and fleshly within us but solely in God.

Faith in Christ: Universal Priesthood

All Christians are "a chosen race, a royal priesthood, a holy nation, and God's own people" (1 Pet 2:9). St. Peter disavows not priesthood but laity. All believers are given the title "a royal priesthood" (1 Pet 2:5), and they exercise their vocational obedience to God through the priestly office. Luther thus dismantles the medieval distinction between the sacred and the secular, viewing everything of the creaturely world as spiritual because it has its origin in God.[14] The distinction of a spiritual estate from a secular one was the first wall of Romanism Luther sought to demolish. In his *Appeal to the Ruling Class of German Nobility* (1520), Luther writes:

> It is pure invention that pope, bishop, priests, and monks are called the spiritual estate while princes, lords, artisans, and farmers are called the temporal estate. This is indeed a piece of deceit and hypocrisy. Yet no one need be intimidated by it, and for this reason: all Christians are truly of the spiritual estate, and there is no difference among them except that of office. Paul says in I Corinthians 12[:12–13] that we are all one body, yet every member has its own work by which it serves others.

This is because we are all Christians alike; for baptism, gospel, and faith alone make us spiritual and a Christian people.[15]

In eliminating this wall, Luther affirms his doctrine of the universal priesthood, that all believers are priests on account of faith in Christ. Luther intends to "restore the little word 'priests' to the common use which the little word 'Christians' enjoys. For to be priest does not belong in the category of an external office; it is exclusively the kind of office that has dealings before God."[16] The universal priesthood is grounded not in the quality of our spiritual life but in baptism, or faith, which Luther describes as the "true priestly office." This occurs as early as in his 1520 *Treatise on the New Testament*, where Luther declares, "Faith must do everything. Faith alone is the true priestly office. It permits no one else to take its place. Therefore all Christian men are priests, all women priestesses, be they young or old, master or servant, mistress or maid, learned or unlearned. Here there is no difference, unless faith be unequal."[17] The holy and spiritual priesthood comprises true Christians who "believe in Christ" and whose faith is built on him, the stone. Luther states plainly, "He who does not believe is no priest."[18] In 1 Peter 2:5, Peter addresses Christians, "Like living stones be yourselves built into a spiritual house." Through one faith and one baptism, we are alike and equal in dignity before God. Christ is in all without distinction. "Before God, however, there is no distinction . . . between laymen and priests, princes and bishops, between religious and secular, except for the sake of office and work, not for the sake of status. They are all the spiritual estate, all are truly priests, bishops, and popes."[19] The difference lies externally, that is, in the office to which one is appointed by the congregation. Anyone could do these tasks, but only a few officiants are chosen from the whole congregation to administer the office on behalf of God's people. Everyone has this office, but no one arrogates it to themself; it must be conferred by the congregation. No one should assume the authority that is common to all without the authorization or consent of the community. Luther elaborates:

> Therefore, when a bishop consecrates it is nothing else than that in the place and stead of the whole community, all of whom have like power, he takes a person and charges him to exercise this power on behalf of the others. It is like ten brothers, all king's sons and equal heirs, choosing one of themselves to rule the inheritance in the interests of all. In one sense they are all kings and of equal power, and yet one of them is charged with the responsibility of ruling.[20]

Luther's theology puts its emphasis, Kolb writes, "on the impact that the work of Christ has on those whom God has chosen to make kings and priests."[21] First Peter 2:9 allows him to stress that believers participate in Christ's benefits primarily through Christ's twofold office, kingship and priesthood, though he does not exclude the office of prophet. The "three offices" of Christ—prophet, priest, and king—Christ bestows on us.[22] Just as Christ is all three, so, too, are we. "For what he has, that I, too, have."[23] We are priests and kings in Christ, both on account of faith in Christ. We reap benefits from Christ's kingly office, just as we do from Christ's priestly office. Christ's twofold office, emphasized in 1 Peter 2:9, appears in *The Freedom of the Christian*, where Luther teaches, "Now just as Christ by his birthright obtained these two prerogatives [kingship and priesthood], so he imparts them to and shares them with everyone who believes in him."[24] As king, every Christian is lord of all things and is preserved from all harm. However, "more excellent than being kings" is being priests, who can boldly approach God through Christ, intercede for people, and teach God's truth. Faith alone, not human works, confers upon the Christian the "lofty dignity" of two prerogatives: first, "his royal power" through which he presides over the contraries of

death, life, and sin; and second, "his priestly glory" through
which he "is omnipotent with God" and can achieve what God
asks; as Paul teaches, "He will fulfill the desire of those who
fear him; he also will hear their cry and save them" (cf. Phil
4:13).[25]

The freedom for which Christ redeems us finds expression
in a community in which all believers are constituted priests
and kings. Justified existence, Helmer writes aptly, "is inherently social." She expands:

> Christ's gift of his two-fold office establishes the new commu-
> nity of those Christ justifies. The justification of the sinner is
> not the final goal; rather, the end of justification is the constitu-
> tion of a new social organization: a royal and holy priesthood
> made up of priests and kings. When the individual is freed
> from their sin they are free to participate in a community in
> which a new kind of rulership applies. Rather than a com-
> munity to which there can only be one king and one priest,
> Christ rules a community in which the leadership is provided
> by all. Christ as king confers his kingship on all members of
> his body; the same holds true for his priestly office.[26]

The benefits of Christ's mediatorial activity are accrued
to the common priesthood so that both men and women can
exercise the priestly ministry of mediating these benefits to
others. Luther avers, "A woman can baptize and administer the
Word of life, by which sin is taken away, eternal death abolished, the prince of the world cast out, heaven bestowed: in
short by which the divine majesty pours itself forth through
all the soul."[27] All are given the authority to preach God's word
except women.[28] They should let men preach and instead submit to their husbands, as 1 Corinthians 14:34 teaches. Luther
stresses, "God does not interfere with the arrangement."[29] Faith
qualifies women to exercise the gift of prophecy, but only in a
situation where there are no men and only women, as in nun-
neries.[30] Luther elaborates:

Children, women, and other persons are not qualified for this office, even though they are able to hear God's word, to receive baptism, the sacrament, absolution, and are also true, holy Christians, as St. Peter says [1 Pet. 3:7]. Even nature and God's creation makes this distinction, implying that women (much less children or fools) cannot and shall not occupy positions of sovereignty, as experience also suggests and as Moses says in Genesis 3:16, "You shall be subject to man." The gospel, however, does not abrogate this natural law, but confirms it as the ordinance and creation of God.[31]

The universal priesthood of believers does not mean the elimination of all external order and discipline in church life. Luther heeds the apostolic teaching on the dispensation of various gifts and the exercise of them for upbuilding the body of Christ (Eph 4:8). Luther endorses, as Lohse notes, the "public character" of the ministerial office for the sake of propriety in the congregation and the entire church.[32] However, the person appointed to the office may be removed if the congregation thinks otherwise. The efficacy of the office is not permanent but is contingent upon the decision of the whole congregation, not upon one's own choice. "Therefore, a priest in Christendom is nothing else but an officeholder. As long as he holds office he takes precedence; where he is deposed, he is a peasant or townsman like anybody else. Indeed, a priest is never a priest when he is deposed."[33] Here Luther parts company with the Romanists' idea of the indelible character of a priest, that a priest, once consecrated, remains a priest, even when deposed from office. Luther writes, "[The Romanists] hold the illusion that a priest can never be anything other than a priest, or ever become a layman. All this is just contrived talk, and human regulation."[34]

Spiritual Rule: A Word of Instruction

Public ministry involves the exercise of various gifts for upbuilding the body of Christ (Eph 4:8): "There must be bishops, or pastors, or preachers."[35] The word "elders," for Luther, is synonymous with "bishops" and "priests"; it refers to those who "administer the spiritual rule," that is, preaching and caring for the flock.[36] The word is central to this particular calling to public office; as Luther writes, "No one should teach or preach anything unless he is sure that it is God's Word, in order that our conscience rests on solid rock."[37] As Peter says, "Whoever speaks [does so] as one who utters oracles of God" (1 Pet 4:11). Each service must be offered in accordance with "the strength which God supplies"; it is an obedience rendered to "God's work and arrangement."[38] So a bishop should proceed with his office, convinced that "God is doing it, and that it is God's Word or work."[39]

Elders: Cruciform Leadership

St. Peter wrote his epistle as an elder, at his time a word used for those with public authority to preach in the church, and "a witness of the sufferings of Christ" (1 Pet 5:1). From the cross, he derived the "cruciform" eldership. Just as "the cruciform God"[40] enters the human plight, suffers, and acts to liberate us from the enemies of life, so the "cruciform" elder must accept "outward poverty, contempt, illnesses, and weakness"[41] as part of their vocational obedience to God. Elders and flocks differ in office but are equal in status before God, as they "have now returned to the Shepherd and Guardian of [their] souls" (1 Pet 2:25). Luther expands:

> Therefore it is a lie when they say today that the office of a bishop implies dignity and that he is a bishop who wears a miter on his head. It is not a position that implies dignity. No, it is an office requiring that the incumbent must take care of us, watch over us, and be our guardian. He must know what kind of weakness there is everywhere. If someone is weak, he must help and comfort. If someone falls, he must buoy him up, etc., in order that the Christians may be adequately provided in body and soul, etc.[42]

Elders are to serve "not for shameful gain but eagerly" (1 Pet 5:2) for the benefit of the flocks. Christ's officials who care for nothing but themselves, for Luther, exhibit "an exceedingly harmful" and "especially disgraceful" vice.[43] Their sole duty is to "tend the flock," that is, to feed them with nothing but the gospel and the word so that they become "fat and fruitful."[44] They must serve, "not as domineering over" those under their care (1 Pet 5:3). They are not "an overlord" who tends the flock by "constraint" (1 Pet 5:2) but a willing servant, leading the sheep to pasture.[45] Only those who are "called" will exercise this office willingly and be "fruitful" in what they do.[46] They are not to serve as "the kings of the Gentiles" (Luke 22:25–26) did, that is, by lording their power over the subjects for the sake of honor; rather, they are to serve as humble servants, as Christ did, and confine themselves only to what benefits the flock. By example, they lead a life that is consistent with their confession so that others will follow them. Otherwise, the flock would soon despise the office of bishop. The "chief Shepherd" will reward the labor of those who care for souls with "the unfading crown of glory" (1 Pet 5:4), not on account of the office itself but because of God's grace.

Humility: God's Exaltation

The cross imposed upon the elder spells the death of self-willed leadership and the illegitimate exertion of one's power. Elders are to endorse "a truly Christ-formed" leadership whose authority lies not in subduing others but in enduring love for others, not in resisting but in risking vulnerability for the sake of others. The cross imposed upon the elder is also imposed upon youths who fall under the ministry of eldership. Spiritually, older people are imbued with "knowledge and understanding of the Holy Spirit," and youths would do well to obey them.[47] In his exposition of the Ten Commandments, Luther teaches that "after the excellent works of the first three commandments there are no better works than to obey and serve all those who are set in authority over us."[48] On the fourth commandment, "Thou shalt honor thy father and mother," Luther praises obedience, from which proceeds many virtues and good works. He stresses, "For everybody must be ruled and subject to other men. So we see here again how many good works are taught in this commandment, for in it all our life is made subject to other men."[49] In his exposition of 1 Peter 5:6, "Humble yourselves therefore before the mighty hand of God," Luther reiterates, "God wants everyone to be subject to the other person. Therefore do this willing and gladly."[50] In particular, Luther impresses upon young people the virtue of humility so that prosperity, discipline, and many good fruits abound everywhere.[51] In exhorting youths to obey the elders who rule over them, St. Peter imposes upon them a strict command;[52] as 1 Peter 5:5 says, "God opposes the proud but gives grace to the humble."[53] However, this command is imposed on all, as Paul teaches in Romans 12:10: "Outdo one another in showing honor." Luther identifies in this verse "a special word" ("hold") when Peter writes, "Hold firmly to humility" (1 Pet 5:5). "That means," Luther explains, "to 'hold' together in a way that is very 'firm,' knotted and tied to each other, or like clothing is sewn and laced most densely through and through so that it cannot rip."[54] All of us are given equal grace and inheritance so that none can exalt himself above others. "If he does that, he loses the grace given to him and falls far below others into damnation."[55] We may differ in gifts and offices but not in humility with which to serve others. "As good stewards of varied grace" (1 Pet 4:10), we do due diligence to fasten to each other by humility so that unity is not broken. There is nothing more beautiful than the virtue of humility with which Christians are clothed (Col 3:12). All offices and estates[56]—household, civil, and spiritual—must be adorned with Christlike humility, the spring of all good works. Luther elaborates:

As far as the spiritual life which is pleasing to God is concerned, no one should seek it elsewhere by running into the
monasteries and wildernesses or putting on a gray coat or a
monk's cowl. St. Peter here admonishes all estates to obtain
this virtue. This preaching about good works applies to all
offices in every house, city, village, church, and school, that
children, servants, and youths should humbly be subject and
obedient to parents, those in authority, superiors, and their
elders. On the other hand, those in authority and the higher
estates are to serve their inferiors, even the least of them.
If people did this, we would be full of good works, for it is
impossible for humility to do evil; rather, it is useful, advanta-
geous, and pleasant to everyone.[57]

God places us under the "impressive power"[58] of his word by
which arrogance is crushed so that God might exalt us at the
proper time; as 1 Peter 5:6 reads, "Humble yourselves therefore
under the mighty hand of God that in due time He may exalt
you." We must yield to the alien work of God's word through
which the "sinful old Adam becomes mellow and soft" in order
that we might experience God's proper work of exaltation.[59]
God bestows his mercy on those who are taken out of themselves and ascribe all things to God; conversely, God pours out
his wrath against those who are left to themselves and thwart
God's purpose. To be taken out of oneself incurs divine pleasure; to be left to oneself incurs divine displeasure. To incite
humility, Luther quotes Daniel 3:55 (Vulgate), "Thou sittest
upon the cherubim and beholdest the depths," to speak of the
salutary aspect of God's "seeing that looks into the depths"
of our miserable condition in order that he might bestow his
grace. Because God is the Most High, he does not look beyond
himself, for there is nothing there; nor does he look at what lies
beside him, as there is no equal to him. He can look "within
him and beneath him; and the farther one is beneath, the better
does He see him."[60] To be seen by God's eyes is to be seized by
the merciful God—"the kind of God," Luther writes, "who does

nothing but exalt those of low degree."[61] God's work is most effective when we leave ourselves out and cleave solely to God, as Mary did, fearing, loving, and trusting him despite appearances to the contrary. For hidden in circumstances where God appears to be against us is God's "sure promise" that "the mighty hand of God" will sustain us and deliver us.[62] For it is, Luther writes, "the nature of this mighty hand to support, comfort and strengthen anew the humbled and frightened."[63]

The Church: The Vehicle of God's Grace

Luther sees in 1 Peter 5:7—"Cast all your anxieties on Him, for he cares about you"—Peter's emphasis on community support as the cure for the human soul. The providential care of God encompasses all offices and estates: household, civil, and spiritual.[64] The church is an instrument of God's grace, but it is not to be confused with the gospel. "The church is a creature of God," Luther writes, "incomparably less than the gospel."[65] The church is both the creature of the gospel and the bearer and proclaimer of the gospel. The gospel creates the church, not vice versa. Yet the gospel cannot be known apart from the community of the word it proclaims. The gospel occupies a magisterial domain, possessed of its own efficacy to create its own adherents; the church plays a ministerial role in making the gospel known. Arand recognizes in Luther "two simultaneous actions" of the Holy Spirit: faith in Christ and incorporation into the church.[66] Through the word, the Spirit breathes faith into us and engrafts us into the body of Christ. The Holy Spirit constitutes the church, which Luther defines as "a holy little flock and community of pure saints" united in Christ, their common head.[67] The Holy Spirit makes us holy through "the Christian church, the forgiveness of sins, the resurrection of the body, and the life everlasting."[68] Lohse points out that Luther explicitly adheres to Cyprian's phrase "outside the church there is no salvation."[69] In the *Large Catechism*, Luther writes,

"Outside this Christian community, however, where there is no gospel, there is also no forgiveness," and hence "no holiness."[70] For Luther, justification occurs "through" the church but "not outside" it, as the fanatics teach.[71] This accounts for the order of the third article in which "immediately after the Holy Spirit is placed the Christian Church, in which all his gifts are to be found."[72]

Luther applies the doctrine of the communion of the saints to his reading of 1 Peter 5:9: "Knowing that the same experience of suffering is required of your brotherhood throughout the world." When assailed by the devil, take comfort that the believer is not forsaken because he is part of Christendom. "He can be certain, as the Sacraments point out, that a great many eyes are upon him: first the eyes of God and of Christ himself; then also, the eyes of the dear angels, of the saints, and of all Christians."[73] We are not alone, for many more must suffer as we do, and they help us fight too. Luther admits a social dimension to the deliverance from trials or sufferings. "In that hour the work of love and the communion of the saints are seriously and mightily active."[74] Here Luther speaks of the maternal care the church provides for nurturing souls. He inherits from Cyprian the functional aspect of the church as "the mother that begets and bears every Christian."[75] Cyprian once said, "You cannot have God for our Father unless you have the church for our mother."[76] The Holy Spirit places us, as Luther puts it, in the "church's lap," where he instructs us and nurtures our faith, as a mother does.[77] Nothing, Luther exults, is "more pleasing and friendly" than a mother's care and comfort.[78] God does not reach us in his naked majesty, which only frightens us away; rather, he hides in the earthly elements of the word and sacraments to reach us, which are by far more friendly and pleasant.

The Creed speaks of the economic action of the triune God in the self-giving of God-self. Mattox writes, "The self-communication of God as Father, Son, and Spirit—the trinitarian self-giving—stands at the very center of the Christian faith, and thus also of Luther's faith."[79] The triune God works together as one God, bestowing upon us all his gifts. In Luther's words, "These are the three persons and one God, who has given himself to us all wholly and completely, with all that he is and has."[80] The first article of faith assures us of the Father's providential care of our physical life through the bountiful provision of creaturely goods. The second article announces that Christ's work of redemption through the cross is complete so that every eternal good he acquired for us is ours by faith. The Holy Spirit of the third article distributes these heavenly blessings to us, lest they remain in ruin. Believers are strengthened, free, and secure in their consciences by the rich measure of God's provision, which, Luther spells out in his *Smalcald Articles*, is conveyed through particular vehicles of God's presence: "first, through the spoken word, in which the forgiveness of sins is preached to the whole world (which is the proper function of the gospel); second, through baptism; third, through the Holy Sacrament of the Altar; fourth, through the power of the keys and also through the mutual conversation and consolation of brothers and sisters."[81] Through the various ministries of the church, the Spirit gathers us, nurtures us, absolves us of sins, and causes our faith to be fruitful. Riddled with faults, sins, and contradictions, the church nonetheless remains God's means of support. Nothing in this world can replace the maternal care and protection the church provides for God's people. The church, Luther stresses, "is completely in God's hands alone, who must preserve it through His divine strength. From the beginning He has always miraculously preserved it in the world, in great weakness, in division through schismatics and heretics, and in persecution by tyrants. It is His own governance alone, and yet He commits the office and service to people, whom he summons and wants to use to distribute His Word and Sacrament through their mouths and hands."[82] To recognize the various ministries of the church is another way of sanctifying God as Lord (1 Pet 3:15). We close our "eyes, senses, and thoughts"[83] to things that contradict God's word, instead clinging to that same word, trusting that God's eyes never avert from us and that he has the best regard for us. The words "Cast all your anxieties on Him, for He cares about you" (1 Pet 5:7) are "exceedingly delightful words," so alluring that they impel us to humble ourselves gladly. "Therefore," Luther exhorts, "forget about all your anxiety, and let Him manage."[84]

Faith's Adversary: The Devil

Peter presented himself, says Luther, "as a faithful servant"[85] who alerts us to the reality of the devil and his regime against God's purpose and his people.[86] Scriptural teaching of the devil and Luther's personal experience of the devil's assaults are essential to Luther's account of faith. Any attempt to excise the devil from his experience of faith, Tomlin avers rightly, "is to emasculate his theology, to render it tame."[87] Luther once confessed that demonic action makes "a real doctor" out of him, causing him to "seek and love God's Word."[88] The word is armor by which we are equipped to combat not only the vices of the old Adam but also conquer the "adversary the devil [who] prowls around like a roaring lion, seeking some to devour" (1 Pet 5:8). The word reveals our adversary so that we know not only of his designs to gain ground but also how we might arm ourselves to triumph over his agency.[89] The words "be sober, be watchful" (1 Pet 5:8) must be written, Luther says, "in golden letters"[90]—not to incite terror but to strengthen the faithful to combat the devil's cunning attacks. Luther is keenly aware of the devil's opposition to God's rule of the created orders. He describes, "The world is nothing but the devil's den of robbers, both in spiritual and physical government and affairs."[91] The devil holds people in his power and constitutes them as agents

of evil. The devil's "sole purpose is to crush and destroy everything that God creates and does through" his created orders.
For instance, the devil opposes "the spiritual rule" by having
"the heretics, false teachers, hypocrites, false brethren; and he
does not rest until he has destroyed this rule. Opposed to the
secular rule he has the rebellious, lawless scoundrels, evil, ven-
omous counselors at the courts of the princes, flatterers, trai-
tors, spies, tyrants, madmen, and everything that promotes
war, discord, and destruction of lands and people."[92]

Luther uses more adjectives to describe the devil: crafty, dil-
igent, cunning, and malicious.[93] The devil is ceaseless in tempting our body into licentiousness and rascality, our mind into
error and blindness, and our soul into contempt and distrust
for God. Therefore we ought to be watchful "physically," for the
devil can entice a lazy body to loosen its rein and give in to evil
lusts. We must guard against the body so that it is given "less
reason to sin."[94] We must be sober "spiritually," for the faithful
are often too frail to face the adversary without adequate provision.[95] The devil lures us to exalt reason above revelation, giving
it a magisterial role that sits in judgment on divine things. In
matters of faith, Luther regards reason negatively, viewing it
as seductive. He claims, "Reason is the devil's prostitute and
can do nothing else but slander and dishonor what God does
and says."[96] But this does not mean Luther denigrates reason
altogether. His positive estimation of reason is apparent in his
exposition of the first article of the Creed, where he writes, "I
hold and believe that I am God's creature, that is, that he has
given me and constantly sustains my body, soul, and life, my
members great and small, all my senses, my reason and understanding, and the like."[97] In his *Disputation Concerning Man*
(1536), Luther acknowledges the positive role reason has in the
ordering of our creaturely existence and affairs. He avers, "Nor
did God after the fall of Adam take away this majesty of reason, but rather confirmed it."[98] Luther assigns divine status to

reason, considering it as "the most important and the highest in rank among all things, and in comparison with other things of this life, the best and something divine."[99] Reason operates well in the social, economic, and political realm over which human beings have dominion. When reason extends into the religious or spiritual world, it is sinful; it fails to grasp the true God and culminates in idolatry instead. Fallen reason has lost its integrity and thus is incapable of appropriating the kingdom of God. It cannot yield true knowledge of God unless by the grace of God's revelation. As Grosshans writes rightly, "Luther's sharp criticism of reason as it relates to true religion and the true God is behind this famous condemnation of reason as a 'whore' who sells itself to anyone—and every religious endeavor—that pays well."[100]

The devil causes us to focus on external works that steer us away from God's word and his grace. He also causes us to turn inward to seek resources for aid where there is none. The devil, to use Oberman's phrase, is the "master of subjectivity,"[101] who prompts us to place our trust in the subjective dictate of what is true or right rather than the objective assurance of God's word. When driven into "melancholy because of sin," St. Peter's remedy, says Luther, is "resist him, firm in your faith" (1 Pet 5:9). Luther quotes St. Paul, who teaches us "to take up the shield of faith" with which we might "extinguish all [the devil's] poisonous, flaming darts" (Eph 6:16).[102] Luther writes, "The true sword is your strong and firm faith. If you take hold of God's Word in your heart and cling to it with faith, the devil cannot win but must flee."[103] When the tempter disappears, so do all vices of the flesh: "aversion, evil lust, anger, greed, melancholy and doubt."[104] Faith places us in Christ and adorns us with all that we need to conquer the edifices of the devil.

We have been called by God and put into the position of Christians so that we would renounce the devil and contend against him, and thus maintain God's name, Word, and king-dom against him. Christ, our Head, has already in Himself defeated and destroyed the devil and his power over us. In addition, He also gives us faith and the Holy Spirit, by which we can completely knock down his remaining wickedness, wrath, and might with which he tempts us.[105]

The "Chief Function of a Priest": Grace and Peace

Luther teaches us how to preach aright, focusing not on human powers but on the impact the work of Christ has on those whom God has distinguished as "a royal priesthood [and] a holy nation" (1 Pet 2:9). "The chief function of a priest" for Peter is to "declare the wonderful deeds of Him who called you out of darkness into His marvelous light" (1 Pet 2:9).[106] This verse highlights the extreme predicament of sinners, that they are in darkness and thus are ignorant of the way of deliverance. "The wonderful deeds of God" refers to the redemptive work that Christ has accomplished for us by which the contraries of death, sin, and hell are vanquished in exchange for life, righ-teousness, and heaven. The priestly office of the church must expend all efforts to uphold God's "true light," namely, what God has achieved for us, and to teach people how they can be liberated from utter darkness into "His marvelous light."[107] No mortal soul can understand the redemptive work of God unless by revelation, nor perform it unless by God's power. Reason can judge about external things but not divine wisdom, Luther avers—not even "one letter" of it.[108] So, it requires "another light, a light that is marvelous," by which God leads us out of dark-ness into his "true light."[109] In this regard, Luther hails Peter as a brave apostle, who names darkness as it really is, contradict-ing what people consider as light.[110] Reason is "stone-blind" and can only grasp the righteousness that proceeds from works.[111] The inefficacy of reason points to the necessity of divine illu-mination. "Consequently," Luther contends, "everything that is not God's Word and faith is darkness."[112] The impoverished and the weak crave the word the priests proclaim and enter the true light; the learned and the powerful shun it and remain in darkness. Implied in 2 Peter 1:19, "God's Word is like a lamp shining in a dark place," is that this light presupposes its opposite, namely, darkness that it exposes and disposes. "For since the Word of God is the light in a pitch-dark place, it is established that everything else is darkness."[113] Apart from the word, Luther avers, everything is "sheer error and darkness."[114]

The word and the Holy Spirit are one; their unity enables Luther to refute the enthusiasts who claim to have an unmediated encounter with God, apart from the external word. Luther rebuts, "How can they have God's Spirit if they do not have God's Word? Therefore they do nothing else than call darkness light and 'put darkness for light,' as Is. 5:20 states."[115] The word of the gospel—that Christ's redemption has annihilated sin, death, and hell—illumines our hearts and eliminates the darkness within. The gospel must be preached so that we can "grasp it . . . with our ears and have it in the Word."[116] Whoever "hears" the word, says Luther, "has lighted the light and the lamp in our hearts to enable us to see."[117] The error and darkness within could only be disposed by the hearing of God's word. The preaching of St. Peter is without effect unless accompanied by the Holy Spirit, Luther avers, "so that he believed in it and confidently preached and confessed it. The former pertains solely to the office of the ministry, not to the soul; the latter, however, pertains to the Spirit."[118]

St. Peter's greeting to Christians is identical to St. Paul's: "May grace and peace be multiplied in you" (1 Pet 1:1; Gal 1:3). "Grace" and "peace" constitute "the whole of Christianity."[119] In his Galatians commentary, Luther regards "grace" and "peace" as the remedy of the "two monsters" that assault the Christian life: "sin and conscience, [and] the power of the Law and the sting of sin" (1 Cor 15:56).[120] Likewise, in his sermons on 1 Peter, Luther considers grace as the foundation of peace; both are essential to the Christian life. Helmer writes, "[Luther] preached that grace is vastly abundant, that divine generosity recognizes persons as just because Christ has clothed them with his righteousness."[121] Grace means "God's goodwill," which is the basis of peace.[122] Luther writes:

> And he who realizes and believes that he has a gracious God, he has Him. Then his heart gains peace, and he fears neither the world nor the devil. For he knows that God, who is omnipotent, is his friend and will rescue him from death, hell, and all adversity. Therefore his conscience has peace and joy.[123]

Once our hearts are seized by a gracious and omnipotent God, they find peace and courage to face the enemies of life. God's grace and peace are ours, but only in part because of the impediment of the old Adam. The afflicted conscience finds relief, not by a recourse to itself for resources but by a reliance upon Christ, the cornerstone. We are daily to advance in grace and peace until the flesh dies completely. Thus, such a greeting is proper, as it spurs believers toward growth in grace and peace.[124]

The subject of proclamation is this: "By grace alone all things come to us who merit nothing."[125] Hordern writes, "The primary aspect of justification is not our faith but God's grace. Because God has acted for us in Jesus Christ, because God's love seeks us, because God forgives our sins, we are justified. This gracious act and attitude of God is received by us through faith, but it is not our faith that saves us, it is God's grace alone."[126] Grace began in eternity but became actual in history. The grace upon which our hope is set is offered in no other way than through the life-giving activities of Jesus Christ; as 1 Peter 1:13 reads, "Set your hope fully upon the grace that is coming to you at the revelation of Jesus Christ." We do not earn God's grace; it is bestowed on us completely without any condition.

Luther conceives grace as the effectual presence of Christ in our lives by which we triumph over all contraries of life—sin, death, the devil, and hell—and become "lord" over them, if we firmly believe.

> Whoever believes in Jesus Christ and clings to the Word has Him with all His blessings, so that he becomes lord over sin, death, the devil, and hell, and is sure of eternal life. This treasure is brought to our door and laid into our laps without our cooperation or merit, yes, unexpectedly and without our knowledge or thoughts. Therefore the apostle wants us to set our hope cheerfully on this grace, for the God who offers it to us will surely not lie to us.[127]

Like Peter, we are commanded to preach grace, not human works or doctrines, which are of no help to people. We are to proclaim "the power of God" by which "Christ has swallowed up death, devoured hell, drunk sin to the dregs, and placed us into eternal life . . . [and] the kind of power that overcomes the devil, sin, and death."[128] And "those who stress most frequently and above all how nothing but faith in Christ justifies," says Luther, "are the best evangelists."[129] So "the first concern" of a justified saint, says Luther, is to abandon "all confidence in works and increasingly to strengthen faith alone and through faith to grow in the knowledge, not of works, but of Christ Jesus, who suffered and rose for him, as Peter teaches in the last chapter of his first Epistle (1 Pet. 5:10)."[130]

Commenting on 1 Peter 5:10—"the God of grace, who has called you to His eternal glory in Christ, will Himself restore, establish, and strengthen you"—Luther recognizes that St. Peter uses several verbs to reinforce the various ways that God provides for us (*pro nobis*): "call," "restore," "establish," and "strengthen." Luther is so thrilled at grace that he stresses "not only little grace but all grace piled up," through which we may increase faith in the gospel.[131] Faith and works are irreconcilable opposites. Quoting Isaiah 28:16 in his exposition of 1 Peter 2:6, Luther declares faith as the immovable stone: "Let all works by which we aim to gain righteousness and all our own merits depart because we are built upon the foundation not by doing works but by believing. Therefore let every godly man, terrified by sin, run to Christ as the Mediator and the Propitiator, and let him leave all his own works behind."[132] The hearts that rest on God's bountiful grace, not on any works or merits, will be able to withstand all storms of life. Luther extols grace over law in thesis 26 of his *Heidelberg Disputation*: "The law says, 'do this,' and it is never done. Grace says, 'believe in this, and everything is already done.'"[133] Just as Peter began his greeting with "grace and peace" (1 Pet 1:2), so he ended his speech with the same: "This is the true grace of God; stand fast in it. . . . Peace to all of you that are in Christ" (1 Pet 5:12, 14). We do well by laying hold of Peter's repeated words in his greeting and farewell, "grace" and "peace"; they are effective words that establish what they say. They are, Luther avers, "words of fire" that inflame the hearts that believe.[134]

The God-imposed Cross and the Sacrifice of Self

All the physical sacrifices of the priesthood foreshadowed in the Old Testament ceased at the advent of Christ. Luther says, "Today everything is new and spiritual."[135] Part of the priestly office is to offer "spiritual sacrifices" to God.[136] The spiritual sacrifices in 1 Peter 2:5 refer not to the external sacrifices of the Old Testament but to the spiritual sacrifice of ourselves to God. "Just as He sacrificed His own body, so, we, too, must sacrifice ourselves."[137] The spiritual sacrifice of self is achieved by the proclamation of the word; through the gospel, every remnant of the old Adam is mortified.[138] The preached word performs an alien work: it "slaughters the calf, namely, the carnal mind; [it] strangles the old Adam. For one must slay with the Gospel" the lust of the flesh and its vices.[139] The old flesh that clings to us hinders the accomplishment of God-pleasing things. "For we have our enemy in our flesh. He is a real rascal, which Paul calls *prudentia carnis*, that is, 'the mind of the flesh' (Rom. 8:6). If this rascality has been subdued, the rest is easily subdued. This rascality commonly harms our neighbor so furtively that one cannot notice it."[140] We are not to be "idle" but instead must be active in "girding the loins of the flesh" (1 Pet 1:13) by nailing it to the cross.[141] We offer up ourselves as sacrifices and allow the cross to crucify our old person.[142] Luther avows, "The true priestly office is practiced when we sacrifice that villainous rogue, the lazy old ass, to God."[143] The death of the old self under the law is the "only sacrifice" God approves of.[144] The more the self-curvedness is fortified, the more the old Adam seeks to dominate the new Adam; conversely, the more the self-curvedness is mortified, the more the old Adam ceases its dominion so that the new Adam rises in power. Apart from Christ, no sacrifice, including the noble task of bearing the cross, counts before God. All our works are vitiated before God unless done through Christ, "the living stone" whom God regards, and who imparts all his blessings to all who are joined to him, as a bride to her groom, through faith.[145]

The cross-shaped vocation constitutes a true mark of the church, characterized by seeking to serve, and by embracing suffering rather than glory as a sign of obedience to God. God-imposed suffering, Wingren intimates, does not mean that "God brings [troubles] upon [a person] from without, through divine direction of affairs and dispensations. They are brought upon him from within, through God's direction of his heart."[146] We embrace the cross only when God determines it, as Peter says, "if that should be God's will" (1 Pet 3:17). If suffering is sent by God, we should thank God, boasting of being made "worthy of becoming like Christ," suffering as he did, without reviling or threatening but even praying for the wicked.[147] In cross-bearing, St. Peter urges us to "sanctify in [our] hearts Christ as Lord" (1 Pet 3:15). To "sanctify" him is to "hallow" his name, as in the Lord's Prayer.[148] Luther quotes Psalm 145:17: "The Lord is just in all His ways, and holy in all His doings." Whatever allotments God sends, shame or honor, we accept them as "not only good but also holy."[149] Luther cites Job as an instance of "the right way" of sanctifying God. After suffering enormous losses, Job said, "The Lord gave, and the Lord has taken away. As it pleased Him, so it has happened. Blessed be the name of the Lord" (Job 1:21).[150] Job attributed all things—good and bad—to God, even when God constitutes the devil as his instrument to reach his goal. Thus, Job hallowed God's name by his confession: "God gave it, and God took it away" rather than "God gave it, and the devil took away."[151] God grants King Nebuchadnezzar the land, though he has no right to it; likewise, the devil has no right to anything that he took away by God's permission. We regard God as holy, clinging to his word that we have a God who shows special regard to those who suffer for his sake.[152] We should derive comfort from these words: "But even if you do suffer for righteousness' sake, you will be blessed" (1 Pet 3:14). In Luther's words, "Then the fact that you are suffering for doing right is a greater blessing for you and makes you happier."[153] Evildoers suffer both "outwardly" in the flesh and "inwardly" with a gnawing conscience; the righteous suffer only "outwardly," being "inwardly" comforted.[154] "For the eyes of the Lord look at the righteous, and His ears [listen] to their prayers" (1 Pet 3:12). There is nothing more comforting than God's gracious eyes that are upon the righteous, and God's earnest ears that attune to their cries and laments. Faith trusts that there is "no lack of [God's] looking at us" and no lack of God's hearing us "with sharp, open ears" to our praying.[155] By contrast, St. Peter writes, "The face of the Lord looks against those who do evil" (1 Pet 3:12). Evildoers encounter a bitterly wrathful face, which incites terror rather than comfort.[156] Their miserable condition ought to motivate us not to avenge and repay evil for evil (1 Pet 3:9) but to pray for them, pleading that God will deliver them from his wrath, as he did with us.

The God-imposed cross differs from the self-imposed cross; the former emanates from faith, while the latter does so from flesh. Self-imposed suffering is another form of Gabriel Biel's premise, of "doing what lies in us,"[157] a sort of a preparatory work for the reception of God's grace; to Luther, this is of the flesh. Quoting Colossians 2:23, Luther repudiates the cross as self-imposed "devotion and self-abasement and severity to the body."[158] For to impose a cross upon oneself is to exalt "reason," which, for Luther, "extols only its own works."[159] To seek the cross ourselves is to "choose our own works" rather than God's.[160] Any self-chosen undertaking, even as noble as cross-bearing, that is not commanded by God is empty of efficacy before God. "For obedience, which depends on God's word," Luther concedes, "is of all works the noblest and best."[161] To perform works on which God has not stamped his approval is to reassert the old self as lord. The performance of works, in whatever form it may assume, does not dispose us to grace. Thesis 30 of Luther's *Disputation against Scholastic Theology* declares his position: "On the part of man, however, nothing precedes grace except ill will and even rebellion against grace."[162] The self-chosen cross is of the flesh and thus is no meritorious work. Suffering that is God-pleasing proceeds from faith, not from vices, scandals, or self; it stems from communion with God.

For Paul, the configuration of the authentic Christian life is "faith, hope, and love"; for Peter, with a minor variation, it is "faith, hope, and the *holy cross*, for one follows from the other."[163] Faith gives rise to hope; it also gives rise to love and the holy cross so that "faith, love, and the holy cross" form an organic unity in the genuine Christian life.[164] The genuineness of faith is tested by "the holy cross," the agent of mortification. "For if faith is present," Luther avers, "a hundred more evil thoughts and a hundred more trials come than there were before."[165] Our faith must be proved true and refined through life's manifold adversities God sends—as 1 Peter 1:9 reads, "so that the genuineness of your faith, more precious than gold which though perishable is tested by fire, may redound to praise and glory and honor at the revelation of Jesus Christ." Peter likens the testing of faith by suffering to the testing of gold by fire. Just as fire purifies gold and causes all alloy to disappear from it, so also God has imposed temptation and afflictions upon believers to cause all impurities and every falsehood to disappear; as the psalmist declares in Psalm 17:3, "Thou hast tried me by fire, and iniquity has not been found in me." The chief purpose of testing, Rittgers rightly points out, is "the purification of the heart, and thus of faith and life, not the production of humility and self-accusation."[166] Of this, Luther avers, "For how can an external work cleanse the heart inwardly? But when faith is tested in this way, all alloy and everything false must disappear. Then, when Christ is revealed, splendid honor, praise, and glory will follow."[167] Suffering is imposed not by a stern judge whose sole purpose is to condemn but by a merciful God whose sole purpose is to exalt. God consecrates suffering as a "sacred cross" through which he sanctifies us and renews us into the image of his Son.[168] Kachelmeier puts it well: "Instead of us forming God into our fallen image, God forms us into His image and likeness."[169] In Luther's own words, "Christ is a tested stone, that is, distressed and afflicted, or He is a testing stone, that is, a stone by whose shape all other stones are tested, so that we may be conformed to the image of the Son of God (Rom. 8:29). As Christ was polished, hewn, and squared by the promise, by death and the cross, so we, in His image, should become well-polished by such suffering and such a cross."[170] The cross God imposes upon his children is God's alien work of killing the sinful identity to achieve his proper work of creating a new identity.

Paul teaches in Galatians 5:24 that "those who belong to Christ have crucified their flesh with all its desires" (Gal 5:24).[171] Likewise, Peter teaches in 1 Peter 4:1–2: "Whoever has suffered in the flesh has ceased from sin, so as to live for the rest of the time in the flesh no longer by passions but the will of God." The word "flesh" refers to the whole person, consisting of "reason and will, internally and externally, together with body and soul."[172] Not only did Christ suffer in his body, he also suffered in his soul (cf. Isa 53:11). Likewise, Christian suffering extends beyond physical pain into assaults, misery, and distress.[173] If these attacks come our way as God permits, God will ensure that they redound to our benefit. God hallows "the holy cross [as] a good means with which to subdue sin. When it attacks you in this way, your tickling, envy, and hatred, and your other rascality, vanish. God has laid the holy cross on us in order that it may drive and compel us, so that we have to believe and to extend a helping hand to one another."[174] Consequently, our new life is no longer governed by "human passions," as the Gentiles are (1 Pet 4:3), but rather by the cross of Christ. The purpose of Christian suffering is so that their faith may be proved true, through which unbelievers may be attracted to it. In his exposition of 1 Peter 4:12—"Beloved, do not be surprised at the fiery ordeal which comes upon you to prove you, as though something strange were happening to you"—Luther stresses again the benefits of suffering, "an oven full of fire and heat," through which God strengthens our faith and renews us into a true, vibrant life to the praise of God. The gospel is most effective in its opposites: not in power but in weakness, not in life but in death, not in ease but in trials. Luther avers, "Were there only peace and no trials, we would never learn to know God Himself. . . . Trouble and distress constrain us and keep us within Christendom. Crosses, troubles, therefore, are as necessary for us as life itself, and much more necessary and useful than all the possessions and honor in the world."[175] Assaults (suffering, trials, darkness, despair, and grief) thus are causally useful, as they cause us to find hope in the power of God's word. Luther expands:

> When faith begins, God does not forsake us; He lays the holy cross on our backs to strengthen us and to make faith powerful in us. The holy Gospel is a powerful Word. Therefore it cannot do its work without trials, and only he who tastes it is aware that it has such power. Where suffering and the cross are found, there the Gospel can show and exercise its power. It is a Word of life. Therefore it must exercise all its power in death. In the absence of dying and death it can do nothing, and no one can become aware that it has such power and is stronger than sin and death. Therefore the apostle says, "to prove you"; that is, God inflicts no glowing fire or heat—cross and suffering, which make you burn—on you for any other purpose than "to prove you," whether you also cling to His Word.[176]

The agency of the cross is set opposite to the agency of sin; each has its own aim. "The cross puts to death everything we have,"[177] says Luther, stripping us of all merits. The cross calls for a radical abandonment of our trust in all created beings. Hope lies not in turning inward to the self for resources or outward to created beings; it lies "outside of ourselves and all other things, in God alone."[178] While distress, "a narrow place," squeezes us and casts us to despair, God's grace, "a large place," liberates us and brings us joy.[179] The cross causes us to despair of ourselves and all creaturely things so that "we learn to believe in God, to trust him, to love him, and to place our hope in him."[180] Faith that has undergone testing, Luther expands,

> does not despair of the God who sends trouble. Faith does not consider Him angry or an enemy, as the flesh, the world, and

the devil strongly suggest. Faith rises above all this and sees God's fatherly heart behind His unfriendly exterior. Faith sees the sun shining through these thick, dark clouds and this gloomy weather. Faith has the courage to call with confidence to Him who smites it and looks at it with a sour face.[181]

On the contrary, "our iniquity tries to keep itself and its possession alive," and "the godless nature of ours," if not subdued by the cross, exudes all kinds of vices and evils by which we perish eternally.[182] The word of life is most effective when our deeply "curved in on itself"[183] nature undergoes the alien work of purification through fire, as through suffering we are reduced to nothing so that we can boast nothing of our own, but only of Christ and his boundless goods.

CHAPTER 6

God's Command and Secular Government
Civil Obedience and External Righteousness

First Peter 2:13–20 presents an occasion for Luther to teach two governments: secular and spiritual.[1] As a human institution, the secular government has no power to rule over faith, which belongs to the spiritual government. The civil government is God's ordained instrument by which he rules the world and promotes external righteousness. It achieves this by wielding the sword—in Peter's words, "to punish those who do wrong and to praise those who do right" (1 Pet 2:14). The same sentiment occurs in Romans 13:3: "Rulers are not a terror to good conduct, but to bad. Would you have no fear of him who is in authority? Then do what is good, and you will receive his approval." If civil government meddles in the spiritual estate, where God alone rules, we in no wise obey it. On the other hand, spiritual government does not interfere with the secular domain, which belongs to princes and kings, whom God appoints as ministers of civil righteousness. We obey human authorities, not because of their command but because of God's word attached to their office, and thus we are duty bound to submit to their domain as a public confession of our faith. We must willingly serve him, not to merit anything before God for this but only to please God without recompense. On 1 Peter 2:7, "Cast all your anxieties on Him, for He cares about you,"[2] Luther affirms all offices and estates as God's gifts for the sustenance of his created world. Like the household and civil orders, the secular estate is the means of God's providential care for us.

In his exposition of 1 Peter 2:13, Luther locates the origin of civil government in the fall, viewing it as a postlapsarian remedy for evil; he writes, "If there were no evil people, one would not need a government."[3] However, elsewhere Luther locates it in the original created order before the fall, that is, prelapsarianly. The logic of Luther's two-realms thinking suggests that community hierarchy and governance belongs to what is essentially good in human life and so must not merely be seen to defend against disorder and sin. On 1 Peter 2:18—"Servants, be submissive to your masters with all respect, not only to the kind and gentle but also to the overbearing"—Luther teaches that civil power extends to the master–slave relationship, which, as Althaus notes, "has a basis antecedent to the dominion of sin."[4] The same appears in his exposition of the phrase "the congregation of God" in Psalm 82:1, where Luther argues that civil government "was not only first founded and created by the word in Genesis 1 but was established and ordered by a special word of God."[5]

Beeke raises an incisive question: "Was there a time when the two kingdoms were not?"[6] While Luther scholars differ on this question, the tension can be resolved depending on the subject to whom civil government is applied, just as the usage of the law is related to the subject to whom it is addressed. In the prelapsarian state, where sin has not entered the scene, the law is not opposed to the promise. The antithesis between law and promise in the postlapsarian state occurs when the subject to whom the law is applied changes. The wicked would come under the negative imposition of the political force against their evil deeds, while the righteous are praised for doing right.

Here the historical context in which Luther was preaching helps sharpen the focus.

The Law's Civil Use: "Gods" but Not "God"

In his treatise on *Temporal Authority* (1522), Luther provides "a sound basis for the civil law and sword so no one will doubt it is in the world by God's will and ordinance."[7] This runs contrary to the view that disregards civil law and denies its godly service. In his commentary on Psalm 82:1, "God stands in the congregation of God and is Judge among the gods," Luther esteems highly the offices of government, "from the least to the highest."[8] Moses calls them "gods" who rule over us, but they do not rule over God because he is the one who appoints them to govern. For God cannot cease to be God; he must remain the supreme God, the judge who rules over all, including the civil gods. Civil authority is a divine ordinance, and kings and rulers in it are rightly called divine or godlike—not on account of their persons but solely on the basis of God's word and command. Accordingly, King Jehoshaphat said to his officials in 2 Chronicles 19, "Consider, and judge rightly; for the judgment is God's." We ought to render obedience to civil servants and honor them with all fear and reverence, as to God himself. This is because "God names [them] with His own name and calls [them] 'gods' and to whom He attaches His own honor."[9] To repudiate the civil order is to repudiate the supreme God who lies hidden in these appointed gods to govern the created order. Government is no terror to the children of Adam; as Paul says, "It is God's minister to you for good" (Rom 13:3). Where civil government is disdained, there will be chaos and disorder. Obedience to civil gods is the exercise of the first commandment. We trust, fear, and love God by rendering an obedience to the government as 1 Peter 2:17 has it, "Fear God. Honor the emperor." We fear God by honoring lords and kings, whom

God places over us, even when they are heathen.[10] Luther writes, "For God's Word appoints them, makes them gods, and subjects everything to them."[11] The creator God "does not leave the world desolate and empty but has made it for men to live in, to till the land and fill it, as it is written in Genesis 1:29–30. Because this cannot happen where there is no peace, He is compelled as a Creator, preserving His own creatures, works, and ordinances, to institute and preserve His own creatures, commit to it the sword and the laws."[12] God wills that God's command to obey the civil government be taken as seriously as the other commands, and he attaches to it a terrifying threat that he will punish the disobedient whom he regards as "not worthy to live."[13] Luther exhorts, "Each citizen, subject, etc., should attend to his activity and work. Whatever else there may be can simply be committed to God."[14]

Civil obedience is limited only when it contradicts God's commandment, as Peter teaches in Acts 5:26: "We must obey God rather than man." This holy office ceases its proper function through either unbelief or pride. When that happens, its respective subjects are exonerated from the duty to obey.[15] This does not mean Luther encourages revolutions and resistance by force. His position is obvious in *Warning to His Dear Christian People* (1531), where he regards the peasants' revolt as rebellion against God's juridical function.[16] In his exposition of 1 Peter 2:19–20, Luther teaches that temporal power "cannot harm the soul," as it does not deal with "the preaching of the gospel, or with faith, or with the first three commandments."[17] Hence secular power "is but a very small matter" in God's sight for anyone to resist or disobey on its own account, irrespective of whether it does right or wrong.[18] God grants King Nebuchadnezzar the land, though he has no right to it; God assumes the right to punish people through him. We hallow God's name by yielding to his "right and truthful judgment,"[19] even when he uses the devil or wicked rulers as his alien work to govern the land. "Hence rascals and wrong are a good thing too."[20] To sanctify God as Lord is to "let Him manage things. He will surely repay."[21] God ordains civil order, and he alone is the judge.[22] Luther adamantly opposes bad governmental practices, promising God's wrath for courtiers and princes who instigate civil disobedience. God imposes judgment upon officials who tyrannize their people, but their subjects bear no authority to resist them. Luther proposes, in Methuen's phrase, "passive or non-violent resistance";[23] as Luther avers, "Outrage is not to be resisted but endured."[24] God restrains the evil passion of the rabble, subjecting them to the law of the sword. They are not allowed to seize the sword and revolt against the rulers. "No, they must leave that alone! It is not God's will, and he has not committed this to them."[25] On the other hand, God restrains self-willed rulers so that they do not abuse "His majesty and power" hidden in their offices but instead use them to promote peace and order, the very purpose for which they are appointed as gods.[26]

The injunction not to resist evil is taught by Jesus in Matthew 5:39: "Yet Christ gave the command not to resist evil, but that if anyone strikes us on one cheek, we should turn to him the other cheek also. How, then, can we strike and kill people?"[27] Jesus's command not to resist evil pertains only to believers. Luther instructs them about their outward life and their obligation to others in the secular realm. They are to conduct themselves in fear of God and not be involved in things pertaining to secular authority, power, or punishment. Quoting Luther: "For we have been transferred to another and a higher existence, a divine and an eternal kingdom, where the things [for instance, 'private acts of revenge'][28] that belong to the world are unnecessary."[29] Instead of resisting their enemies, Christians subject themselves to the civil government, which holds the power of the sword. However, Christians may exercise the sword, not for themselves but for the sake of their neighbors.

Johansson writes, "Where [a Christian's] own matters are concerned, he should follow the Sermon on the Mount. But when it comes to public responsibility or 'office,' he is not only allowed to use force but even commanded to use it for the common good."[30] Such action, says Luther, still is "a work of Christian love."[31] Where there is a lack of officials in the government, he must offer his services and occupy the position; he does all he can to uphold the government in honor and fear. Civil office is external, just as the other offices and estates are. It falls outside the purview of Christ's office so that both Christians and non-Christians can occupy the civil office.[32] By this, Luther highlights the opposite of what society could become, were it not for secular power, which God uses to promote order and peace.

Though Christ was free and lord above all, he submitted himself to Caesar, rendering to him what was rightly his (Matt 22:21); he, too, placed himself under the scrutiny of Pilate, who was granted the power to rule "from above" (John 19:11). His obedience to secular rule was pleasing to the Father.[33] This was what the prophets of the Old Testament did, too, as they prostrated beneath the feet of the kings of Babylon.[34] Christians in whom Christ lives and reigns have been transplanted into the dominion of the Holy Spirit, and thus are not in need of any law to compel them to serve others; as Paul writes in 1 Timothy 1:9, "The Law is not laid down for the just." To be possessed of Christian freedom is not to be relieved of obligations to obey civil power. Though the Christian does not need the sword, they willingly work with the secular state for the common good of their neighbors. "Because the sword is most beneficial and necessary for the whole world in order to preserve peace, punish sin, and restrain the wicked, the Christian submits most willingly to the rule of the sword, pays his taxes, honors those in authority, serves, and helps, and does all he can to assist the governing authority, that it may continue to function and be held in honor and fear."[35] Having been freed from all laws, we serve not out of compulsion, nor by coercion from secular authorities, but willingly. "All their works are performed without compulsion and for nothing; they flow from a happy and cheerful heart, which thanks, praises, and lauds God for all the good things it has received from Him."[36]

Civil and Spiritual Regiments: The Law and Gospel Distinction

The distinction between the two kingdoms stems from two distinct actions of the one and same God. It is, DeJonge writes, "ultimately about the twofold way that God preserves the sinful world from falling into unfettered chaos while ushering it toward redemption."[37] One must observe a limit to temporal authority: "No one shall or can command the soul unless he is able to show it the way to heaven; but this no man can do, only God alone."[38] It cannot extend into God's kingdom and government, a domain reserved for God alone. "For God cannot and will not permit anyone but himself to rule the soul."[39] Secular rule does not interfere with the office of Christ; it has no causal power to make us Christian or otherwise. We should obey secular power so long as it gives commands that deal only with external matters and do not infringe the Christian's conscience. As a "human institution" (1 Pet 2:13), the secular government does not possess any power in matters related to faith, and in such instances, believers are absolved of the duty to yield. Luther expands:

> Therefore if an emperor or a prince were to ask me now what my faith is, I would have to tell him, not because of his command, but because it is my duty to confess my faith publicly before everybody. But if he wanted to go beyond this and commanded me to believe this or that, I would have to say: "My dear lord, attend to your secular rule. You have no authority

to meddle in God's kingdom. Therefore I refuse to obey you.
You surely cannot put up with any meddling in your domain.
If anyone trespasses on your territory without your consent,
you shoot at him with guns. Do you suppose that God should
tolerate your desire to dethrone Him and to put yourself in
His place?"[40]

Not everybody shows regard for God and gladly obeys him,
thus the institution of the secular sword and authority is "necessary."[41] Luther avers, "Since we cannot all be pious, Christ
has entrusted the wicked to the government to be ruled as they
must be ruled. But the pious He keeps for Himself and rules
them Himself with His Word alone."[42] God imposes political
force upon the bad, those who refuse to yield to civil authority. Hence civil government is primarily instituted for the sake
of unbelievers.[43] Spiritual and secular rules are not opposed to
each other. Both governments are required for the preservation
of the unity and peace in the world. "Neither one is sufficient
in the world without the other."[44] Where only the secular rules,
Christian righteousness would not occur; but where only the
spiritual rules, all kinds of vices or evils would dominate. God
works in both kingdoms, achieving his own purpose. "In brief,"
Beeke summarizes, "the operation of the Holy Spirit in the spiritual government produces righteousness in Christians before
God (*coram Deo*), whereas the temporal government merely
ensures righteousness before humans (*coram hominibus*)."[45]

The church is, Nestingen notes, "where the two kingdoms
overlap."[46] A believer must live in both kingdoms and continually perform works of love in both. The church is, Wannenwetsch writes, "both mediator of the duality of the regiments
and bearer of the tension that their simultaneity brings with
it."[47] When believers gather at church to hear God's word and to
have the Spirit seize their hearts via the created means of grace,
they are empowered to concretize their righteous identity in
the civil realm. As DeJonge writes, "The character of their

participation in the spiritual kingdom sends them to action in the temporal kingdom."[48] The civil sphere is where Christians not only express their righteous identity but also grow in "proper righteousness," though they are completely clothed with "alien righteousness."[49] "Because believers remain sinful," DeJonge writes, "temporal forms of authority still play a role in their lives even after justification. Because justification creates a *simul* situation, the believer is a citizen of both worlds, the spiritual and temporal."[50] The dual citizenship that a believer is expected to exemplify, Johansson notes, is not "mutually exclusive"; it is incorporated into the *simul* dimension of Luther's theology.[51] Justification makes her a new creature, though the old creature remains. As an old creature, she must be "subject to secular law"; as a new creature, she must serve her neighbor with "the instrument of the secular order."[52]

The distinction between the two kingdoms corresponds to the distinction between law and gospel. Wannenwetsch argues accurately, "Yet this distinction must not amount to separation where the two are seen as unrelated and without any mutual effect on each other."[53] The two regiments or realms are always a part of everyone's life.[54] McCain writes, "For Luther, any attempt to impose the Law in the realm of the Gospel is to undo everything. If the bishops attempt to use the Law to enforce the Gospel, they err; just so, the secular rulers cannot use the Gospel to rule where the Law is given to do its work among men."[55] Luther cautions against the collapse of the distinction between the two kingdoms, a work he attributes to the devil. The devil works incessantly to merge them into each other, and he works tirelessly on both sides. "In the devil's name the secular leaders always want to be Christ's masters and teach Him how He should run His church and spiritual government. Similarly, the false clerics and schismatic spirits always want to be the masters, though not in God's name, and to teach people how to organize the secular government."[56] The two

kingdoms, Bornkamm observes, "are not rigidly fixed prov-
inces into which the Christian's existence is divided."[57] In his
exegesis of Psalm 102:5, "I destroy him who secretly maligns
his neighbor," Luther underscores King David as the luminary
who shows us "a proper Christian way" of living in the two
basic relations without confusion.[58] David led God's people
"vertically toward God," bringing them God's eternal goods
such as righteousness, forgiveness, and eternal life so that they
are saved; politically, he governed his people "horizontally"
with justice, ensuring that all creaturely goods such as the
body, property, children, home and house, and every temporal
thing are securely preserved.[59] The bishops, priests, and pope of
Luther's days had succumbed to the devil's lure, meddling with
temporal duties such as governing lands, castles, and cities outwardly at the expense of ruling souls inwardly by the gospel. In
so doing, Beeke recognizes, they confused the two kingdoms,
and thus dissolved the distinction between law and gospel.[60]
Like the law, temporal authority has no power to bestow eternal
goods; only spiritual authority does. While temporal goods—
"the righteousness, wisdom, and power of this world"—will
cease, the eternal goods—"the righteousness of Christ and
of those who are in His kingdom"—will last forever.[61] Keenly
aware of the devil's scheme to blur the line between the secular
and spiritual realms, Luther labors painstakingly to "pound in
and squeeze in and wedge in this difference between the two
kingdoms."[62] In Nestingen's assessment:

> As with law and gospel, the distinction of the two kingdoms is
> made for the sake of both. By their very nature, earthly insti-
> tutions are tempted to claim ultimacy for themselves, be they
> families, social organizations, churches, or governments. The
> ultimacy of Christ's kingdom reduces such claims to their
> proper penultimate order. By the same token, when the pious
> claim religious entitlements to transcend the legal order, the
> rule of law is undermined. The distinction cuts both ways,

against those who in the name of the gospel wish to dominate and those who in the name of Christ would seek to withdraw from earthly relations.[63]

In external, physical matters, reason, law, and the teachings of the heathen may be consulted; in internal, spiritual matters, faith, the gospel, and the teachings of Scripture must reign. "God is a gentle and wealthy Lord" who provides for all people, Christians and heathens, bountiful, creaturely gifts for the preservation of the world.[64] Christians ought to render obedience to pagan rulers, the God-appointed sword of justice, just as they do the Christian governments, the God-appointed sword of the word. In so doing, they silence the critiques of the enemies, as in 1 Peter 2:15: "For it is God's will that by doing right you should put to silence the ignorance of foolish men."[65] God gives eternal dominion to able, wise, and faithful teachers to rule the Christian church; he also passes temporal dominion to the heathen, equipping them with courage, wisdom, and natural skills to govern society. "God wants the government of the world to be a symbol of true salvation and of His kingdom of heaven, like a pantomime or a mask."[66] God hides in secular government, as he does in spiritual government, to preserve the created order and mediate his presence.

Though reason is dignified as a means of civil governing, it is not deified as a goddess. Blind and ignorant of God and his work, the world transfers the victory of a kingdom to its own wisdom, reason, and power, regarding them as its goddesses. The heathen cannot perceive the difference and thus attribute their success to fortune or luck; only the eyes of faith perceive the hidden act of God in their rulers, these masks, causing their works to flourish. David, for one, knew that his kingdom gained victory not by his own edifice but by "God's directing."[67] The fruits of his labor stemmed primarily from God's creative power and did not count as merits for justification. Unless God's blessing follows, no human efforts can bear fruits, as taught in Psalm 127:1: "Unless the Lord keeps the city, the watchman guards in vain."

The New and Old Adams: In Tension

First Peter 4:6—"For this is why the Gospel was preached to the dead, that though judged in the *flesh* like men, they might live in the *spirit* like God"—speaks of a twofold distinction within each human agent. The words "flesh" and "spirit" designate the whole person, each with its peculiar orientation. "Flesh" refers to "the whole man (person)" in rebellion against God; "spirit" refers to "the whole man (person)" in conformity to God.[68] The human agent perishes according to their "outward being," that is, according to the flesh; they live according to the "inner being," that is, according to the spirit.[69] The justified saint comprises a twofold nature in the one person: a spiritual nature or soul, referring to "a spiritual, inner, or new man," and a bodily nature, or flesh, denoting "a carnal, outward, or old man."[70] These two persons—the outer man and the inner man—exist in contradiction within the same human agent. The antithesis between the outer and inner being corresponds to the antithesis between flesh and Spirit, as taught in Galatians 5:17: "for the desires of the flesh are against the Spirit, and the desires of the Spirit are against the flesh."[71]

The believer's dialectical nature consists in his existence as "a differentiated unity" of "two persons," exemplifying a "Christian-in-relation"[72] before God and the world. Luther writes, "According to your own person you are a Christian; but in relation to your servant you are a different person, and you are obliged to protect him."[73] Of this, Stephenson explains, "Luther accordingly distinguishes between the two persons in each believer: the Christian as he exists before God and for himself (*Christperson*), and the Christian in society (*weltperson*),

clad in a particular office (amt)—for example, that of parenthood or governmental authority—which entails responsibili-
ties for others."[74] Luther's conception of a duality between the
two identities in the *simul* does not imply, Durheim contends,
"schizophrenic theological anthropology."[75] It simply reflects
the twofold relation between flesh and spirit within a whole
person. The "coincidental opposites"—the inner and outer
man—in the same person do not, Wannenwetsch argues,

> represent anthropological provinces within "man." Yet Luther
> thought of both those designations as assignable to man as a
> whole, only in different perspectives, either facing God (*coram
> Deo*) or facing the world (*coram mundo*). Likewise, freedom
> and bondage are not to be divided between the inner and the
> outer man, but belong to both. Liberated from the bondage
> of sin, the inner man is the slave of God and the outer is the
> slave of his neighbor; yet both bondages amount not to a new
> antinomy to freedom, but to its proper *Gestalt*.[76]

Both bondages—to God and to the neighbor—are freedom's
proper forms. The inner person is "perfectly free lord of all, subject to none," and the outer person is a "perfectly dutiful servant
of all, subject to all."[77] While freedom in the vertical dimension
of life is acquired by the passive reception of faith apart from
any merit of works, freedom in the horizontal dimension of life
is displayed in the active performance of works to serve others.
Justifying faith not only frees us from everything that holds us
in captivity (sin, death, and the devil), it also frees us for everything we might contribute through our different life stations to
benefit others.

The contrast between spirit and flesh, Kolb notes, is not
between "the spiritual 'inner person' and the sinful 'outer person.'"[78] Rather it is a distinct characteristic of the reborn child of
God who is now caught in tension between the old "I" in Adam
and the new "I" in Christ. Thus, the contrast between the new

and old person, Kolb notes, is between "the believer's assurance of forgiveness and restoration of a trusting relationship with God" and "external blessings from God and physical exhibitions of religiosity."[79] It reflects the struggle between believers' new identity as God's children, equally loved with Christ, and their old identity, together with its residual enmity against God's grace. Justified saints feel the opposition between the depraved nature of the old and the renewed nature of the Spirit, the accusation of the law and the consolation of the gospel, the assault of sin and the assurance of grace. Quoting Holl, Helmer writes, "The self feels the contrast between the former sinful self and the new self that 'God has raised . . . up and regarded . . . as worthy of perpetual community with himself.'"[80] This tension constitutes, Helmer notes, "the paradox of subjectivity between the self-under-judgment [that is, under law] and the self-forgiven-by-God [that is, under gospel]."[81] The contrary of wrath and mercy inheres in the paradoxical experience of justification: only the self that surrenders to God's judgment and feels the godforsakenness is prepared to cling to God's mercy, accompanied by a new awareness of "belonging-to-God."[82] Faith grasps this new reality of belonging to him created by the spoken word. The contradiction and tension between the inner and outer persons we endure on earth will be resolved at the end of time when the freedom of the Christian, which we enjoy partially here, reaches its consummate expression.

The "coincidental opposites" of the two men in one person must not be taken to mean that they are weighted equally; the inner person reigns above and dominates the outer person. Luther avers, "The spirit must busy itself daily to tame the flesh and to bring it into subjection, must wrestle with it incessantly, and must take care that it does not repel faith."[83] For the justified saint, the spirit takes "precedence" over the flesh. This is apparent in Luther's exegesis of 1 Peter 4:6, where he illustrates the asymmetrical relation between them by an analogy.

Now this is mixed up, just as I say of a person who is wounded that he is in good health and yet is wounded, but in such a way that the part that is in good health is larger than the part that is wounded. He may be termed wounded only according to the part that has been smitten. Thus here, too, the spirit should have precedence.[84]

Where the Spirit reigns, there is true freedom. Kolb writes, "True freedom exists for the inner person only in total dependence on God. In parallel fashion, bondage of various kinds for the outer person does not affect that freedom at the core of one's humanity, the believer's 'inner identity.'"[85] The freedom accrued to the inner person does not proceed from external or worldly circumstances. "No external thing has any influence in producing Christian righteousness or freedom."[86] No external matters or works of piety can endanger the inner soul; they do no harm to a person's justified status, which is a new reality created and cemented by God's justifying word. This in no wise means the outer person does whatever it wills, leading to licentious abuse of freedom externally. The inner person dominates the outer person, just as the spirit dominates the flesh. Mannermaa asserts "that in faith these [carnal desires] no longer dominate; however, they do not die, either, but are still there, smoldering."[87] Luther describes the believer's two modes of existence, placing the Spirit above our flesh, righteousness above sin: "the Spirit rules and the flesh is subordinate, [and] righteousness is supreme and sin is a servant."[88] Thus, Wannenwetsch's proposal of relating the new to the old has merit; he writes, "The inner man of faith motivates the outward man to do what the outward man has rationally identified as the good thing to do, and insures that he does it with a happy mind."[89] Nonetheless, the law's curbing function continues to discipline the sinner in the believer as well. Luther's twofold relation does not promote ethical passivity, as the inner person takes "precedence" over the outer person, but in such a way that it does not abandon the outer person to its own devices; instead, the inner person gains control over the outer, just as faith has "power over the flesh."[90] Helmer avers, "The new self, while in relation to but distinct from the old self, is re-created as oriented to God's will, and ultimately to service to neighbour."[91] Faith alone equips believers with a proper assessment of reality, declaring, "'This life is right. That one is not. This work is good and well done. That one is evil.' What such a person concludes is right and true; for he cannot be misled but is preserved and protected, and he remains a judge of all doctrine."[92] While efficacious faith permeates the old self, subduing it and its vices, it, too, impels the new self, as Wannenwetsch argues, to "discover the right ways to act by virtue of the creative potential of love."[93] "Love," Bornkamm opines, "is the clamp which holds together God's dealings with the world and the corresponding responsibility of the Christian in spiritual as in secular affairs."[94]

"Was There a Time When the Two Kingdoms Were Not?"

"The law of this temporal sword," for Luther, is a created dispensation that "existed from the beginning of the world."[95] Luther cites the slaying of Abel by Cain in Genesis 4:14–15, to prove his point that because Cain, after having killed his brother, was frightened for his life, God imposed a ban on the sword so that his life would be spared from it. The fact that he was stricken with fear of being slain in return shows that he would have known the word from Adam concerning the fate of murderers that they die by the sword.[96] This was later confirmed in Genesis 9:6: "Whoever sheds the blood of man, by man shall his blood be shed." The law of the sword also emerges in Jesus's teaching in Matthew 26:52: "He who takes the sword will perish by the sword." As in the *Temporal Authority*,[97] Luther, in his commentary on Psalm 82, also holds that government belongs to the original created order rather than to the fall. He writes, "[It] was not only first founded and created by the word in Genesis 1 but was established and ordered by a special order of God."[98] In his sermons on 1 Peter, Luther seems to contradict himself, teaching that government emerges as a postlapsarian device to curb evil. He writes, "If there were no evil people, one would not need a government."[99] This raises an important question: Is civil government located before or after the fall? To use Beeke's phrase, "Was there a time when the two kingdoms were not?"

Scholars differ on the question of the location of civil government. Beeke contends that "Luther's two kingdoms reveals it to be a postlapsarian reality; although Luther himself at times wrote to the contrary, his overall presentation must necessarily recognize that Adam's paradise-kingdom was singularly spiritual, one that was maintained and guaranteed by his active obedience to God's law, Adam's fulfillment of the *mandatum Dei*."[100] Nestingen sees civil order as a postlapsarian solution to evil, saying, "More provisionally in that it was instituted after the fall, government's defining characteristic is not a particular form but a function: it exists to restrain the effects of sin in public life, to work out the provisions necessary to approximate peace and justice in a fallen world."[101] Lohse holds that the sword is "the external disciplinary means against the consequences of sin. To that extent we may appropriately describe *politia* as a *regnum peccati* (kingdom of sin)."[102] Along the same line, Parsons writes, "Commenting on Genesis 2:16–17, [Luther] shows how the church was established first, then the government of the home and the state, in that order. . . . Civil government (as a remedy, in contrast to the human society which was formed at Eve's creation) [comes into existence] only when the pair rebel against God."[103] Bayer contends that "Luther did not recognize the third order—government or politics—as an order of creation, seeing it rather merely as an expedient made necessary only by the fall, although Luther was definitely aware that politics is grounded in economy, and thus has to be considered from the outset as a consequence of the household order of creation, so that in a sense it belongs to it and to its governance."[104] His view is drawn from Luther's exposition of the fourth commandment in the *Large Catechism*: "All other authority flows and spreads out from the authority of the parents."[105] Elsewhere, he quotes Luther: "The household is the source of all public affairs";[106] and "parents are the source and well-spring from which the temporal realm comes."[107] The rationale behind Bayer's assertions is that if the secular authority comes from the household authority, it would have coexisted with the household estate as a created order.[108] With Bayer, Althaus writes, "And this is especially true which Luther includes in the secular government, such as marriage, the household, property, the relationship between master and servant—those do not have their basis in humanity's fall into sin."[109] In this regard, the political estate, Wannenwetsch discerns, is what Luther calls "a con-creature,"[110] that is, created by God together with human beings prelapsarianly. It was, says Luther, "instituted from the beginning of creation."[111] Wright also asserts that "the two kingdoms were part of God's creation ordinance."[112] His position is drawn from Luther's understanding of creation in which Adam "was created for his physical life in such a way that he was nevertheless made according to the image and likeness of God—this is an indication of another and better life than the physical life. Thus, Adam had a two-fold life: a physical life and an immortal life" (Gen 1:26).[113] Kolb and Arand add, "In his earlier years, Luther tended to treat this order [temporal government] as a postlapsarian necessity. But in his later years he recognized the human need for organization in society."[114]

Undoubtedly, there abides in Luther scholarship a tension between viewing secular authority as a postlapsarian measure and secular authority as a created dispensation. Yeago proposes

a way to resolve it by referring to God's command as a way
of being for Adam and Eve prior to the fall. God's word, he
argues, was initially framed within the distinction between
God's promise and his threat.[115] The promise of life—"you may
freely eat" (Gen 2:16)—is safeguarded, Luther writes, by the
threat of death: "But of the tree of the knowledge of good and
evil you shall not eat, for in the days that you eat of it you shall
die" (Gen 2:17). In Luther's own words, "For Adam this Word
was Gospel and Law; it was his worship; it was his service and
the obedience he could offer God in this state of innocence."[116]
The command of God (law) not to eat of the forbidden tree was
given to the righteous Adam in order for him to have "an outward form of worship by which [he would] show his obedience
and gratitude toward God."[117] Luther elaborates:

> There is now created a new tree for the distinguishing of good
> and evil, so that Adam might have a definite way to express
> his worship and reverence toward God. After everything has
> been entrusted to him to make use of it according to his will,
> whether he wished to do so by necessity or for pleasure, God
> finally demands from Adam that at this tree of the knowledge
> of good and evil he demonstrate his reverence and obedience
> toward God and that he maintains this practice, as it were, of
> worshipping God by not eating anything from it.[118]

Luther differentiates between "the law before sin," which the
Lord God gave to Adam in his pristine state, and "the law given
after sin," which he applies to the sinful and wicked nature.[119]
Adam, who is without sin, is commanded by God to refrain
from eating of the forbidden tree.[120] Created with the gift of
"the original righteousness," Luther argues, Adam gladly loved
God and readily obeyed this command until Satan deceived
him.[121] Adam was created in God's image, which for Luther
means "he not only knew God and believed that He was good,
but that he also lived a life that was wholly godly; that is, he

was without the fear of death or of any other danger, and was content with God's favor."[122] Already in his innocence, Adam had the word of God, both in promise and command, which makes obedience to God possible. In the original created order, Luther reasons, "there are no good works except those works God has commanded, just as there is no sin except that which God has forbidden."[123] The command to obey God occurs in the context where sin is not; thus the negative function of the law, either to restrain or accuse, is not in view. "The existence of the law," Wannenwetsch argues, "presupposes grace, not sin."[124] He elaborates:

> Surprisingly, the law is not envisaged as a postlapsarian device, a makeshift repair provoked by the fall, but rather as belonging to Adam's original righteousness, and as such, it could not be opposed to his spontaneous love of God. Indeed, Luther understands the original purpose of the law as being to provide Adam with a means of giving concrete form to this love through his responsive obedience to God's explicit command.[125]

With Wannenwetsch, Yeago affirms that the "original and proper function of the law"[126] was not given, to borrow Hütter's phrase, "under the condition of sin."[127] The law was first bestowed, Luther asserts, when Adam was "intoxicated with rejoicing toward God and was delighted also with all the other creatures."[128] The command thus is an enactment of his righteous identity in concrete form, not an acquisition of it. Our creatureliness is fundamentally bestowed upon us and not something of our making, just as righteousness is given to us and not acquired by our efforts. Both creation and re-creation are grounded in God's prior action, that is, in his initiating grace before which we can only respond with gratitude. Kolb explains that in relationship to God, only the passive righteousness that he gave Adam and Eve counts. Their righteous activities in the garden flow only from God's gift of righteousness. Kolb expands:

> They were human in God's sight not because they had proved their humanity through specific activities which had won God's favor. Instead, they had been created by his breath and hand because he wanted them to be his children. His love and mercy expressed themselves by forming his creatures as right and righteous in his sight. He formed them with the expectation that they would perform as his children in relationship to the rest of his creation as they trusted in him and showed him their love.[129]

The law given to an innocent nature is positive, and it offers an occasion for a historical concretization of Adam's identity as God's child, to whom God has attached his promise. "The commandments of God," Laffin writes, are "an invitation to formed creaturely life";[130] or in Hütter's words, "God's commandments are a welcome help to form the freedom of the Christian life."[131] They are given neither for the purpose of attaining righteousness (for Adam was already righteous), nor to level an accusation of sin (for this had not yet emerged).[132]

Luther makes use of the Pauline text "the Law has not been given for the just person, but for murderers, adulterers, [etc.]" (1 Tim 1:9-10), not to deny the existence of law before sin appeared in the world but to speak of the negative function of law, as the subject under God's rule is no longer a righteous person but a sinner.[133] The proper meaning of Paul's negative injunction on law in 1 Timothy is located within Luther's distinction between the law's function before sin and after sin. Prior to the fall, the law is positive; posterior to it, the law is punitive. In the first instance, the law that is addressed to the righteous Adam is not antithetical to the gospel. The law when addressed to a sinner kills and is opposed to the gospel. Yeago elucidates, "The negativity of the law is not located in its formal character as commandment, as a proposal of form and order; its ground is rather in our disorder, our sin, our non-conformity to Christ."[134] The law takes on a meaning different from the original, now that Adam changes from being innocent to being guilty. Luther states, "After sin Adam is not the same person he was before sin in the state of innocence."[135] In either context, the law abides. What is changed is not the substance of law itself but the subject to whom it is applied. Thus, Yeago concludes, the same word "law" is used analogously; the meaning of "law" in each case is not identical to the other due to the change in subject.[136]

The political order, before and after the fall, remains and is constitutive of God's unitary rule. What is changed is not the substance of the civil order that has, Luther avers, "already existed from the beginning of the world" but the subject to whom political force is to be administered. As Laffin discerns rightly, "There is only one political order, only one rule of God, which is experienced differently depending on the human subject of this rule, whether as innocent Adam, fallen humans, or reconciled in Christ to receive the gift of God's rule in its proper and original sense."[137] If the sword assumes the wicked as its subject, the negative, punitive aspect of politics becomes operative, just as the law does the opposite of saving when it deals with the guilty. In this case, the fall makes the state necessary, without which society would degenerate into complete chaos and corruption.[138] This in no way implies that the state per se does not exist as a "con-creature"; it means its coercive function was not in force because there was no sin. The oppressiveness of secular government, not secular government itself, is required by human wickedness. Just as God is provoked into wrath by the sinful predicament of human beings, so, too, is the state compelled into coercion by human disobedience. Luther writes, "[One] may correctly call civil government the rule of sin."[139] "The one and foremost function of government" is coercive, says Luther, "to hold sin in check, as Paul says in Romans 13:4: 'Government bears the sword for the punishment of the wicked.'"[140] Parallelism occurs between the first, negative function of the law and the law's opposition to the gospel, except that the law, in the second, theological sense, serves the gospel. The imposition of the sword of justice is not predicated upon the secular institution itself, a created good, but upon human rebellion, just as the law's "opposition to the gospel," Laffin asserts, "is not grounded in the law itself but rather in human disobedience."[141] When civil government meets with evil deeds, it necessarily is wrathful against them, just as when law meets with sin, it inevitably opposes it. Consequently, Luther's assertion "If there were no evil people, one would not need a government" (cf. 1 Pet 2:13)[142] need not be taken strictly as a postlapsarian remedy for evil, for the subject Peter had in mind was not the righteous, who are praised for doing right, but the wicked, who must be restrained from the destructive power of evil lust through the law's coercive function.

Luther's homiletical undertaking underscores community hierarchy and governance in human life as essentially good; they are not to be conceived merely as defenses against chaos and evil. Luther's sermon on 1 Peter 2:18—"Servants, be submissive to your masters with all respect, not only to the kind and gentle but also to the overbearing"—sheds light on the question of whether there was a time when civil kingdom was not. Civil power pertains to "a community," that everyone must obey it; it also extends to "particular" people who are placed in different life stations or positions to do God's will and abound in good works.[143] Earthly life must comply with God's allotment: "The gifts of God are manifold and different, so that one person is in a higher position than another. But no one knows who is the highest before God. For one who is in the very lowest position here He can easily elevate to the highest position there."[144] Earthly relationships include the superior and the subordinate,

those who command and those who obey, leaders and followers; that is the way God intends it to be, not because of the fall.
Obedience is highly prized so that good works abound; Luther
insists, "God wants everyone to be subject to the other person.
Therefore do this willing and gladly" (cf. 1 Pet 5:6).[145] Secular
government, Althaus writes, "includes everything that contrib-
utes to the preservation of this earthly life, especially marriage
and family, the entire household, as well as property, business,
and all the stations and vocations which God has instituted."[146]
These things, including the relationship the slave has with their
master, are not grounded in the fall. Inwardly before God, both
masters and servants are equal in dignity; but outwardly before
the world, the slaves occupy "an inferior station and must
serve others."[147] Just as Christ became a humble servant for our
sake and was found pleasing to God, so, too, the servants must
fulfill their call to this estate "with all respect" (1 Pet 2:18). As
support, Luther quotes Psalm 123:2: "Behold, as the eyes of
the servants look to the hand of their master, as the eyes of
the maid to the hand of her mistress, so our eyes look to the
Lord our God."[148] Servants obey their earthly masters, as to the
Lord, not to people; they serve not "as men-pleasers, but as servants of Christ," doing their bidding in honor of him (cf. Eph
6:5–7).[149] The works they do in faith, small or great, are equally
holy and done well before God, not because people institute it
but because God commands it. We should have regard only for
God's word and command, irrespective of the person for whom
service is done. "Then the most significant work, if it is done
properly, is better in the sight of God than the works of all the
priests and monks put together."[150] With this, the apostle consoles the slaves who suffered pain and injustice from their abu-
sive masters that "they have God's approval" (1 Pet 2:20). Civil
authorities are not necessitated by the fall; they are simply part
of the creaturely order that works good in human life. They
do more than merely restrain evil and violence; they preserve

the people whom God has created. The virtue of the civil order is not derived from its negative function of restraining evil. "Rather," Althaus insists, "it comprehends all the orders of life."[151] Secular government thus coexisted with spiritual government in paradise, antecedent to the fall; apart from it, creaturely existence will not endure.

Conclusion

The basic elements of Luther's evangelical way of thinking embedded in his *Heidelberg Disputation* receive further development in his sermons. Evangelical seeds sown earlier come to fruition in homiletics. Luther's sermons on 1 Peter are the exercise of his hermeneutical principle—the theology of the cross—in which God's redeeming work in Christ and human participation in it by faith become central. The knowledge of "how or where or in what condition" God does his justifying acts for us (*pro nobis*) is to be found in "no other God than this Man Jesus Christ. Take hold of Him; cling to Him with all your heart, and spurn all speculation about the Divine majesty; for whoever investigates the majesty of God will be consumed by His glory."[1] Luther regards Moses as a theologian of glory who aspires to "see" God as he is hidden "in his glory and majesty."[2] Such knowledge, which incites terror, is forbidden to Moses; rather, he was permitted by God to see "the manifest and visible things of God," that is, God "as he is hidden in his suffering."[3] A theologian of the cross does not gaze at what lies, to borrow Forde's word, "behind"[4] the cross but at "the humility and shame of the cross" in which God's mercy shines.[5] Forde captures Luther well: "Apart from Jesus, God is indistinguishable from the devil."[6] In Christ, the distance, both cognitively and affectively, between God and sinners is abolished. Hence, God ceases to be an angry judge or a neglectful parent but is our gracious Father.

The proclamation of the gospel is not a recitation of the story of "the old rugged cross" but an inculcation of its saving significance for us (*pro nobis*). It does not merely convey some

information about God; it announces Christ and all his goods
for those who believe. Preaching becomes an occasion of God's
power: it vanquishes the terror of "the absolute God," that is,
the majestic God before whom we are crushed. Preaching creates faith in us, causing us to cling to "his promises and blessings shown in Christ" through which our despair is healed.[7]
The oceanic depth of God's being remains an ineffable mystery, hidden from us, from which we are led by the preached
word to the revealed God of mercy. We follow the preached
word, as Peter did, and allow it to achieve its saving purpose
in us. Proclamation actually delivers God's conquering action
in Christ through which both the haunting voices—the law
and God's wrath—come to an end for those who believe. The
word performs an alien work of annihilating reason, flesh, and
all human efforts to apprehend the hidden God and his ways.
We are not to conceive any other idea of God but instead must
"receive the Son, so that Christ is welcome in your heart in His
birth, miracles, and cross."[8] The word Peter preached is the true
gospel, that "Jesus Christ . . . died and rose from the dead," and
that he did so "in order that people may come to faith through
such preaching and be saved through faith."[9] Any deviation
from this preaching, Luther writes, "is not the Gospel, no matter who does it."[10]

The word creates faith by which we grasp God's promise. Faith
is not an innate quality of the soul; nor is it a natural endowment.
Rather, Bornkamm affirms, "Faith is something that must be
presented to us," working in us an evangelical "breakthrough to
liberty before God. . . . It is our grateful amen to God's friendly
promise."[11] God is precious to faith, but not so to unbelief. Faith
and unbelief are causal agents as they cause something to exist
that formerly did not. Bayer elucidates further:

> Faith and unbelief are more than merely explanations about
> reality. In both cases, concerning both faith and unbelief,

something actually *happens*: the judgment of God makes a determination about the existence of the human being; the judgment of the human being concerning God makes a determination as well—though admittedly not about the nature of God; it determines something about the human being instead.[12]

Both faith and unbelief have their own opposing goals. While faith makes God real in us, unbelief does the opposite, converting him into a nonreality. Faith, Luther writes, "is the creator of the Deity, not in the substance of God but in us."[13] This is a point that Luther makes in detail in his explanation of the first commandment in his *Large Catechism*. Faith alone, Luther contends, "make[s] both God and an idol": where your faith is right, there you have the true God; if otherwise, you have an idol.[14] Faith reckons God as truthful and trustworthy, and consequently believers become as truthful and as reliable as he is through faith. Conversely, unbelief reckons God a liar and unreliable, and consequently unbelievers themselves become identical to their (false) perception of God, as well as vitiating all things and reducing them to nothing through their unbelief. The causal agency of faith and its consequent is contrasted with the causal agency of unbelief and its resultant. This is borne out in Luther's exposition of Isaiah 7:9, "If you are not firm in faith, you will not be firm at all."

> Hence faith alone makes certain and has a solid foundation. But the promise becomes useless unless faith is added. Hebraically in this way: If you do not believe, you will not be truthful. For those who believe God make and reckon Him to be true, which is giving glory to God, as Rom. 4:20 says, and they themselves also become truthful through faith. On the contrary, to the unbelieving all things become deceptive, unreliable, and unsure. . . . This must be taught everywhere, because he who believes nothing accomplishes nothing. But whatever the godly man does will always prosper (Ps 1:3).[15]

Luther's theology does not eliminate the experience of uplifting emotions such as joy and peace but locates it in its proper context, viewing it as the outcome of God's justifying action rather than the prerequisite for justification. Experience is in constant flux and thus is no measure of validity of faith. The antidote to changing inner feelings is not introspection—that is, by turning inward for aid—but ex-centricity, that is, by turning outward, outside us (*extra nos*), to the objective word and its various created forms. The justified saint, in Hampson's phrase, "lives excentrically to himself"[16] so that his true identity is no longer a self-determining entity. His real self is not defined by any prior action or pious feelings of his but by the word that addresses him from outside, assuring him with the knowledge of "the great distinction"[17] to be God's beloved through Christ despite appearances to the contrary. The voice we hear ends all human efforts to seek righteousness in themselves and for themselves. All other voices—reason, conscience, sin, death, and hell—vanish so that nothing remains but the loving embrace of Christ, a created reality that corresponds to the justifying word. Hampson captures the performative character of the gospel: "For it is in hearing and grasping the fact that we are accepted without desert that we become new persons, set free to serve the world. Lutherans are simply speaking of human change relationally, not in terms of an interior quality of righteousness."[18]

True faith ignores "everything it sees, hears, and feels"; it clings completely to God's word, which cannot lie, and proceeds "joyfully on its way."[19] Apparently "Luther's emphasis on the passive receptivity of faith," Kim writes, "does not imply any sterility or infecundity."[20] St. Peter, Luther contends, proposes "a proper way to preach": begin with faith, "what it does and what its power and nature are, namely, that it gives us enough of everything necessary for piety and salvation, that one can do nothing except through faith, and that through it we have everything God has."[21] But a living faith does not remain alone; it necessarily works through love, its instrument of serving and giving oneself to the neighbor as God does. Lohrmann writes:

> Far from ignoring good works or turning human love into a source of salvation, Luther used the distinction between faith and love both to preach the evangelical freedom that comes through faith alone and to keep a strong emphasis on the fruits of faith expressed as love of neighbor. In this way, Luther gave preachers and parishioners clarity about how faith in Christ transforms hearts and daily lives through God's grace.[22]

The faith of our relationship with God and the works of our active righteousness are closely linked; the former is causative of the latter. Three realms of human life—the household, civil, and spiritual orders—are where "faith is active through love." They are life stations where God mediates his power and provides bountifully for us in all aspects of our creaturely life. Veith intimates, "And even when we resist God's project of working through us, there is something about vocation itself that makes good things happen despite ourselves."[23] Vocations are where the old and new creatures often collide; yet it is precisely where God hides to effect his saving purpose. The virtue of vocations thus lies not in the vocations themselves but in the masked God who works in them. For instance, marriage as a vocation is where, in Wingren's estimation,

> we come across what for Luther is the decisive contrast between God's self-giving love and man's egocentricity. The human being is self-willed, desiring that whatever happens shall be to his advantage. When husband and wife, in marriage, serve one another and their children, this is not due to the heart's spontaneous and undisturbed expression of love, every day and hour. Rather, in marriage as an institution something compels the husband's selfish desires to yield and likewise inhibits the egocentricity of the wife's heart. At work

in marriage is a power which compels self-giving to spouse and children. So it is the "station" itself which is the ethical agent, for it is God who is active through the law on earth.[24]

Each vocation we practice represents a holy obedience to God because they have the word of God. Luther upholds the holy character of every life station and regards every vocation as God-pleasing.[25] He writes, "A servant, maid, son, daughter, man, woman, lord, subject, or whoever else may belong to a station ordained by God, as long as he fills his station, is as beautiful and glorious in the sight of God as a bride adorned for her marriage or as the image of a saint decorated for a high festival."[26] The fulfillment of a vocation requires the concurrence of divine and human agency. "Man must work," but that alone does not sustain itself; so "God must do it."[27] Luther stresses again: "God must be over all and nearest to all, to preserve this ring or circle against the devil, and to do everything in all of life's vocations, indeed, in all creatures."[28] No creature creates anything; only God does. The Hebrew word for "create," Bayer notes rightly, is the exclusive predicate of the creator himself, not to be shared with his creatures.[29] God constitutes his creatures as "his coworkers" (*cooperatores Dei*), not his "co-creators" (*concreatores*).[30] God and human beings work together to bring about an action. In matter of order, Luther opines, "God is there first, secretly laying his blessing therein," which awaits our reception of it by labor.[31] God bestows on the human subject the power of "responsivity"[32] through which God's gifts are to be received, not acquired through merit or achievement. Tranvik summarizes Luther's paradox: "As God was active in creation, upholding and sustaining humanity, so were God's 'masks' (those living out their callings) constantly at work (labor, parenting, governing) in love and service of their neighbors."[33]

Christians possess dual citizenship simultaneously, and thus, Althaus writes, have "two lords: one in the earthly kingdom and one the spiritual kingdom. He is obligated to the emperor and to Christ at the same time; to the emperor for his outward life, to Christ inwardly with his conscience and in faith."[34] God is lord of both, but he appoints subordinate lords to exercise dominion within the earthly realm. The power of "responsivity" is given to Christians, who dwell in both kingdoms, rendering them capable of receiving God's gifts within their dual identity: gifts of peace and order from his left-hand kingdom of civil government, and gifts of forgiveness and grace from his right-hand kingdom of spiritual government.

One becomes a true theologian not by idle speculation but by suffering the fire of trials and the assaults of the devil; as Luther claims, "For as soon as God's Word takes root and grows in you, the devil will harry you, and will make a real doctor of you, and by his assaults will teach you to seek and love God's Word."[35] The devil and his dominion St. Peter alerts us to is no figment of his imagination—for Luther, it is as certain as Christ himself. "Without a recognition of Satan's power," Oberman comments, "belief in Christ is reduced to an idea about Christ," devoid of the experience of faith.[36] The assaults of life in God's hands work good in us, as they expose the futility of self-justification so that we would seek only the certainty of God's justification. In Hamm's formulation, "Only those who have been broken on the illusion of their *iustitia activa* (active righteousness) will recognize salvation in the *iustitia passiva* (passive righteousness) received from Jesus Christ."[37]

Luther's homiletical undertaking of this epistle is an instance of the exercise of his calling as a preacher of the word. As Hans-Martin Barth asserts, "God's Word is the primal reality, which underlies all reality. Therefore, we must not orient ourselves to superficial reality or allow ourselves to be blinded by it."[38] The word, when declared, performs its own task; it begets new life and produces its own fruits. Luther avows that "by speaking God created all things and worked through his

Word. All his works are words of God, created by the uncreated Word."[39] God's word is a creative power that brings about a new reality, that which has not existed before. Trueman writes, "Reality, we might say, is what God says it is."[40] The prolific nature of the word so thrills Luther that he never wavers from it. Nor does Luther weary in finding delight in the word, as wine delights the heart. Readers will benefit from his sermons on 1 Peter, which is simply "the good news that was preached to us," the same gospel the prophets foretold and proclaimed in times past by the Holy Spirit. Interlaced with the rigor of biblical and theological content that undergirds his homiletical task, these sermons portray Luther as a theologian who interfaces theology and spirituality. The Reformer's depths and insights into the biblical text will continue to be generative in the hearts of anyone who has tasted the sweetness of God's word and thus permits it to dwell in them and perform its causative work there. What more fitting epilogue to this volume than Luther's own words with which he instructs *Concerning the Order of Public Worship*: "Spare everything except the Word!"[41]

Notes

Foreword

1 Martin Luther, *D. Martin Luthers Werke* (Weimar: Böhlau, 1883–1993), *Deutsche Bibel* 6: 10, *Luther's Works* (Philadelphia: Fortress, 1958–1986), 35: 361–62.

2 Reinhard Schwarz, *Martin Luther, Lehrer der christlichen Religion* (2nd ed., Tübingen: Mohr Siebeck, 2016), 22–23.

3 Dennis Ngien, *Fruit for the Soul: Luther on the Lament Psalms* (Minneapolis: Fortress Press, 2015).

4 Dennis Ngien, *Luther's Theology of the Cross: Christ in Luther's Sermons on John* (Eugene: Cascade Books, 2018).

5 Dennis Ngien, *Grace and Law in Galatians: Justification in Luther and Calvin* (Eugene: Cascade Books, 2023).

Introduction

1 See Martin Hengel, *Saint Peter: The Underestimated Apostle*, trans. Thomas H. Trapp (Grand Rapids, MI: Eerdmans, 2010), ix, italics original.

2 This study is largely based on *Luther's Works, Volume 30: The Catholic Epistles*, ed. Jaroslav Pelikan (St. Louis: Concordia, 1967), and *Luther's Works, Volume 78: Church Postil IV*, ed. Benjamin T. G. Mayes and James L. Langebartels (St. Louis: Concordia, 2015), which contains a few sermons on 1 Peter.

3 LW 35:362.

4 LW 35:361–62.
5 LW 30:9; WA 12:265.
6 See foreword, LW 30:4; WA 12:260.
7 See foreword to *Sermons on the First Epistle of St. Peter*, LW 30:3; WA 12:260.
8 See foreword, LW 30:3; WA 12:260.
9 See foreword, LW 30:3; WA 12:260.
10 LW 35:362.
11 See foreword, LW 30:4; WA 12:260.
12 Tim Saleska, "The Clarity of Paradox: A Meditation on Exodus 34:6–7," in *Simul: Inquiries into Luther's Experience of the Christian Life*, ed. Robert Kolb, Torbjörn Johansson, and Daniel Johansson (Göttingen: Vandenhoeck & Ruprecht, 2021), 195.
13 Gerhard O. Forde, *On Being a Theologian of the Cross: Reflections on Luther's Heidelberg Disputation, 1518* (Grand Rapids, MI: Eerdmans, 1997), 31.
14 Robert Kolb, *Martin Luther: Confessor of the Faith* (Oxford: Oxford University Press, 2009), 42.
15 Lewis W. Spitz, "Luther's Ecclesiast: A Historian's Angle," in *Seven-Headed Luther: Essays in Commemoration of a Quincentenary, 1483–1983*, ed. Peter Newman Brooks (Oxford: Clarendon, 1983), 117.
16 James M. Kittelson, "Luther and Modern Church History," in *The Cambridge Companion to Martin Luther*, ed. Donald K. McKim (Cambridge: Cambridge University Press, 2003), 261.
17 LW 30:10; WA 12:265.
18 LW 30:10–11; WA 12:266.
19 LW 30:15–16; WA 12:271.
20 LW 30:15–16; WA 12:271; LW 75:395; WA 40.1.1:377.
21 LW 30:11; WA 12:266.
22 Augustine, *De trinitate* 4.3, as cited in Bernhard Lohse, *Martin Luther's Theology: Its Historical and Systematic Development*, trans. and ed. Roy A. Harrison (Minneapolis: Fortress Press, 1999), 222n19.
23 LW 27:238; WA 2:501.
24 LW 30:117; WA 12:371.
25 Lohse, *Martin Luther's Theology*, 48. Contrary to Lohse, Norman Nagel, in his "*Sacramentum et Exemplum* in Luther's Understanding of Christ" in *Luther for an Ecumenical Age: Essays in Commemoration of the 450th Anniversary of the Reformation*, ed. Carl S. Meyer (St. Louis: Concordia, 1967), argues for the contrary view that Luther abandons Augustine's Sacrament–Example Christology in his "mature" theology (175, 183, 188). This is pointed out by Dietmar Lage, *Martin Luther's Christology and Ethics* (Lewiston, NY: Edwin Mellen Press, 1990), 104n29.

26 WA 39.1:356, as cited in Lage, *Martin Luther's Christology and Ethics*, 105n29. Lage's translation.

27 WA 39.1:462, as cited in Lage, *Martin Luther's Christology and Ethics*, 105n29. Lage's translation.

28 WA 57.3:114, as cited in Lage, *Martin Luther's Christology and Ethics*, 101.

29 LW 35:120.

30 LW 35:120.

31 LW 35:120.

32 Berndt Hamm, *The Early Luther: Stages in a Reformation Reorientation*, trans. Martin J. Lohrmann (Grand Rapids, MI: Eerdmans, 2014), 216–17n86.

33 LW 30:69; WA 12:324.

34 LW 26:90; WA 40.1:167.

35 Benjamin M. Durheim, *Christ's Gift, Our Response: Martin Luther and Louis-Marie Chauvet on the Connection between Sacraments and Ethics* (Collegeville, MN: Liturgical Press, 2015), 70.

36 Hamm, *Early Luther*, 217.

37 Hamm, *Early Luther*, 78.

38 LW 30:50; WA 12:304.

39 Christine Helmer, "The Experience of Justification," in *Justification in a Post-Christian Society*, Church of Sweden Research Series, vol. 8, ed. Carl-Henric Grenholm and Goran Gunner (Eugene, OR: Pickwick, 2014), 52. Helmer shares the conviction of the Swedish linguist Birgit Stolt, who argues for a diverse range of lifting emotions as part of the experience of freedom in Christ.

40 Brian L. Kachelmeier, *Reading Isaiah with Luther* (St. Louis: Concordia, 2018), 115.

41 LW 30:32; WA 12:287.

42 LW 44:24.

43 LW 26:25; WA 40.1:70.

44 LW 26:25; WA 40.1:70.

45 LW 30:109; WA 12:364.

46 LW 30:34; WA 12:290.

47 LW 30:34; WA 12:290.

48 LW 26:255; WA 40.2:402.

49 Craig L. Nessan, *Free in Deed: The Heart of Lutheran Ethics* (Minneapolis: Fortress Press, 2022), 1.

50 LW 25:291; WA 56:305.

51 LW 31:367.

52 Hans J. Iwand, *The Righteousness of Faith According to Luther*, ed. Virgil F. Thompson, trans. Randi H. Lundell (Eugene, OR: Wipf & Stock, 2008), 61–62.

53 LW 31:57, where Luther draws from the Song of Solomon to speak of the dynamism of an "exceedingly attractive" love in human actions. He cites Song of Solomon 1:4: "Draw me after you, let us make haste" toward the fragrance "of your anointing oils" (Song of Sol 1:3), that is, "your works."

54 LW 30:30; WA 12:285, my italics.

55 LW 26:29; WA 40.1:78.

56 LW 26:30; WA 40.1:78–79.

57 LW 30:30; WA 12:285.

58 LW 33:140.

59 LW 30:45; WA 12:299.

60 LW 26:29; WA 40.1:78.

61 Mark C. Mattes, *Martin Luther's Theology of Beauty: A Reappraisal* (Grand Rapids, MI: Baker Academic, 2017), 102.

62 Scott R. Swain, *The Trinity and the Bible: On Theological Interpretation* (Bellingham, WA: Lexham Academic, 2021), 88.

63 Wolfhart Pannenberg, "God of the Philosophers," *First Things* 174 (June 2007): 33.

64 LW 30:24; WA 12:279.

65 LW 30:23–24; WA 12:279.

66 LW 22:528.

67 LW 22:528.

68 Christoph Schwöbel, "'We are All God's Vocabulary': The Idea of Creation as a Speech-Act of the Trinitarian God and its Significance for the Dialogue between Theology and Science," in *Knowing Creation: Perspectives from Theology, Philosophy, and Science*, ed. Andrew B. Torrance and Thomas H. McCall (Grand Rapids, MI: Zondervan, 2018), 47.

69 LW 1:22; WA 42:17.

70 Marc Cortez, *Christological Anthropology in Historical Perspective* (Grand Rapids: Zondervan, 2016), 91.

71 Carl E. Trueman, "What Luther Teaches Us Today," in *The Beauty and Glory of the Reformation*, ed. Joel R. Beeke (Grand Rapids, MI: Reformation Heritage Books, 2018), 107–8.

72 Helmer, "Experience of Justification," 46.

73 LW 30:31; WA 12:286; LW 29:223; WA 57:221.

74 LW 30:45; WA 12:300.

75 LW 31:348–49.

76 Oswald Bayer, *Martin Luther's Theology: A Contemporary Interpretation*, trans. Thomas H. Trapp (Grand Rapids, MI: Eerdmans, 2008), 180, italics original.

77 Bayer, *Martin Luther's Theology*, 180.

78 LW 37:364–65.

79 LW 41:177.

80 LW 54:446, no. 5533, as quoted in Oswald Bayer, "Nature and Institution: Luther's Doctrine of the Three Orders," *Lutheran Quarterly* 12 (1998): 127.

81 LW 14:114.

82 Cortez, *Christological Anthropology*, 105.

83 See Bayer, *Martin Luther's Theology*, 140–41.

84 Kolb, *Martin Luther*, 172.

85 LW 43:200.

86 LW 43:200.

87 Robert Kolb and Timothy J. Wengert, eds., "The Small Catechism," in *The Book of Concord: The Confessions of the Evangelical Lutheran Church* (Minneapolis: Fortress Press, 2000), 351.

88 Robert Kolb and Timothy J. Wengert, eds., "The Large Catechism," in *The Book of Concord: The Confessions of the Evangelical Lutheran Church* (Minneapolis: Fortress Press, 2000), 392.

89 Michael Parsons, *Reformation Marriage: The Husband and Wife Relationship in the Theology of Luther and Calvin* (Edinburgh: Rutherford House, 2005), 137.

90 LW 44:52.

91 LW 44:52.

92 LW 45:326.

93 LW 45:326.

94 LW 45:325.

95 Niels Henrik Gregersen, "Introduction: Ten Theses on the Future of Lutheran Theology," in *The Gift of Grace: The Future of Lutheran Theology*, ed. Niels Henrik Gregersen, Bo Holm, Ted Peters, and Peter Widmann (Minneapolis: Fortress Press, 2005), 13.

96 Risto Saarinen, *Luther and the Gift* (Tubingen: Mohr Siebeck, 2017), 118.

97 Saarinen, *Luther and the Gift*, 119.

98 LW 3:217; WA 43:30.

99 LW 31:198; WA 31.2:601.

100 Hermann Sasse, *We Confess Jesus Christ*, trans. Norman Nagel (St. Louis: Concordia, 1984), 52.

101 LW 30:110; WA 12:346.

102 Gustaf Wingren, *Luther on Vocation*, trans. Carl C. Rasmussen (Philadelphia: Muhlenberg Press, 1957), 66.

103 LW 31:198; WA 31.2:601.

104 LW 31:10.

105 LW 31:50.

106 LW 31:50.

107 LW 31:50, 53.

108 LW 31:50.

109 LW 31:51.

110 LW 31:51.

Chapter 1

1 David Steinmetz, *Luther in Context*, 2nd ed. (Grand Rapids, MI: Baker Academic, 2002), 115.
2 Steinmetz, *Luther in Context*, 115.
3 Gerhard O. Forde, "The Word That Kills and Makes Alive," in *The Marks of the Body of Christ*, ed. Carl E. Braaten and Robert W. Jenson (Grand Rapids, MI: Eerdmans, 1999), 8.
4 LW 1:21–22; WA 42:17.
5 Jaroslav Pelikan, *Luther the Expositor: Introduction to the Reformer's Exegetical Writings*, companion volume to *Luther's Works* (St. Louis: Concordia, 1959), 54.
6 Pelikan, *Luther the Expositor*, 54.
7 LW 12:33. Also cited in Pelikan, *Luther the Expositor*, 58.
8 LW12:32–33; also quoted in Robert Kolb, *Martin Luther and the Enduring Word of God: The Wittenberg School and Its Scripture-Centered Proclamation* (Grand Rapids, MI: Baker Academic, 2016), 47.
9 Oswald Bayer, *Theology the Lutheran Way*, ed. and trans. Jeffrey G. Silcock and Mark C. Mattes (Grand Rapids, MI: Eerdmans, 2007), 129.
10 WA TR 4:666 (no. 5106), Table Talk, 1540, as cited in Oswald Bayer, "Preaching the Word," *Lutheran Quarterly* 23 (2009): 266n9. I follow Bayer's translation.
11 Bayer, *Martin Luther's Theology*, 51.
12 Robert Kolb and Charles P. Arand, *The Genius of Luther's Theology* (Grand Rapids, MI: Baker Academic, 2008), 129–59.
13 LW 30:43; WA 12:298.
14 See Ralph W. Doermann, "Luther's Principles of Biblical Interpretation," in *Interpreting Luther's Legacy: Essays in Honor of Edward C. Fendt*, ed. Fred W. Meuser and Stanley D. Schneider (Minneapolis: Augsburg, 1969), 18.
15 LW 30:43; WA 12:297.
16 LW 30:43; WA 12:297.
17 LW 26:392; WA 40.1:597.
18 LW 30:48–49; WA 12:302.
19 LW 30:44; WA 12:298.
20 LW 30:44; WA 12:298.
21 LW 26:392; WA 40.1:597.
22 Dennis Bielfeldt, "Luther's Late Trinitarian Disputations: Semantic Realism and the Trinity," in *The Substance of Faith: Luther's Doctrinal Theology for Today*, ed. Paul R. Hinlicky (Minneapolis: Fortress Press, 2008), 91.
23 LW 17:11; WA 31:2.268.
24 LW 17:11; WA 31:2.268.

25 LW 30:45; WA 12:299.
26 Kolb and Arand, *Genius*, 156.
27 LW 30:48; WA 12:302.
28 LW 30:50; WA 12:301.
29 LW 21:302.
30 LW 21:303.
31 LW 30:50; WA 12:304.
32 LW 30:49; WA 12:302.
33 LW 30:50; WA 12:304.
34 LW 30:49; WA 12:303.
35 LW 30:50; WA 12:304; cf. LW 21:346–47.
36 Beth Kreitzer, "The Magnificat, 1521," in *The Annotated Luther, Volume 4: Pastoral Writings*, ed. Mary Jane Haemig (Minneapolis: Fortress Press, 2016), 310.
37 LW 21:348.
38 Beth Kreitzer, "Luther Regarding the Virgin Mary," in *The Pastoral Luther: Essays on Martin Luther's Practical Theology*, ed. Timothy J. Wengert (Grand Rapids, MI: Eerdmans, 2009), 242.
39 For a study of Mary's piety, see George H. Tavard, "Medieval Piety in Luther's Commentary on the Magnificat," in *Ad fontes Lutheri: Toward the Recovery of the Real Luther; Essays in Honor of Kenneth Hagen's Sixty-Fifth Birthday*, ed. Timothy Maschke, Franz Posset, and Joan Skocir (Milwaukee, WI: Marquette University Press, 2001), 281–301.
40 LW 21:342.
41 LW 30:50; WA 12:304.
42 LW 53:68.
43 LW 30:49; WA 12:303.
44 LW 15:230; WA 31.2:684.
45 LW 30:49; WA 12:303.
46 LW 15:208; WA 31.2:628.
47 LW 15:208; WA 31.2:628.
48 LW 30:45; WA 12:300.
49 LW 30:45; WA 12:300.
50 H. S. Wilson, "Luther on Preaching as God Speaking," in Wengert, *The Pastoral Luther*, 102.
51 Gustaf Wingren, *The Living Word: A Theological Study of Preaching and the Church* (Philadelphia: Muhlenberg, 1960), 19.
52 LW 30:30; WA 12:285, my italics.
53 LW 1:262; WA 42:194.
54 LW 9:41; WA 14:578.
55 Trueman, "What Luther Teaches Us Today," 113.
56 LW 30:45; WA 12:300.
57 Trueman, "What Luther Teaches Us Today," 123.

58 LW 53:14.
59 LW 30:5; WA 12:261.
60 John Headley, *Luther's View of Church History* (New Haven, CT: Yale University Press, 1963), 23.
61 Steinmetz, *Luther in Context*, 115.
62 LW 30:45; WA 12:300.
63 LW 30:41; WA 12:296.
64 LW 1:21; WA 42:17.
65 LW 31:346.
66 Stephen Chester, "'Abba! Father!' (Gal. 4:6): Justification and Assurance in Martin Luther's Lectures on Galatians (1535)," *Biblical Research* 63 (2018): 18.
67 LW 30:45; WA 12:300.
68 LW 30:45; WA 12:299.
69 LW 9:277; WA 14:729.
70 LW 9:277–78; WA 14:729.
71 LW 9:278; WA 14:729.
72 LW 25:291; WA 41:305.
73 LW 9:278; WA 14:729.
74 LW 9:278; WA 14:730.
75 Hamm, *Early Luther*, 235.
76 WA 5:537.10, as cited in Daphne Hampson, *Christian Contradictions: The Structures of Lutheran and Catholic Thought* (Cambridge: Cambridge University Press, 2001), 47.
77 LW 9:278; WA 14:730.
78 See chapter 2 for an expansion of the "ears" as the vehicles of faith.
79 LW 9:278; WA 14:730.
80 LW 9:278; WA 14:730.
81 LW 9:279; WA 14:731.
82 Hampson, *Christian Contradictions*, 47.
83 LW 16:82; WA 31.2:57.
84 LW 9:278; WA 14:730.
85 LW 9:279; WA 14:731.
86 LW 9:279; WA 14:731.
87 LW 9:279; WA 14:731.
88 LW 9:279; WA 14:731.
89 Swain, *The Trinity and the Bible*, 88.
90 LW 30:24; WA 12:279.
91 Philip S. Watson, *Let God Be God: An Interpretation of the Theology of Martin Luther* (Philadelphia: Fortress Press, 1947), 167.
92 Timothy Maschke, "Contemporaneity: A Hermeneutical Perspective in Martin Luther's Work," in Maschke, Posset, and Skocir, *Ad fontes Lutheri*, 178.

94 LW 30:49; WA 12:303.
95 LW 30:49; WA 12:302.
96 LW 29:223; WA 57.3:220.
97 LW 30:30; WA 12:286.
98 Robert Kolb, *Luther's Treatise on Christian Freedom and Its Legacy* (Lanham, MD: Lexington/Fortress Academic, 2020), 57–58.
99 Jeffrey G. Silcock, "Theology and Proclamation: Towards a Lutheran Framework for Preaching," *Lutheran Theological Journal* 42, no. 3 (December 2008): 135.
100 LW 30:49; WA 12:303.
101 LW 30:49; WA 12:303.
102 LW 30:49; WA 12:303.
103 LW 30:49; WA 12:303.
104 LW 9:138; WA 14:651.
105 LW 9:138; WA 14:651.
106 LW 30:49; WA 12:303.
107 LW 30:140; WA 12:394.
108 LW 42:13.
109 LW 42:13.
110 LW 5:45; WA 43:459.
111 Eberhard Jüngel, *God as the Mystery of the World: On the Foundation of the Theology of the Crucified God in between Theism and Atheism*, trans. Darrell L. Guder (Grand Rapids, MI: Eerdmans, 1983), 346.
112 Jüngel, *God as the Mystery of the World*, 346.
113 B. A. Gerrish, "'To the Unknown God': Luther and Calvin on the Hiddenness of God," in *The Old Protestantism and the New: Essays on the Reformation Heritage* (Chicago, IL: University of Chicago Press, 1982), 136.
114 Robert Bertram, "Again on the Trinity: Bertram Responds," *Dialog* 29 (1990): 60. See discussions on the Trinity in these articles: Robert Bertram, "When is God Triune?," *Dialog* 28 (Spring 1989): 123–32; Paul Hinlicky, "Some Questions to Bertram on the Trinity," *Dialog* 28 (Autumn 1989): 307–8; and Anne Pederson, "A Question to Bertram and Luther on the Trinity," *Dialog* 28 (Autumn 1989): 308–9.
115 Bertram, "Again on the Trinity," 61. See Luther's exposition of Galatians 3:13 in LW 26:281–82; WA 40:440–41.
116 LW 26:278; WA 40:434.
117 LW 31:52.
118 LW 33:140. Also cited in Gerhard O. Forde, *The Preached God: Proclamation in Word and Sacrament*, ed. Mark C. Mattes and Steven D. Paulson (Minneapolis: Fortress Press, 2017), 51.
119 Forde, *Preached God*, 50.

120   LW 33:140.

121   LW 33:140.

122   LW 12:312.

123   Mattes, *Martin Luther's Theology of Beauty*, 102.

124   Volker Leppin, "God in Luther's Life and Thought: The Lasting Ambivalence," in *The Global Luther: A Theologian for Modern Times*, ed. Christine Helmer (Minneapolis: Fortress Press, 2009), 93–94.

125   Gerrish, "'To the Unknown God,'" 136–37.

126   Forde, *Preached God*, 2.

127   Forde, *Preached God*, 52.

128   Otto Weber, *Foundations of Dogmatics*, vol. 1, trans. and annot. Darrell L. Guder (Grand Rapids, MI: Eerdmans, 1981), 401.

129   Alister E. McGrath, *Luther's Theology of the Cross: Martin Luther's Theological Breakthrough* (Oxford: Wiley-Blackwell, 1985), 165.

130   McGrath, *Luther's Theology of the Cross*, 165.

131   John T. Pless, *Pastor Craft: Essays and Sermons* (Irving, CA: New Reformation, 2020), 80.

132   Kolb and Wengert, eds., "The Small Catechism," 355.

133   Douglas Harink, *1 & 2 Peter*, Brazos Theological Commentary on the Bible (Grand Rapids, MI: Brazos Press, 2009), 41.

134   LW 30:6; WA 12:262.

135   Harink, *1 & 2 Peter*, 42.

136   Timothy J. Wengert, *Martin Luther's Catechisms: Forming the Faith* (Minneapolis: Fortress Press, 2009), 67.

137   Wengert, *Martin Luther's Catechisms*, 46.

138   Wengert, *Martin Luther's Catechisms*, 67.

139   LW 30:30; WA 12:286n21; cf. LW 25:5; WA 56:5.

140   LW 30:7; WA 12:263.

141   LW 30:7; WA 12:263.

142   LW 30:6; WA 12:262.

143   LW 30:8; WA 12:263.

144   LW 30:8; WA 12:263.

145   LW 30:32; WA 12:287.

146   Harink, *1 & 2 Peter*, 55, italics original.

147   LW 30:7; WA 12:262.

148   LW 30:30; WA 12:286.

149   LW 30:32; WA 12:287.

150   LW 30:32; WA 12:287.

151   LW 30:32; WA 12:287.

152   LW 30:32; WA 12:287.

153   LW 30:32; WA 12:287.

154   LW 26:25; WA 40.1:70.

155 John Kleinig, "Luther on the Reception of God's Holiness," *Pro Ecclesia* 17, no. 1 (2008): 79.

156 LW 26:25; WA 40.1:70. Also cited in Kleinig, "Reception of God's Holiness," 79.

157 LW 30:32; WA 12:287.

158 LW 26:352; WA 40.1:542.

159 LW 26:352; WA 40.1:542.

160 LW 26:353; WA 40.1:542.

161 Mark D. Tranvik, "Diluting Luther: Baptism in Sixteenth-Century Catechisms," in *Teaching Reformation: Essays in Honor of Timothy J. Wengert*, ed. Luka Ilić and Martin J. Lohrmann (Minneapolis: Fortress Press, 2021), 204.

162 LW 30:32; WA 12:287.

163 LW 26:353; WA 40.1:540.

164 LW 30:58; WA 12:312.

165 Kolb and Wengert, eds., "The Small Catechism," 359.

166 Kolb and Wengert, eds., "The Small Catechism," 359.

167 LW 30:26; WA 12:281.

168 LW 30:26; WA 12:281.

169 LW 30:26; WA 12:281.

170 LW 30:41; WA 12:295.

171 LW 30:27; WA 12:282.

172 LW 30:41; WA 12:296.

173 LW 30:41; WA 12:296.

174 LW 30:41; WA 12:295.

175 Theodore Dieter, "Why Does Luther's Doctrine of Justification Matter Today?," in Helmer, *Global Luther*, 199.

176 LW 31:10.

177 Gerhard Ebeling, *Luther: An Introduction to His Thought*, trans. R. A. Wilson. (Philadelphia: Fortress Press, 1970), 121.

178 LW 30:143; WA 12:398.

Chapter 2

1 LW 30:10; WA 12:265.

2 LW 33:140, as cited in Forde, *Preached God*, 51.

3 LW 31:52.

4 LW 30:10; WA 12:265.

5 LW 30:45; WA 12:300.

6 LW 30:51; WA 12:304.

7 LW 30:51; WA 12:304.

8 LW 14:45; WA 31:66. Also cited in Robert Kolb, *Martin Luther as Prophet, Teacher, and Hero: Images of the Reformer, 1520–1620* (Grand Rapids, MI: Baker Academic, 1999), 172.

9 LW 14:45–46; WA 31:66–67.

10 LW 14:46; WA 31:67.

11 LW 14:290; WA 5:34.

12 LW 26:266; WA 40.1:416.

13 LW 14:96; WA 31:171. For a study of Luther's exposition of Psalm 118, see my *Fruit for the Soul: Luther on the Lament Psalms* (Minneapolis: Fortress Press, 2015), 229–97.

14 LW 14:96; WA 31:172.

15 LW 14:97; WA 31:172.

16 LW 14:97; WA 31:172.

17 LW 30:58; WA 12:311.

18 LW 30:58; WA 12:311.

19 LW 14:97; WA 31:172.

20 LW 14:97; WA 31:172.

21 LW 30:52; WA 12:306.

22 LW 30:57; WA 12:310.

23 LW 30:63; WA 12:316.

24 LW 30:57; WA 12:311.

25 LW 30:57; WA 12:311.

26 LW 30:13; WA 12:268.

27 LW 31:52.

28 LW 30:60; WA 12:314.

29 LW 30:60; WA 12:314.

30 LW 30:61; WA 12:315.

31 LW 31:49, 55.

32 LW 31:51.

33 LW 30:60; WA 12:314.

34 LW 30:59; WA 12:313.

35 LW 30:60; WA 12:314.

36 LW 16:91; WA 31:264.

37 "This stone is no *joke*" could be understood as "the stone is nothing for child's play."

38 LW 30:61; WA 12:315.

39 LW 30:61; WA 12:316.

40 LW 30:58; WA 12:312.

41 LW 30:58; WA 12:312.

42 LW 30:60; WA 12:314.

43 LW 31:41.

44 Ebeling, *Luther: An Introduction*, 99.

45 David S. Yeago, "Gnosticism, Antinomianism, and Reformation Theology: Reflections on the Costs of a Construal," *Pro Ecclesia* 2, no. 1 (1993): 48.

46 Hampson, *Christian Contradictions*, 12.
47 LW 30:59; WA 12:312.
48 LW 30:68; WA 12:333.
49 LW 30:68; WA 12:323.
50 LW 30:68; WA 12:323.
51 The term "coincidental opposites" (*coincidentia oppositorum*) also appears in Oswald Bayer, "Luther's 'Simul Iustus et Peccator,'" in *Simul: Inquiries into Luther's Experience of the Christian Life*, ed. Robert Kolb, Torbjörn Johansson, and Daniel Johansson (Göttingen: Vandenhoeck & Ruprecht, 2021), 35.
52 LW 30:68–69; WA 12:323.
53 LW 30:69; WA 12:324.
54 LW 30:69; WA 12:324.
55 LW 14:191; WA 18:518.
56 Brian Cummings, *The Literary Culture of the Reformation: Grammar and Grace* (Oxford: Oxford University Press, 2002), 98.
57 Cummings, *Literary Culture*, 98.
58 LW 26:387; WA 40.1:589.
59 Berndt Hamm, *The Reformation of Faith in the Context of Late Medieval Theology and Piety* (Leiden: Brill, 2004), 203–4. He quotes WA 5, 408, 4f: "Entering into Christ is the faith that gathers us together into the wealth of divine righteousness."
60 Hamm, *Early Luther*, 79.
61 LW 30:71; WA 12:326.
62 LW 30:71; WA 12:326.
63 LW 30:47; WA 12:300.
64 LW 30:71; WA 12:326.
65 LW 30:27; WA 12:282.
66 LW 30:71; WA 12:326.
67 LW 30:71; WA 12:326.
68 See Kolb and Wengert, eds., "The Small Catechism," 360.
69 LW 30:71; WA 12:326.
70 Timothy J. Wengert, *Word of Life: Introducing Lutheran Hermeneutics* (Minneapolis: Fortress Press, 2019), 78.
71 Hamm, *Early Luther*, 217.
72 Mary J. Streufert, *Language for God: A Lutheran Perspective* (Minneapolis: Fortress Press, 2022), 103.
73 LW 49:359. Also cited in Streufert, *Language for God*, 103.
74 LW 30:50; WA 12:304.
75 Here I follow Stolt's translation of *eine frohliche Wirtschaft* as "a happy wedding feast"; see Birgit Stolt, "Luther's Faith of 'the Heart': Experience, Emotion, and Reason," in *The Global Luther: A Theologian for Modern Times*, ed. Christine Helmer (Minneapolis: Fortress Press, 2009), 148–49. See also Bertram Lee Woolf, *Reformation*

Writings of Martin Luther, vol. 1 (New York: Philosophical Library, 1953), 363, where *eine frohliche Wirtschaft* is translated as "a happy household." Cf. LW 31:352.

76 LW 31:357, my italics.

77 LW 21:301.

78 LW 21:301.

79 LW 21:299.

80 LW 21:309.

81 LW 21:299.

82 LW 21:301.

83 LW 21:301.

84 LW 21:309.

85 Helmer, "Experience of Justification," 52.

86 LW 21:300. Also quoted in Stolt, "Luther's Faith of 'the Heart," 147.

87 LW 31:357, my italics.

88 LW 29:223; WA 57.3:220. Also quoted in Erik H. Hermann, "Luther and the Importance of the Hebrew Language for His World of Thought," in *Simul: Inquiries into Luther's Experience of the Christian Life*, ed. Robert Kolb, Torbjörn Johansson, and Daniel Johansson (Göttingen: Vandenhoeck & Ruprecht, 2021), 57. See Bayer, *Martin Luther's Theology*, 106–12, where he analyzes Luther's sermon on Mark 7:31–37 to speak of "the power of unbelief and the still stronger power of faith."

89 LW 29:223; WA 57.3:221.

90 See Dieter, "Why Does Luther's Doctrine," 205.

91 Carl E. Braaten, *Justification: The Article by Which the Church Stands or Falls* (Minneapolis: Fortress Press, 1990), 26.

92 Bayer, "Preaching the Word," 251.

93 LW 9:278; WA 14:729.

94 LW 29:223; WA 57.3:220.

95 LW 30:30; WA 12:286; LW 29:223; WA 57:221.

96 LW 29:224; WA 57.3:221.

97 WA 12:259; 37, 207, as cited in Doermann, "Luther's Principles," 19.

98 Robert Jenson, *Systematic Theology* (Oxford: Oxford University Press, 1999), 2:286. Also cited in Michael Richard Laffin, *The Promise of Martin Luther's Political Theology: Freeing Luther from the Modern Political Narrative* (Bloomsbury: T & T Clark, 2018), 62–63.

99 Pelikan, *Luther the Expositor*, 50.

100 Laffin, *Promise*, 63.

101 LW 30:45; WA 12:299.

102 LW 30:164; WA 14:28.

103 LW 31:349.

104 Hamm, *Early Luther*, 217.

105 LW 30:39; WA 12:293.
106 LW 30:14; WA 12:269.
107 LW 30:11; WA 12:267.
108 LW 30:14; WA 12:270.
109 LW 30:14; WA 12:270.
110 LW 30:14; WA 12:270.
111 LW 30:15; WA 12:271.
112 LW 30:15; WA 12:271.
113 LW 26:430; WA 40.1:649.
114 LW 12:322.
115 LW 36:42.
116 Dieter, "Why Does Luther's Doctrine of Justification Matter Today?," 204.
117 LW 30:52; WA 12:306.
118 LW 30:52; WA 12:306.
119 LW 27:28; WA 40.2:35.
120 LW 30:57; WA 12:311.
121 LW 30:32–33; WA 12:288.
122 LW 35:120.
123 LW 27:30; WA 40.2:37.
124 LW 30:32; WA 12:287.
125 LW 30:32–33; WA 12:288.
126 LW 27:59; WA 40.2:75.
127 LW 30:99; WA 12:354.
128 LW 30:99; WA 12:354.
129 LW 30:34; WA 12:290.
130 LW 44:27.
131 Bernd Wannenwetsch, "Luther's Moral Theology," in *The Cambridge Companion to Martin Luther*, ed. Donald McKim (Cambridge, UK: Cambridge University Press, 2006), 129. He quotes LW 44:26: "In this faith all works become equal, and one work is like the other; all distinctions between works fall away, whether they be great, small, short, long, many, or few."
132 LW 44:26. Also cited in Wannenwetsch, "Luther's Moral Theology," 129.
133 LW 44:27.
134 LW 44:26–27.
135 LW 44:27.
136 LW 30:98; WA 12:353.
137 LW 30:78; WA 12:333.
138 Bayer, "Nature and Institution," 132.
139 LW 30:43; WA 12:297.
140 LW 30:79; WA 12:333.

141 LW 30:78; WA 12:333.

142 LW 30:42; WA 12:296.

143 LW 30:42; WA 12:296.

144 LW 30:43; WA 12:297.

145 LW 31:57.

146 LW 31:57.

147 LW 31:57.

148 LW 31:57.

149 LW 27:113; WA 40.2:145.

150 LW 31:57.

151 LW 31:57.

152 LW 31:367.

153 LW 31:367.

154 Steinmetz, *Luther in Context*, 120. His analysis is based on LW 31:367.

155 LW 30:123; WA 12:377.

156 LW 27:29; WA 40.2:36.

157 The distinction between "abstract faith" and "incarnate faith" appears in Luther's commentary on Galatians; see LW 26:264; WA 40.1:414.

158 Hamm, *Early Luther*, 79.

159 LW 51:71.

160 LW 30:33; WA 12:289.

161 LW 31:367.

162 LW 31:367.

163 LW 30:67; WA 12:331.

164 LW 30:99; WA 12:354.

165 LW 30:34–35; WA 12:290.

166 LW 14:190; WA 18:518.

167 LW 30:34; WA 12:289.

168 LW 30:34; WA 12:289.

169 LW 30:34; WA 12:289.

170 LW 30:33; WA 12:289.

171 LW 30:130; WA 12:385.

172 LW 30:130; WA 12:385. See Forde, "The Word That Kills," for more discussion of the task of proclamation in relation to what the word does.

173 LW 30:130; WA 12:385.

174 LW 12:32.

175 LW 30:35; WA 12:290.

176 LW 30:34; WA 12:290.

177 LW 30:130; WA 12:386.

178 LW 44:81.

179 LW 44:81.
180 LW 44:81.
181 LW 44.81.
182 LW 30:130; WA 12:385.
183 LW 30:35; WA 12:290.
184 LW 30:67; WA 12:332.
185 LW 30:67; WA 12:332.

Chapter 3

1 LW 30:117; WA 12:371.
2 LW 30:110; WA 12:364.
3 LW 30:118; WA 12:373.
4 LW 30:117; WA 12:371.
5 LW 31:52.
6 Forde, *On Being a Theologian*, 86.
7 Marc Lienhard, *Luther: Witness to Jesus Christ*, trans. Edwin H. Robertson (Minneapolis: Augsburg Publishing, 1982), 137.
8 LW 27:34; WA 40.2:43.
9 LW 30:34; WA 12:289.
10 LW 30:84; WA 12:338.
11 LW 30:18–19; WA 12:274.
12 LW 30:19; WA 12:274.
13 Pelikan, *Luther the Expositor*, 85.
14 LW 30:19; WA 12:274.
15 LW 30:19; WA 12:274.
16 LW 30:29; WA 12:285.
17 LW 30:24; WA 12:280.
18 LW 30:24; WA 12:280.
19 WA 10.2:423, 17–18, as cited in Kolb, *Treatise*, 46.
20 LW 30:15–16; WA 12:271.
21 LW 30:10; WA 12:266.
22 LW 30:25; WA 12:281.
23 Gerhard O. Forde, "Luther's Theology of the Cross," in *Christian Dogmatics*, 2 vols., ed. Carl E. Braaten and Robert W. Jenson (Minneapolis: Fortress Press, 1984), 2:49.
24 Kolb and Wengert, eds., "The Large Catechism," 434.
25 LW 31:53.
26 LW 30:36; WA 12:291.
27 LW 30:36; WA 12:291. See note 24 of LW 30, where it says that the medieval idea "one drop [of the blood of Christ] can save the whole world from every crime" appears in Thomas Aquinas's hymn *Adoro te devote*.

28 LW 30:36; WA 12:291.
29 LW 30:37; WA 12:292.
30 LW 30:38; WA 12:292.
31 LW 30:38; WA 12:292.
32 LW 30:38; WA 12:292.
33 LW 30:38; WA 12:293.
34 LW 30:38; WA 12:293.
35 LW 30:38; WA 12:293.
36 Norman E. Nagel, "Heresy, Doctor Luther, Heresy! The Person and Work of Christ," in *Seven-Headed Luther. Essays in Commemoration of a Quincentenary 1483–1983*, ed. Peter Newman Brooks (Oxford: Clarendon Press, 1983), 38.
37 Nagel, "Heresy, Doctor Luther, Heresy!", 38.
38 LW 30:116; WA 12:370.
39 LW 30:12; WA 12:267.
40 LW 30:12; WA 12:268.
41 LW 30:39; WA 12:293.
42 LW 31:10. See note 5 of this volume has this translation "to do what is in one."
43 LW 17:40; WA 31.2:292.
44 LW 31:10.
45 LW 20:9; WA 13:550.
46 LW 30:10; WA 12:266.
47 LW 26:152; WA 40.1:262.
48 LW 30:10–11; WA 12:266.
49 LW 30:10; WA 12:266.
50 LW 30:33; WA 12:289.
51 LW 30:39; WA 12:293.
52 LW 30:12; WA 12:267.
53 LW 30:12; WA 12:268.
54 LW 35:396.
55 LW 30:12; WA 12:268.
56 Randall C. Zachman, *The Assurance of Faith: Conscience in the Theology of Martin Luther and John Calvin* (Minneapolis: Augsburg Fortress, 1993), 172.
57 LW 26:21–22; WA 40.1:65.
58 LW 30:116; WA 12:371.
59 LW 30:30; WA 12:285.
60 John Webster, *Christ Our Salvation: Expositions and Proclamation* (Bellingham, WA: Lexham Press, 2020), 64.
61 LW 30:12; WA 12:268.
62 LW 30:12; WA 12:268.
63 LW 30:30; WA 12:285, my italics.

64   Kolb, *Treatise*, 41.

65   LW 42:8.

66   LW 30:60; WA 12:313.

67   LW 30:60; WA 12:313.

68   LW 30:33; WA 12:289.

69   LW 23:149; WA 33:233.

70   LW 30:67; WA 12:331. See note 16 of LW 30, where LW 23:149 is cited.

71   LW 42:23.

72   Kolb and Wengert, eds., "The Small Catechism," 355.

73   Kolb and Wengert, eds., "The Small Catechism," 345. Here Tappert translates "that I may be His."

74   Hamm, *Early Luther*, 218.

75   Hamm, *Early Luther*, 218.

76   LW 14:106.

77   LW 43:200.

78   Steinmetz, *Luther in Context*, 144.

79   LW 31:57.

80   LW 18:13; WA 12:11.

81   Steven D. Paulson, *Lutheran Theology* (New York: T & T Clark, 2011), 53.

82   LW 30:60; WA 12:313.

83   LW 30:10; WA 12:266.

84   See Vincent Evener, "Wittenberg's Wandering Spirits: Discipline and the Dead in the Reformation," *Church History* 84 (2015): 531–55, where Luther counsels Christians to exercise discipline in the vision of seeing Christ rather than the devil, and in hearing the word rather the dead.

85   LW 30:113; WA 12:368.

86   LW 30:113; WA 12:368.

87   LW 30:112; WA 12:368.

88   LW 30:114; WA 12:368.

89   LW 30:114; WA 12:369.

90   LW 30:114; WA 12:369.

91   LW 30:114; WA 12:369.

92   LW 30:114; WA 12:369.

93   LW 30:114; WA 12:369.

94   LW 30:115; WA 12:369.

95   LW 30:121; WA 12:376.

96   LW 30:121; WA 12:376.

97   LW 30:121; WA 12:376.

98   LW 57:130; WA 37:65.

99   LW 57:132; WA 37:66.

100 LW 57:128; WA 37:63.

101 Kolb and Wengert, eds., "Article IX, Formula of Concordia," in *The Book of Concord: The Confessions of the Evangelical Lutheran Church*, 635.

102 Kolb and Wengert, eds., "The Creed," in *The Book of Concord: The Confessions of the Evangelical Lutheran Church*, 434–35.

103 LW 30:116; WA 12:371.

104 LW 30:115; WA 12:370.

105 LW 42:14.

106 Lienhard, *Luther*, 25.

107 Forde, *On Being a Theologian*, 86.

108 LW 30:111; WA 12:365.

109 Ronald K. Rittgers, *The Reformation of Suffering: Pastoral Theology and Lay Piety in Late Medieval and Early Modern Germany* (Oxford: Oxford University Press, 2012), 207.

110 LW 69:128.

111 LW 69:252; WA 28:384. See my *Luther's Theology of the Cross: Christ in Luther's Sermons on John* (Eugene, OR: Cascade Books, 2018), 263–64.

112 See Jean Gerson, *Oeuves Completes*, ed. Palemon Glorieux (Paris: Desclee, 1960), 102; Nicholas of Lyra, *Postilla super totam Bibliam*, (Strassburg, 1492; repr., Frankfurt am Main: Minerva, 1971); John 19:17, "Et baiulans sibi crucem," Matt. 27:32, "Exeuntes autem," as cited in LW 69:253n102.

113 Ludolph of Saxony, *Vita Jesu Christi* 2.57.3 (vol. 4:3), as cited in LW 69:127–28.

114 Augustine, *Harmony of the Gospels* 3:10, as cited in LW 69:253.

115 LW 30:127; WA 12:381.

116 LW 30:126; WA 12:380.

117 LW 30:127; WA 12:381.

118 LW 41:165.

119 Rittgers, *Reformation of Suffering*, 366n98.

120 LW 30:111; WA 12:365.

121 LW 30:23; WA 12:279.

122 LW 30:129; WA 12:385.

123 LW 30:129; WA 12:385.

124 Rittgers, *Reformation of Suffering*, 115.

125 LW 41:165.

126 LW 41:165.

127 LW 30:23; WA 12:279.

128 LW 30:24; WA 12:279.

129 This theme of righteous suffering, or the God-imposed cross, will recur in chapter 5.

130 LW 30:127; WA 12:383.

131 LW 30:128; WA 12:384.

132 LW 31:371.

133 LW 30:34; WA 12:290.

134 Kolb and Arand, *Genius*, 26.

135 LW 31:299.

136 LW 31:300.

137 LW 31:300.

138 LW 27:34–35; WA 40.2:43–44.

139 Douglas John Hall, *Lighten Our Cross: Toward an Indigenous Theology of the Cross* (Philadelphia: Westminster, 1976), 117.

140 LW 42:14.

141 LW 30:85; WA 12:340.

142 LW 42:14.

143 LW 42:9.

144 Graham Tomlin, *Luther's Gospel: Reimagining the World* (London: Bloomsbury T & T Clark, 2017), 62.

145 LW 30:118; WA 12:373.

146 The phrase "a truly Christ-formed" person appears in LW 14:201; WA 18:526.

147 LW 26:353; WA 40.1:542.

148 LW 31:56.

149 Forde, *On Being a Theologian*, 110.

150 LW 31:57.

151 LW 31:57.

152 LW 31:57.

153 LW 15:198; WA 31.2:606.

154 LW 27:30; WA 40.2:38.

155 LW 31:56–57. Also quoted in Forde, *On Being a Theologian*, 111.

156 LW 31:57.

157 I will discuss the God-imposed cross in chapter 5.

158 LW 31:57.

Chapter 4

1 Timothy Shaun Price, "Luther's Use of Aristotle in the Three Estates and Its Implications for Understanding Oeconomia," *Journal of Markets and Morality* 18, no. 2 (2015): 385.

2 LW 45:322n17, where Aristotle's *Politics* I, 3–13 is cited. The household economy includes three types of relationships: master-slave, husband-wife, and father-children. Personal relationships take precedence over material possessions.

3   For a detailed study of the Reformation view of marriage, see Parsons, *Reformation Marriage*.
4   Oswald Bayer, "Luther's View of Marriage," in *Freedom in Response: Lutheran Ethics; Sources and Controversies*, trans. Jeffrey F. Cayzer (Oxford: Oxford University Press, 2007), 179.
5   LW 5:140; WA 43:525. Also cited in Bayer, *Theology the Lutheran Way*, 269n211. I follow Bayer's translation.
6   LW 45:42.
7   LW 14:201; WA 18:526.
8   LW 14:192; WA 18:519.
9   LW 75:393; WA 10.1.1:394.
10 LW 45:42.
11 LW 42:13.
12 LW 30:89; WA 12:344.
13 LW 30:89; WA 12:344.
14 LW 30:90; WA 12:344.
15 LW 30:89; WA 12:344.
16 LW 30:90; WA 12:344.
17 LW 30:90; WA 12:344.
18 LW 30:89; WA 12:344.
19 LW 30:90; WA 12:344.
20 Augustine, *Confessions*, Book IX, chap. 9, para. 22, as cited in LW 30:88; WA 12:342n1.
21 LW 30:90; WA 12:344.
22 LW 30:88; WA 12:343.
23 LW 3:174; WA 42:673.
24 LW 30:89; WA 12:343.
25 LW 30:87; WA 12:343; Kolb and Wengert, eds., "The Small Catechism," 366n118. See Mickey Leland Mattox, *Defender of the Most Holy Matriarchs: Martin Luther's Interpretation of the Women of Genesis in the "Enarrationes in Genesin," 1535–1545*, Studies in Medieval and Reformation Traditions, vol. 92 (Leiden: Brill, 2003), chapter 3, where he shows Luther's familiarity with the Patristic exegesis of the story of Sarah.
26 Wengert, *Martin Luther's Catechisms*, 160–61.
27 LW 3:208; WA 43:24.
28 LW 3:209; WA 43:25.
29 LW 3:209; WA 43:25.
30 LW 3:208; WA 43:24.
31 LW 3:208; WA 43:24.
32 LW 3:208; WA 43:24.
33 LW 3:208; WA 43:24.
34 Kolb, *Martin Luther: Confessor*, 183.

35 LW 30:91; WA 12:345.
36 LW 3:177; WA 43:2.
37 LW 3:217; WA 43:30.
38 LW 3:201; WA 43:18–19.
39 LW 3:201; WA 43:18.
40 LW 30:91; WA 12:345.
41 Parsons, *Reformation Marriage*, 103.
42 LW 3:354; WA 43:129.
43 LW 5:32; WA 43:450–51.
44 LW 30:92; WA 12:346.
45 Kolb and Wengert, eds., "The Small Catechism," 366.
46 LW 30:93; WA 12:347.
47 LW 30:88; WA 12:343.
48 LW 30:92; WA 12:346.
49 LW 30:92; WA 12:346.
50 LW 30:92; WA 12:347.
51 LW 30:92; WA 12:347.
52 See LW 12:308–9: "Through the fall his will, understanding, and all natural powers were so corrupted that man was no longer whole, but was diverted by sin, lost his correct judgement before God, and thought everything perversely against the will and law of God."
53 Paul R. Hinlicky, *Luther and the Beloved Community: A Path for Christian Theology after Christendom* (Grand Rapids, MI: Eerdmans, 2010), 207.
54 LW 3:353; WA 43:129.
55 LW 30:92; WA 12:347.
56 John Witte Jr., "'The Mother of All Earthly Laws': The Lutheran Reformation," in *Encounters with Luther: New Directions for Critical Studies*, ed. Kirsi I. Stjerna and Brooks Schramm (Louisville, KY: Westminster John Knox Press, 2016), 119. Witte takes the quotation from Steven Ozment, *Ancestors: The Loving Family in Old Europe* (Cambridge, MA: Harvard University Press, 2000), 37.
57 LW 30:93; WA 12:348. See chapter 5 for a discussion of the devil's works.
58 LW 15:198; WA 31.2:601.
59 Martin Marty, *The Hidden Discipline* (St. Louis: Concordia, 1962), 80.
60 LW 25:365; WA 56:375.
61 Bruce G. McNair, "Luther and the Pastoral Theology of the Lord's Prayer," *Logia* 14, no. 4 (2005): 44.
62 Marty, *Hidden Discipline*, 82.
63 LW 25:365; WA 56:375.
64 LW 25:365; WA 56:375.

65 LW 30:93; WA 12:347.

66 Kolb and Wengert, eds., "The Large Catechism," 453.

67 Kolb and Wengert, eds., "The Large Catechism," 453.

68 LW 51:178–79.

69 Marty, *Hidden Discipline*, 82.

70 LW 2:302; WA 42:477.

71 LW 2:302; WA 42:477.

72 LW 2:302; WA 42:477.

73 LW 2:301; WA 42:477.

74 WA 34:52.12–21, as quoted in Scott Hendrix, "Luther on Marriage," *Lutheran Quarterly* 14 (Autumn 2000): 347. Hendrix's translation.

75 Bayer, "Luther's View of Marriage," 179.

76 WA 34.1:52, as cited in Bayer, "Luther's View of Marriage," 223.

77 LW 36:92.

78 Bayer, "Luther's View of Marriage," 180.

79 WA 40.3:275, as cited in Paul Althaus, *The Ethics of Martin Luther*, trans. Robert C. Schultz (Minneapolis: Augsburg Fortress, 1972), 93.

80 WA 34.1:64, as cited in Bayer, "Luther's View of Marriage," 175.

81 WA 34.1:64, as cited in Bayer, "Luther's View of Marriage," 175.

82 LW 3:228; WA 43:38.

83 LW 3:228; WA 43:38.

84 Tomlin, *Luther's Gospel*, 130.

85 LW 4:154–55; WA 43:247.

86 LW 4:154–55; WA 43:247.

87 LW 4:6–7; WA 42:140. Also cited in Kolb, *Martin Luther*, 183, and Parsons, *Reformation Marriage*, 157–58.

88 LW 14:190; WA 18:518.

89 Hinlicky, *Luther and the Beloved Community*, 207.

90 LW 45:34.

91 William H. Lazareth, *Luther on the Christian Home: An Application of the Social Ethics of the Reformation* (Philadelphia: Muhlenberg Press, 1960), 129.

92 James Arne Nestingen, "Luther on Marriage, Vocation, and the Cross," *Word and World* 23, no. 1 (Winter 2003): 38.

93 LW 14:191; WA 18:518.

94 LW 14:191; WA 18:518. Also quoted in Michael Parsons, *Luther and Calvin on Grief and Lament: Life-experience and Biblical Text* (Lewiston, NY: Mellen, 2013), 122.

95 LW 14:191; WA 18:518.

96 LW 45:42.

97 LW 45:42.

98 Bayer, *Theology the Lutheran Way*, 126.

99 LW 45:42.
100 LW 45:323.
101 LW 14:201; WA 18:526.
102 Kolb, *Martin Luther*, 183.
103 LW 45:39.
104 LW 45:39.
105 LW 45:39–40.
106 LW 45:40.
107 LW 30:91; WA 12:345.
108 LW 44:27.
109 LW 44:27.
110 LW 44:27.
111 LW 44:27.
112 LW 75:393; WA 10.1.1:394.
113 LW 3:177; WA 43:2.
114 LW 3:176; WA 43:1.
115 LW 3:212; WA 43:26.
116 LW 3:212; WA 43:26.
117 LW 3:211; WA 43:26.
118 LW 3:208; WA 43:23.
119 LW 3:177; WA 43:2.
120 LW 3:211; WA 43:26.
121 Mattox, *Defender of the Most Holy Matriarchs*, 123.
122 LW 3:216; WA 43:29.
123 LW 3:216; WA 43:29.
124 LW 3:216; WA 43:29.
125 LW 3:216; WA 43:29.
126 LW 3:212; WA 43:27.
127 LW 3:177; WA 43:2.
128 LW 3:211; WA 43:26.
129 LW 3:211; WA 43:14.
130 Bielfeldt, "Luther's Late Trinitarian Disputations," 86. Bielfeldt labels "semantic realism" (the word creates reality, just as it says) as "most accurate" of Luther (98).
131 LW 3:212; WA 43:26.
132 Paul Althaus, *The Theology of Martin Luther*, trans. Robert C. Schultz (Philadelphia: Fortress Press, 1966), 259. Althaus quotes WA 39.1:446: "And so the law ought to be interpreted by the gospel and to be led back through that which is impossible to that which is salutary; it ought to be brought back to Christ and the gospel, which by its power makes a disciplinarian out of a robber and takes the man who was killed by the law and brings him back to Christ; this is what the law cannot do" (259n58).

Chapter 5

1 LW 41:148–65.
2 LW 41:154. Also quoted in Lohse, *Martin Luther's Theology*, 293.
3 Allen G. Jorgenson, "Contours of the Common Priesthood," in *The Global Luther: A Theologian for Modern Times*, ed. Christine Helmer (Minneapolis: Fortress Press, 2009), 253.
4 LW 30:54; WA 12:308.
5 LW 30:64–65; WA 12:318.
6 LW 44:92–93.
7 See chapter 6 for a discussion of secular power.
8 LW 44:93.
9 LW 44:92.
10 LW 41:164–65.
11 LW 43:63.
12 Michael J. Gorman, *Paul's Narrative Spirituality of the Cross* (Grand Rapids, MI: Eerdmans, 2001), 18n29.
13 LW 45:109.
14 Kolb, *Martin Luther: Confessor*, 172.
15 LW 44.127; WA 6:407.
16 LW 30:63; WA 12:317.
17 LW 35:101.
18 LW 30:53; WA 12:307; LW 30:62; WA 12:316.
19 LW 30:55; WA 12:309; LW 44:128.
20 LW 44:128.
21 Kolb, *Treatise*, 57.
22 LW 30:54; WA 12:308.
23 LW 30:64; WA 12:317.
24 LW 31:354.
25 LW 31:355.
26 Christine Helmer, "The Common Priesthood: Luther's Enduring Challenge," in *Remembering the Reformation: Martin Luther and Catholic Theology*, ed. Declan Marmion, Salvador Ryan, and Gesa E. Thiessen (Minneapolis: Fortress Press, 2017), 223.
27 LW 40:25.
28 LW 30:55; WA 12:309.
29 LW 30:55; WA 12:309.
30 LW 30:55; WA 12:309.
31 LW 41:154–55.
32 Lohse, *Martin Luther's Theology*, 293; cf. Timothy J. Wengert, *Priesthood, Pastors, Bishops: Public Ministry for the Reformation and Today* (Minneapolis: Fortress Press, 2008), 27.
33 LW 44:129; cf. LW 30:55; WA 12:309.
34 LW 44:129.

35 LW 44:129.
36 LW 30:132; WA 12:387.
37 LW 30:132; WA 12:387.
38 LW 30:125; WA 12:380.
39 LW 30:125; WA 12:380.
40 See Michael J. Gorman, *Inhabiting the Cruciform God: Kenosis, Justification, and Theosis in Paul's Narrative Soteriology* (Grand Rapids, MI: Eerdmans, 2009).
41 LW 41:164–65.
42 LW 30:136; WA 12:390.
43 LW 30:140; WA 12:394.
44 LW 30:140; WA 12:394.
45 LW 30:133; WA 12:387.
46 LW 30:136; WA 12:390.
47 LW 30:138; WA 12:392.
48 LW 44:80.
49 LW 44:82.
50 LW 30:140; WA 12:393.
51 LW 78:97; WA 22:21.
52 LW 78:98; WA 22:22.
53 LW 78:98; WA 22:22.
54 LW 78:101; WA 22:25.
55 LW 78:101; WA 22:25.
56 See chapter 6 for a discussion of the estate of civil government as part of God's providential care.
57 LW 78:102; WA 22:26.
58 LW 14:94; WA 18:170.
59 LW 14:94; WA 31:170.
60 LW 21:299.
61 LW 21:299.
62 LW 30:140; WA 12:394.
63 LW 78:106; WA 22:29.
64 See chapter 6.
65 WA 2:430, 6–7, as cited in Lohse, *Martin Luther's Theology*, 280.
66 Charles Arand, "Luther on the Creed," in *The Pastoral Luther: Essays on Martin Luther's Practical Theology*, ed. Timothy J. Wengert (Grand Rapids, MI: Eerdmans, 2009), 157.
67 Kolb and Wengert, eds., "The Large Catechism," 437.
68 Kolb and Wengert, eds., "The Large Catechism," 436.
69 Cyprian, Ep. 73.21: "salus extra ecclesiam non est," as cited in Lohse, *Martin Luther's Theology*, 64n63.
70 Kolb and Wengert, eds., "The Large Catechism," 438.
71 LW 51:168.

72 LW 51:168.
73 LW 42:112.
74 LW 42:112.
75 Kolb and Wengert, eds., "The Large Catechism," 436.
76 Cyprian, *On the Unity of the Catholic Church* vi (CSEL. 3.i.214; tr. LCC V. 127 f).
77 Kolb and Wengert, eds., "The Large Catechism," 436.
78 LW 30:140; WA 12:394.
79 Mickey L. Mattox, "Luther's Interpretation of Scripture: Biblical Understanding in Trinitarian Shape," in *The Substance of Faith: Luther's Doctrinal Theology for Today*, ed. Dennis Bielfeldt, Mickey L. Mattox, and Paul R. Hinlicky (Minneapolis: Fortress Press, 2008), 17.
80 LW 37:366.
81 Robert Kolb and Timothy J. Wengert, eds., "Smalcald Articles," in *The Book of Concord: The Confessions of the Evangelical Lutheran Church* (Minneapolis: Fortress Press, 2000), 319.
82 LW 78:108; WA 22:32.
83 LW 78:108; WA 22:31.
84 LW 30:140; WA 12:394.
85 LW 30:141; WA 12:394.
86 For a study of Luther's view on the devil, see Volker Leppin, "Luther on the Devil," in *Encounters with Luther: New Directions for Critical Studies*, ed. Kirsi I. Stjerna and Brooks Schramm (Louisville, KY: Westminster John Knox Press, 2016), 30–41.
87 Tomlin, *Luther's Gospel*, 145.
88 LW 34:287.
89 LW 30:141; WA 12:395.
90 LW 30:140; WA 12:394.
91 LW 78:113; WA 22:36.
92 LW 20:173.
93 LW 30:141; WA 12:395.
94 LW 30:142; WA 12:395.
95 LW 30:140–41; WA 12:394.
96 LW 40:175–76; LW 75:116n26.
97 Kolb and Wengert, eds., "The Large Catechism," 432.
98 LW 34:137.
99 LW 34:137. Also quoted in Hans-Peter Grosshans, "Luther on Faith and Reason: The Light of Reason at the Twilight of the World," in Helmer, *The Global Luther*, 180.
100 Grosshans, "Luther on Faith and Reason," 175.
101 Heiko A. Oberman, *Luther: Man Between God and the Devil* (New Haven, CT: Yale University Press, 1989), 227. Also quoted in Tomlin, *Luther's Gospel*, 138.

102 LW 78:120; WA 22:44.
103 LW 30:142; WA 12:395.
104 LW 30:142; WA 12:395.
105 LW 78:121; WA 22:45.
106 LW 30:64; WA 12:318.
107 LW 30:65; WA 12:319.
108 LW 30:65; WA 12:319.
109 LW 30:65; WA 12:319.
110 LW 30:65; WA 12:320.
111 LW 30:65; WA 12:320.
112 LW 30:65; WA 12:320.
113 LW 30:165; WA 14:30.
114 LW 30:165; WA 14:30.
115 LW 14:165; WA 14:30.
116 LW 30:164; WA 14:28.
117 LW 30:164; WA 14:29.
118 LW 30:164; WA 14:29.
119 LW 26:26; WA 40.1:73.
120 LW 26:26; WA 40.1:73.
121 Christine Helmer, *How Luther Became the Reformer* (Louisville, KY: Westminster John Knox Press, 2019), 122.
122 LW 30:8; WA 12:264.
123 LW 30:8; WA 12:264.
124 LW 30:8; WA 12:264.
125 LW 17:141.
126 William E. Hordern, *Living by Grace* (Philadelphia: Westminster Press, 1975), 25–26.
127 LW 30:29; WA 12:284.
128 LW 30:65; WA 12:320.
129 LW 30:4; WA 12:260.
130 LW 31:347.
131 LW 30:143; WA 12:398.
132 LW 16:230–31; WA 31.2:166.
133 LW 31:56.
134 LW 30:12; WA 12:268.
135 LW 30:54; WA 12:308.
136 LW 30:54; WA 12:308.
137 LW 30:54; WA 12:308.
138 LW 30:64; WA 12:318.
139 LW 30:54; WA 12:309.
140 LW 30:120; WA 12:374.
141 LW 30:120; WA 12:374.
142 LW 30:54; WA 12:309.

143 LW 30:54; WA 12:309.
144 LW 30:54; WA 12:309.
145 LW 30:56; WA 12:309.
146 Wingren, *Luther on Vocation*, 66.
147 LW 30:85; WA 12:339.
148 LW 30:103; WA 12:358.
149 LW 30:103; WA 12:358.
150 LW 30:104; WA 12:358.
151 LW 30:105; WA 12:359.
152 LW 78:202; WA 22:73.
153 LW 30:110; WA 12:364.
154 LW 30:109; WA 12:364.
155 LW 78:199; WA 22:70.
156 LW 78:200; WA 22:70.
157 LW 31:10n5, where the scholastic phrase "to do what is in one" appears.
158 LW 30:110; WA 12:364.
159 LW 30:16; WA 12:272.
160 LW 30:16; WA 12:272.
161 LW 35:239.
162 LW 31:11.
163 LW 30:16; WA 12:271.
164 LW 30:71; WA 12:325.
165 LW 30:71; WA 12:325.
166 Rittgers, *Reformation of Suffering*, 123.
167 LW 30:17; WA 12:273.
168 LW 41:164.
169 Kachelmeier, *Reading Isaiah*, 170.
170 LW 16:229–330; WA 31.2:165. Also cited in Kachelmeier, *Reading Isaiah*, 170.
171 LW 42:14.
172 LW 30:119; WA 12:374.
173 LW 30:119; WA 12:374.
174 LW 30:119; WA 12:373.
175 LW 14:60.
176 LW 30:126; WA 12:381.
177 LW 25:292; WA 41:305–6.
178 LW 25:292; WA 41:305–6.
179 LW 14:59.
180 LW 41:165.
181 LW 14:59.
182 LW 25:292; WA 56:305.
183 LW 25:291; WA 56:305.

Chapter 6

1 LW 44:92. For discussions on the Two Kingdoms, see Matthew C. Harrison and John T. Pless, eds., *One Lord, Two Hands: Essays on the Theology of the Two Kingdoms* (St. Louis: Concordia, 2021).
2 See LW 78:108–9; WA 22:32.
3 LW 30:74; WA 12:329.
4 Althaus, *Ethics*, 48.
5 LW 13:47.
6 See further discussion in Jonathon David Beeke, "Martin Luther's Two Kingdoms, Law and Gospel, and the Created Order: Was There a Time When the Two Kingdoms Were Not?," *Westminster Theological Journal* 73 (2011): 191–214.
7 LW 45:85.
8 LW 13:44.
9 LW 13:44.
10 LW 30:80; WA 12:334.
11 LW 13:48.
12 LW 13:45.
13 LW 13:45.
14 LW 75:109; WA 22:32.
15 See WA 28:24; WA 43:507; LW 5:113–14, as cited in Althaus, *Ethics*, 127n94.
16 See LW 47:30ff.
17 LW 44:92.
18 LW 44:93.
19 The words quoted are Luther's, based on his reading of Daniel 9:5, 7, 14. See note 8 of LW 30:104.
20 LW 30:104; WA 12:358.
21 LW 30:104; WA 12:359.
22 LW 13:45.
23 Charlotte Methuen, *Luther and Calvin: Religious Revolutionaries* (Oxford: Lion Hudson, 2011), 103.
24 LW 45:112; WA 11:267; LW 46:36; WA 18:322.
25 LW 13:45.
26 LW 13:45.
27 LW 30:75; WA 12:329.
28 LW 78:34.
29 LW 21:108.
30 Torbjörn Johansson, "The Simul Dimension of Lutheran Theology," in *Simul: Inquiries into Luther's Experience of the Christian Life*, ed. Robert Kolb, Torbjörn Johansson, and Daniel Johansson (Göttingen: Vandenhoeck & Ruprecht, 2021), 26–27; cf. LW 45:97.
31 LW 30:76; WA 12:330.

32   LW 30:76; WA 12:331. See also LW 45:114–17.

33   LW 30:78; WA 12:332.

34   LW 30:80; WA 12:334. See LW 30:80n27, which says that it is not clear which passages of the Old Testament Luther has in mind. The note cites Daniel 2:46 as the most plausible text.

35   LW 45:94.

36   LW 30:77; WA 12:332.

37   Michael P. DeJonge, *Bonhoeffer's Reception of Luther* (Oxford: Oxford University Press, 2017), 86.

38   LW 45:106.

39   LW 45:105.

40   LW 30:81; WA 12:335.

41   LW 30:76; WA 12:330.

42   LW 30:76; WA 12:329.

43   LW 30:74; WA 12:329.

44   LW 45:92.

45   Jonathan David Beeke, *Duplex Regnum Christi: Christ's Twofold Kingdom*, Studies in Reformed Theology, vol. 40 (Leiden: Brill, 2020), 51; cf. LW 45:92.

46   James Arne Nestingen, "The Two Kingdoms Distinction: An Analysis with Suggestion," *Word and World* 19, no. 3 (Summer 1999): 271.

47   Bernd Wannenwetsch, "The Simultaneity of Two Citizenships: A Theological Reappraisal of Luther's Account of the 'Two Regiments' for our Times," in *Simul*, ed. Robert Kolb, Torbjörn Johansson, and Daniel Johansson (Göttingen: Vandenhoeck & Ruprecht, 2021), 183.

48   DeJonge, *Bonhoeffer's Reception of Luther*, 87.

49   LW 31:297, 299.

50   DeJonge, *Bonhoeffer's Reception of Luther*, 87.

51   Johansson, "Simul Dimension," 27.

52   Heinrich Bornkamm, *Luther's Doctrine of the Two Kingdoms in the Context of His Theology*, trans. Karl H. Herz (Philadelphia: Fortress Press, 1966), 36.

53   Wannenwetsch, "Simultaneity," 182.

54   Wannenwetsch, "Simultaneity," 182. In the Chalcedonian creed, the two natures of Christ, human and divine, are one, each retaining its own distinctiveness. Analogously, Wannenwetsch argues, the two regiments, spiritual and secular, are distinguished but inseparably one.

55   Paul T. McCain, "Receiving the Gifts of God in His Two Kingdoms: The Development of Luther's Understanding," in Harrison and Pless, *One Lord, Two Hands*, 342.

56   LW 13:194.

57   Bornkamm, *Luther's Doctrine*, 8.

58 LW 13:193.
59 LW 13:197.
60 Beeke, *Duplex Regnum Christi*, 54–55.
61 LW 13:72.
62 LW 13:194.
63 Nestingen, "Two Kingdoms," 271.
64 LW 13:198.
65 LW 30:75; WA 12:329.
66 LW 13:199.
67 LW 13:200.
68 LW 30:121; WA 12:375.
69 LW 30:121; WA 12:375.
70 LW 31:344.
71 LW 31:344.
72 LW 45:109.
73 LW 45:109. See note 45, where it indicates the edition of 1534 has "child, servant, and subject" in addition to "servant."
74 John R. Stephenson, "The Two Governments and the Two Kingdoms in Luther's Thought," *Scottish Journal of Theology* 34, no. 4 (1981): 328.
75 Durheim, *Christ's Gift*, 66.
76 Wannenwetsch, "Luther's Moral Theology," 127. The word "Gestalt" means "form" or "configuration of freedom."
77 LW 31:344.
78 Kolb, *Treatise*, 40.
79 Kolb, *Treatise*, 40.
80 Karl Holl, *What Did Luther Understand by Religion?*, ed. James Luther Adams and Walter F. Bense, trans. Fred W. Meuser and Walter R. Wietzke (Minneapolis: Augsburg, 1979), 86, as cited in Christine Helmer, *How Luther Became the Reformer* (Louisville, KY: Westminster John Knox Press, 2019), 59.
81 Helmer, *How Luther Became the Reformer*, 58.
82 Holl, *What Did Luther Understand by Religion?*, 80, as cited in Helmer, *How Luther Became the Reformer*, 58.
83 LW 30:27; WA 12:282.
84 LW 30:121; WA 12:376.
85 Kolb, *Treatise*, 40.
86 LW 31:344–45.
87 Tuomo Mannermaa, *Christ Present in Faith: Luther's View of Justification* (Minneapolis: Fortress Press, 2005), 70.
88 LW 27:74; WA 40.2:93; cf. LW 26:189; WA 40.1:312: "The Spirit . . . dominates them [the flesh and it desires] so that they do not rule."

89 Wannenwetsch, "Luther's Moral Theology," 127.

90 LW 30:68; WA 12:323.

91 Holl, *What Did Luther Understand by Religion?*, 59.

92 LW 30:15; WA 12:271.

93 Wannenwetsch, "Luther's Moral Theology," 128.

94 Bornkamm, *Luther's Doctrine*, 33.

95 LW 45:86.

96 LW 45:86.

97 LW 45:86.

98 LW 13:47–48.

99 LW 30:74; WA 12:328; cf. LW 1:104; WA 42:79: "Moreover, there was no government of the state before sin, for there was no need of it. Civil government is a remedy required by our corrupted nature."

100 Beeke, "Martin Luther's Two Kingdoms," 195.

101 Nestingen, "Luther on Marriage," 35.

102 Lohse, *Martin Luther's Theology*, 323.

103 Parsons, *Reformation Marriage*, 108.

104 Bayer, "Nature and Institution," 128; cf. Bayer, *Martin Luther's Theology*, 148: "The political estate is rooted within the economic or household estate."

105 Kolb and Wengert, eds., "The Large Catechism," 405.

106 WA 40.3:220.4f (on Ps. 127:1; 1532–33), as cited in Bayer, *Martin Luther's Theology*, 148.

107 WA 47:854:7f ("Sermon of September 29, 1539"), as cited in Bayer, *Martin Luther's Theology*, 148.

108 Bayer, *Martin Luther's Theology*, 148.

109 Althaus, *Ethics*, 48.

110 WA 49:237, 142, as cited in Bernd Wannenwetsch, *Political Worship*, trans. Margaret Kohl (Oxford: Oxford University Press, 2004), 62n5; cf. WA 40.3:222, 35f, as cited in Bayer, *Martin Luther's Theology*, 149n99.

111 WA 47:242, as cited in Althaus, *Theology of Martin Luther*, 48.

112 William J. Wright, *Martin Luther's Understanding of God's Two Kingdoms: A Response to the Challenge of Skepticism* (Grand Rapids, MI: Baker Academic, 2010), 119.

113 LW 1:57; WA 42:42, as cited in Wright, *God's Two Kingdoms*, 119.

114 Kolb and Arand, *Genius*, 61.

115 David S. Yeago, "Martin Luther on Grace, Law and Moral Life: Prolegomena to an Ecumenical Discussion of *Veritatis Splendor*," *The Thomist* 61, no. 2 (1998): 178. Trueman shares Yeago's view; see Trueman, "What Luther Teaches Us Today," 108.

116 LW 1:146; WA 42:110.
117 LW 1:101; WA 42:77.
118 LW 1:94; WA 42:71. Also quoted in Richard Hütter, "The Two-fold Center of Lutheran Ethics: Christian Freedom and God's Commandments," in *The Promise of Lutheran Ethics*, ed. Karen L. Bloomquist and John R. Stumme (Minneapolis: Fortress Press, 1998), 42.
119 LW 1:109–10; WA 42:83.
120 LW 1:109: WA 42:82.
121 LW 1:113: WA 42:85.
122 LW 1:62–63; WA 42:47.
123 LW 44:23.
124 Wannenwetsch, "Luther's Moral Theology," 126.
125 Wannenwetsch, "Luther's Moral Theology," 125.
126 Yeago, "Grace, Law and Moral Life," 177.
127 Hütter, "Twofold Center," 186n44.
128 LW 1:94; WA 42:71.
129 Robert Kolb, "Luther on the Two Kinds of Righteousness: Reflections on His Two-Dimensional Definition of Humanity at the Heart of His Theology," *Lutheran Quarterly* 13 (1999): 463.
130 Laffin, *Promise*, 161.
131 Hütter, "Twofold Center," 44.
132 See Yeago, "Grace, Law and Moral Life," 177; Laffin, *Promise*, 161.
133 LW 1:107; WA 42:81.
134 Yeago, "Gnosticism," 48. Also cited in Laffin, *Promise*, 161.
135 LW 1:109; WA 42:82.
136 Yeago, "Grace, Law and Moral Life," 176.
137 Laffin, *Promise*, 184.
138 LW 46:238.
139 LW 1:104; WA 41:79, 11.
140 LW 1:104; WA 41:79, 11.
141 Laffin, *Promise*, 161.
142 LW 30:74; WA 12:329.
143 LW 30:81; WA 12:336.
144 LW 30:79; WA 12:334.
145 LW 30:140; WA 12:393.
146 Althaus, *Ethics*, 47; cf. LW 21:29.
147 LW 30:82; WA 12:337.
148 LW 30:82; WA 12:336.
149 LW 30:82; WA 12:337.
150 LW 30:83; WA 12:338.
151 Althaus, *Ethics*, 48.

Conclusion

1 LW 26:29; WA 40.1:78.
2 LW 31:53.
3 LW 31:52.
4 Forde, *On Being a Theologian*, 76–77.
5 LW 31:52–53.
6 Gerhard O. Forde, *The Captivation of the Will: Luther vs. Erasmus on Freedom and Bondage* (Grand Rapids, MI; Cambridge: Eerdmans, 2005), 45.
7 LW 12:312.
8 LW 5:44; WA 43:559.
9 LW 30:10; WA 12:265.
10 LW 30:10; WA 12:265.
11 Heinrich Bornkamm, *Luther's World of Thought*, trans. Martin H. Bertram (St. Louis: Concordia, 1965), 136.
12 Bayer, *Martin Luther's Theology*, 180.
13 LW 26:227; WA 40.1:361.
14 Kolb and Wengert, eds., "The Large Catechism," 386.
15 LW 16:82–83; WA 31.2:48.
16 Hampson, *Christian Contradictions*, 12.
17 LW 30:33; WA 12:289.
18 Hampson, *Christian Contradictions*, 47.
19 LW 30:28; WA 12:284.
20 Sun-young Kim, *Luther on Faith and Love: Christ and the Law in the 1535 Galatians Commentary* (Minneapolis: Fortress Press, 2014), 139.
21 LW 30:67; WA 12:321.
22 Martin J. Lohrmann, "Faith and Love in Luther's *Small Catechism*," in *Teaching Reformation: Essays in Honor of Timothy J. Wengert*, ed. Luka Ilić and Martin J. Lohrmann (Minneapolis: Fortress Press, 2021), 224.
23 Gene Edward Veith Jr., *The Spirituality of the Cross: The Way of the First Evangelicals*, 3rd ed. (St. Louis: Concordia, 2021), 137.
24 Wingren, *Luther on Vocation*, 6. Also cited in Veith, *Spirituality*, 137–38.
25 For a major study of Luther's view of vocation, see Mark D. Tranvik, *Luther and the Called Life* (Minneapolis: Fortress Press, 2016).
26 LW 13:368.
27 LW 45:325.
28 LW 41:176–77.
29 Bayer, *Martin Luther's Theology*, 175.

30 See WA 47:857.35, as quoted in Bayer, *Martin Luther's Theology*, 176.
    The distinction between coworkers and cocreators appears in LW
    33:242–43.

31 LW 45:327.

32 Risto Saarinen, "Communicating the Grace of God," in *The Gift of
    Grace: The Future of Lutheran Theology*, ed. Niels Henrik Gregersen,
    Bo Holm, Ted Peters, and Peter Widmann (Minneapolis: Fortress
    Press, 2005), 72. The word "responsivity" is Saarinen's.

33 Mark D. Tranvik, "Celebrating the Reformation: The Lutheran
    Foundation of a Called Life," *Intersections* 46 (2017): 14.

34 Althaus, *Ethics*, 61–62.

35 LW 34:287.

36 Oberman, *Luther*, 104.

37 Hamm, *Early Luther*, 33.

38 Hans-Martin Barth, *The Theology of Martin Luther: A Critical
    Assessment* (Minneapolis: Fortress Press, 2013), 437.

39 LW 1:47; WA 42:353.

40 Trueman, "What Luther Teaches Us Today," 113.

41 LW 53:14.

Bibliography

Primary Sources

Kolb, Robert, and Timothy J. Wengert, eds. *The Book of Concord: The Confessions of the Evangelical Lutheran Church*. Minneapolis: Fortress Press, 2000.

Luther, Martin. *The Annotated Luther*. Edited by Hans J. Hillerbrand, Kirsi I. Stjerna, and Timothy J. Wengert. 6 vols. Minneapolis: Fortress Press, 2015–17.

———. *Luther's Works: American Edition*. Edited by Jaroslav Pelikan. Vols. 1–30. St. Louis: Concordia, 1955–73.

———. *Luther's Works: American Edition*. Edited by Helmut T. Lehman. Vols. 31–55. Philadelphia: Fortress Press, 1957–86.

———. *Luther's Works: American Edition*, new series. Edited by Christopher Boyd Brown, Benjamin T. J. Mayes, and James L. Langebartels. Vols. 56–82. St. Louis: Concordia, 2009–15.

Tappert, Theodore G., trans. and ed. *The Book of Concord: The Confessions of the Evangelical Lutheran Church*. Philadelphia: Fortress Press, 1959.

Secondary Sources

Althaus, Paul. *The Theology of Martin Luther*. Translated by Robert C. Shultz. Philadelphia: Fortress Press, 1966.

———. *The Ethics of Martin Luther*. Translated by Robert C. Schultz. Minneapolis: Augsburg Fortress, 1972.

Barth, Hans-Martin. *The Theology of Martin Luther: A Critical Assessment.* Minneapolis: Fortress Press, 2013.

Bayer, Oswald. *Freedom in Response: Lutheran Ethics; Sources and Controversies.* Translated by Jeffrey F. Cayzer. Oxford: Oxford University Press, 2007.

———. *Living by Faith: Justification and Sanctification.* Grand Rapids, MI: Eerdmans, 2003.

———. *Martin Luther's Theology: A Contemporary Interpretation.* Translated by Thomas H. Trapp. Grand Rapids, MI: Eerdmans, 2008.

———. "Nature and Institution: Luther's Doctrine of the Three Orders." *Lutheran Quarterly* 12 (1998): 129–59.

———. "Preaching the Word." *Lutheran Quarterly* 23 (2009): 249–69.

———. *Theology the Lutheran Way.* Edited and translated by Jeffrey G. Silcock and Mark C. Mattes. Grand Rapids, MI: Eerdmans, 2007.

Beeke, Joel R., ed. *The Beauty and Glory of the Reformation.* Grand Rapids, MI: Reformation Heritage Books, 2018.

Beeke, Jonathon David. *Duplex Regnum Christi: Christ's Twofold Kingdom.* Studies in Reformed Theology, vol. 40. Leiden: Brill, 2020.

———. "Martin Luther's Two Kingdoms, Law and Gospel, and the Created Order: Was There a Time When the Two Kingdoms Were Not?" *Westminster Theological Journal* 73 (2011): 191–214.

Bertram, Robert. "Again on the Trinity: Bertram Responds." *Dialog* 29 (1990): 60–61.

———. "When is God Triune?" *Dialog* 28 (Spring 1989): 123–32.

Bielfeldt, Dennis, Mickey L. Mattox, and Paul R. Hinlicky. *The Substance of Faith: Luther's Doctrinal Theology for Today.* Minneapolis: Fortress Press, 2008.

Bloomquist, Karen L., and John R. Stumme, eds. *The Promise of Lutheran Ethics.* Minneapolis: Fortress Press, 1998.

Bornkamm, Heinrich. *Luther's Doctrine of the Two Kingdoms in the Context of His Theology.* Translated by Karl H. Herz. Philadelphia: Fortress Press, 1966.

———. *Luther's World of Thought.* Translated by Martin H. Bertram. St. Louis: Concordia, 1965.

Braaten, Carl E., and Robert W. Jenson. *Christian Dogmatics.* 2 vols. Minneapolis: Fortress Press, 1984.

———. *Justification: The Article by Which the Church Stands or Falls.* Minneapolis: Fortress Press, 1990.

———, ed. *Our Naming of God: Problems and Prospects of God-Talk Today.* Minneapolis: Fortress Press, 1989.

Braaten, Carl E., and Robert W. Jenson, eds. *The Marks of the Body of Christ.* Grand Rapids, MI: Eerdmans, 1999.

Chester, Stephen. "'Abba! Father!' (Gal. 4:6): Justification and Assurance in Martin Luther's Lectures on Galatians (1535)." *Biblical Research* 63 (2018): 15–22.

Cortez, Marc. *Christological Anthropology in Historical Perspective: Ancient and Contemporary Approaches to Theological Anthropology.* Grand Rapids, MI: Zondervan, 2016.

Cummings, Brian. *The Literary Culture of the Reformation: Grammar and Grace.* Oxford: Oxford University Press, 2002.

DeJonge, Michael P. *Bonhoeffer's Reception of Luther.* Oxford: Oxford University Press, 2017.

Durheim, Benjamin M. *Christ's Gift, Our Response: Martin Luther and Louis-Marie Chauvet on the Connection between Sacraments and Ethics.* Collegeville, MN: Liturgical Press, 2015.

Ebeling, Gerhard. *Luther: An Introduction to His Thought.* Translated by R. A. Wilson. Philadelphia: Fortress Press, 1970.

Estes, James M. *Peace, Order, and the Glory of God: Secular Authority and the Church in the Thought of Luther and Melanchthon, 1518–1559.* Studies in Medieval and Reformation Traditions, vol. 111. Leiden: Brill, 2005.

Evener, Vincent. "Wittenberg's Wandering Spirits: Discipline and the Dead in the Reformation." *Church History* 84 (2015): 531–55.

Farrow, Douglas. *Theological Negotiations: Proposals in Soteriology and Anthropology.* Grand Rapids, MI: Baker Academic, 2018.

Forde, Gerhard O. *On Being a Theologian of the Cross: Reflections on Luther's Heidelberg Disputation, 1518.* Grand Rapids, MI: Eerdmans, 1997.

———. *The Captivation of the Will: Luther vs. Erasmus on Freedom and Bondage.* Edited by Steven D. Paulson. Grand Rapids, MI: Eerdmans, 2005.

———. *The Preached God: Proclamation in Word and Sacrament.* Edited by Mark C. Mattes and Steven D. Paulson. Grand Rapids, MI: Eerdmans, 2007.

Gerrish, B. A. "'To the Unknown God': Luther and Calvin on the Hiddenness of God." In *The Old Protestantism and the New: Essays on the Reformation Heritage.* Chicago: University of Chicago Press, 1982.

Gorman, Michael J. *Inhabiting the Cruciform God: Kenosis, Justification, and Theosis in Paul's Narrative Soteriology.* Grand Rapids, MI: Eerdmans, 2009.

———. *Paul's Narrative Spirituality of the Cross.* Grand Rapids, MI: Eerdmans, 2001.

Gregersen, Niels Henrik, Bo Holm, Ted Peters, and Peter Widmann. *The Gift of Grace: The Future of Lutheran Theology.* Minneapolis: Fortress Press, 2005.

Hall, Douglas John. *Lighten Our Cross: Toward an Indigenous Theology of the Cross.* Philadelphia: Westminster, 1976.

Hamm, Berndt. *The Early Luther: Stages in a Reformation Reorientation.* Translated by Martin J. Lohrmann. Grand Rapids, MI: Eerdmans, 2014.

———. *The Reformation of Faith in the Context of Late Medieval Theology and Piety*. Leiden: Brill, 2004.

Hampson, Daphne. *Christian Contradictions: The Structures of Lutheran and Catholic Thought*. Cambridge: Cambridge University Press, 2001.

Harink, Douglas. *1 & 2 Peter*. Brazos Theological Commentary on the Bible. Grand Rapids, MI: Brazos Press, 2009.

Harrison, Matthew C., and John T. Pless, eds. *One Lord, Two Hands: Essays on the Theology of the Two Kingdoms*. St. Louis: Concordia, 2021.

Headley, John. *Luther's View of Church History*. New Haven, CT: Yale University Press, 1963.

Helmer, Christine. "The Experience of Justification." In *Justification in a Post-Christian Society*. Church of Sweden Research Series, vol. 8. Edited by Carl-Henric Grenholm and Goran Gunner, 36–56. Eugene, OR: Pickwick, 2014.

———, ed. *The Global Luther: A Theologian for Modern Times*. Minneapolis: Fortress Press, 2009.

———. *How Luther Became the Reformer*. Louisville, KY: Westminster John Knox Press, 2019.

Hendrix, Scott. "Luther on Marriage." *Lutheran Quarterly* 14 (Autumn 2000): 335–50.

Hengel, Martin. *Saint Peter: The Underestimated Apostle*. Translated by Thomas H. Trapp. Grand Rapids, MI: Eerdmans, 2010.

Hinlicky, Paul R. *Luther and the Beloved Community: A Path for Christian Theology after Christendom*. Grand Rapids, MI: Eerdmans, 2010.

———. "Some Questions to Bertram on the Trinity." *Dialog* 28 (Autumn 1989): 307–8.

———, ed. *The Substance of Faith: Luther's Doctrinal Theology for Today*. Minneapolis: Fortress Press, 2008.

Holl, Karl. *What Did Luther Understand by Religion?* Edited by James Luther Adams and Walter F. Bense. Translated by Fred W. Meuser and Walter R. Wietzke. Minneapolis: Augsburg, 1979.

Hordern, William E. *Experience and Faith: The Significance of Luther for Understanding Today's Experiential Religion*. Minneapolis: Augsburg, 1983.

———. *Living by Grace*. Philadelphia, PA: Westminster Press, 1975.

Ilić, Luka, and Martin J. Lohrmann, eds. *Teaching Reformation: Essays in Honor of Timothy J. Wengert*. Minneapolis: Fortress Press, 2021.

Iwand, Hans J. *The Righteousness of Faith According to Luther*. Edited by Virgil F. Thompson. Translated by Randi H. Lundell. Eugene, OR: Wipf & Stock, 2008.

Jenson, Robert. *Systematic Theology*. 2 vols. Oxford: Oxford University Press, 1997–99.

Jüngel, Eberhard. *The Freedom of a Christian: Luther's Significance for Contemporary Theology*. Translated by Roy A. Harrisville. Minneapolis: Augsburg, 1988.

———. *God as the Mystery of the World: On the Foundation of the Theology of the Crucified God in between Theism and Atheism*. Translated by Darrell L. Guder. Grand Rapids, MI: Eerdmans, 1983.

Kachelmeier, Brian L. *Reading Isaiah with Luther*. St. Louis: Concordia, 2018.

Kim, Sun-young. *Luther on Faith and Love: Christ and the Law in the 1535 Galatians Commentary*. Minneapolis: Fortress Press, 2014.

Kleinig, John. "Luther on the Reception of God's Holiness." *Pro Ecclesia* 17, no. 1 (2008): 76–91.

Kolb, Robert. "Christ's Descent into Hell as Christological Locus in the Era of the 'Formula of Concord': Luther's 'Torgau Sermon' Revisited." In *Lutherjahrbuch* 69: 101–18. Göttingen: Vandenhoeck & Ruprecht, 2002.

———. *Luther's Treatise on Christian Freedom and Its Legacy*. Lanham, MD: Lexington/Fortress Academic, 2020.

———. "Luther on the Two Kinds of Righteousness: Reflections on His Two-Dimensional Definition of Humanity at the Heart of His Theology." *Lutheran Quarterly* 13 (1999): 449–66.

———. *Martin Luther: Confessor of the Faith*. Oxford: Oxford University Press, 2009.

———. *Martin Luther and the Enduring Word of God: The Wittenberg School and Its Scripture-Centered Proclamation*. Grand Rapids, MI: Baker Academic, 2016.

———. *Martin Luther as Prophet, Teacher, and Hero: Images of the Reformer, 1520–1620*. Grand Rapids, MI: Baker Academic, 1999.

———. *Teaching God's Children His Teaching: A Guide for the Study of Luther's Catechism*. New ed. St. Louis: Concordia Seminary Press, 2012.

Kolb, Robert, and Charles P. Arand. *The Genius of Luther's Theology*. Grand Rapids, MI: Baker Academic, 2008.

Kolb, Robert, Irene Dingel, and L'ubomír Batka, eds. *The Oxford Handbook of Martin Luther's Theology*. Oxford: Oxford University Press, 2014.

Kolb, Robert, Torbjörn Johansson, and Daniel Johansson, eds. *Simul: Inquiries into Luther's Experience of the Christian Life*. Göttingen: Vandenhoeck & Ruprecht, 2021.

Laffin, Michael Richard. *The Promise of Martin Luther's Political Theology: Freeing Luther from the Modern Political Narrative*. Bloomsbury: T & T Clark, 2018.

Lage, Dietmar. *Martin Luther's Christology and Ethics*. Lewiston, NY: Edwin Mellen Press, 1990.

Lazareth, William H. *Luther on the Christian Home: An Application of the Social Ethics of the Reformation*. Philadelphia: Muhlenberg Press, 1960.

Lienhard, Marc. *Luther: Witness to Jesus Christ.* Translated by Edwin H. Robertson. Minneapolis: Augsburg, 1982.

Loewenich, Walther von. *Luther's Theology of the Cross.* Translated by Herbert Bouman. Minneapolis: Augsburg, 1976.

———. *Martin Luther: The Man and His Work.* Translated by Lawrence W. Denef. Minneapolis: Augsburg, 1986.

Lohse, Bernhard. *Martin Luther's Theology: Its Historical and Systematic Development.* Translated and edited by Roy A. Harrisville. Minneapolis: Augsburg Fortress, 1999.

Mannermaa, Tuomo. *Christ Present in Faith: Luther's View of Justification.* Minneapolis: Fortress Press, 2005.

Marmion, Declan, Salvador Ryan, and Gesa E. Thiessen, eds. *Remembering the Reformation: Martin Luther and Catholic Theology.* Minneapolis: Fortress Press, 2017.

Marty, Martin. *The Hidden Discipline.* St. Louis: Concordia, 1962.

Maschke, Timothy. "The Authority of Scripture: Luther's Approach to Allegory in Galatians." *Logia* 4, no. 2 (1995): 25–31.

Maschke, Timothy, Franz Posset, and Joan Skocir, eds. *Ad fontes Lutheri: Toward the Recovery of the Real Luther; Essays in Honor of Kenneth Hagen's Sixty-Fifth Birthday.* Milwaukee, WI: Marquette University Press, 2001.

Mattes, Mark C. *Martin Luther's Theology of Beauty: A Reappraisal.* Grand Rapids, MI: Baker Academic, 2017.

Mattox, Mickey Leland. *Defender of the Most Holy Matriarchs: Martin Luther's Interpretation of the Women of Genesis in the "Enarrationes in Genesin," 1535–1545.* Studies in Medieval and Reformation Traditions, vol. 92. Leiden: Brill, 2003.

McGrath, Alister E. *Iustitia Dei: A History of the Christian Doctrine of Justification.* 4th ed. Cambridge: Cambridge University Press, 2020.

———. *Luther's Theology of the Cross: Martin Luther's Theological Breakthrough.* Oxford: Wiley-Blackwell, 1985.

McKim, Donald, ed. *The Cambridge Companion to Martin Luther.* Cambridge: Cambridge University Press, 2006.

McNair, Bruce G. "Luther and the Pastoral Theology of the Lord's Prayer." *Logia* 14, no. 4 (2005): 41–46.

Methuen, Charlotte. *Luther and Calvin: Religious Revolutionaries.* Oxford: Lion Hudson, 2011.

Meuser, Fred W., and Stanley D. Schneider, eds. *Interpreting Luther's Legacy: Essays in Honor of Edward C. Fendt.* Minneapolis: Augsburg, 1969.

Meyer, Carl S., ed. *Luther for an Ecumenical Age: Essays in Commemoration of the 450th Anniversary of the Reformation.* Saint Louis: Concordia, 1967.

Nagel, Norman E. "Heresy, Doctor Luther, Heresy! The Person and Work of Christ." In *Seven-Headed Luther: Essays in Commemoration of a Quincentenary, 1483-1983*. Edited by Peter Newman Brooks, 25-49. Oxford: Clarendon Press, 1983.

Nessan, Craig L. *Free in Deed: The Heart of Lutheran Ethics*. Minneapolis: Fortress Press, 2022.

Nestingen, James Arne. "Luther on Marriage, Vocation, and the Cross." *Word and World* 23, no. 1 (Winter 2003): 31-39.

———. "The Two Kingdoms Distinction: An Analysis with Suggestion." *Word and World* 19, no. 3 (Summer 1999): 268-75.

Ngien, Dennis. *Fruit for the Soul: Luther on the Lament Psalms*. Minneapolis: Fortress Press, 2015.

———. *Luther's Theology of the Cross: Christ in Luther's Sermons on John*. Eugene, OR: Cascade Books, 2018.

Oberman, Heiko A. *Luther: Man between God and the Devil*. New Haven, CT: Yale University Press, 1989.

Pannenberg, Wolfhart. "God of the Philosophers." *First Things* 174 (June 2007): 31-34.

Parsons, Michael. *Luther and Calvin on Grief and Lament: Life-experience and Biblical Text*. Lewiston, NY: Mellen, 2013.

———. *Reformation Marriage: The Husband and Wife Relationship in the Theology of Luther and Calvin*. Edinburgh: Rutherford House, 2005.

Paulson, Steven D. *Lutheran Theology*. New York: T & T Clark, 2011.

Pederson, Ann. "A Question to Bertram and Luther on the Trinity." *Dialog* (Autumn 1989): 308-9.

Pelikan, Jaroslav. *Luther the Expositor: Introduction to the Reformer's Exegetical Writings*. St. Louis: Concordia, 1959.

Pless, John T. *Pastor Craft: Essays and Sermons*. San Clemente, CA: New Reformation, 2020.

Price, Timothy Shaun. "Luther's Use of Aristotle in the Three Estates and Its Implications for Understanding Oeconomia." *Journal of Markets and Morality* 18, no. 2 (2015): 373-89.

Rittgers, Ronald K. *The Reformation of Suffering: Pastoral Theology and Lay Piety in Late Medieval and Early Modern Germany*. Oxford: Oxford University Press, 2012.

Saarinen, Risto. *Luther and the Gift*. Tübingen: Mohr Siebeck, 2017.

Sasse, Hermann. *We Confess Jesus Christ*. Translated by Norman Nagel. St. Louis: Concordia, 1984.

Siggins, Ian D. Kingston. *Martin Luther's Doctrine of Christ*. New Haven, CT: Yale University Press, 1970.

Silcock, Jeffrey G. "Theology and Proclamation: Towards a Lutheran Framework for Preaching." *Lutheran Theological Journal* 42, no. 3 (December 2008): 131-40.

Steinmetz, David. *Luther in Context*. 2nd ed. Grand Rapids, MI: Baker Academic, 2002.

Stephenson, John R. "The Two Governments and the Two Kingdoms in Luther's Thought." *Scottish Journal of Theology* 34, no. 4 (1981): 321–37.

Stjerna, Kirsi I., and Brooks Schramm, eds. *Encounters with Luther: New Directions for Critical Studies*. Louisville, KY: Westminster John Knox Press, 2016.

Streufert, Mary J. *Language for God: A Lutheran Perspective*. Minneapolis: Fortress Press, 2022.

Swain, Scott R. *The Trinity and the Bible: On Theological Interpretation*. Bellingham, WA: Lexham Academic, 2021.

Tomlin, Graham. *Luther's Gospel: Reimagining the World*. London: Bloomsbury T & T Clark, 2017.

Torrance, Andrew B., and Thomas H. McCall. *Knowing Creation: Perspectives from Theology, Philosophy, and Science*. Grand Rapids, MI: Zondervan, 2018.

Tranvik, Mark D. "Celebrating the Reformation: The Lutheran Foundation of a Called Life." *Intersections* 46 (2017): 11–16.

———. *Luther and the Called Life*. Minneapolis: Fortress Press, 2016.

Veith, Gene Edward, Jr. *The Spirituality of the Cross: The Way of the First Evangelicals*. 3rd ed. St. Louis: Concordia, 2021.

Wannenwetsch, Bernd. *Political Worship*. Translated by Margaret Kohl. Oxford: Oxford University Press, 2004.

Watson, Philip S. *Let God Be God: An Interpretation of the Theology of Martin Luther*. Philadelphia: Fortress Press, 1947.

Weber, Otto. *Foundations of Dogmatics*. Vol. 1. Translated and annotated by Darrell L. Guder. Grand Rapids, MI: Eerdmans, 1981.

Webster, John. *Christ Our Salvation: Expositions and Proclamation*. Bellingham, WA: Lexham Press, 2020.

Wengert, Timothy J. *Martin Luther's Catechisms: Forming the Faith*. Minneapolis: Fortress Press, 2009.

———, ed. *The Pastoral Luther: Essays on Martin Luther's Practical Theology*. Grand Rapids, MI: Eerdmans, 2009.

———. *Priesthood, Pastors, Bishops: Public Ministry for the Reformation and Today*. Minneapolis: Fortress Press, 2008.

———. *Word of Life: Introducing Lutheran Hermeneutics*. Minneapolis: Fortress Press, 2019.

Wingren, Gustaf. *The Living Word: A Theological Study of Preaching and the Church* Philadelphia: Muhlenberg Press, 1960.

———. *Luther on Vocation*. Translated by Carl C. Rasmussen. Philadelphia: Muhlenberg Press, 1957.

Woolf, Bertram Lee. *Reformation Writings of Martin Luther*, vol. 1. New York: Philosophical Library, 1953.

Wright, William J. *Martin Luther's Understanding of God's Two Kingdoms: A Response to the Challenge of Skepticism.* Grand Rapids, MI: Baker Academic, 2010.

Yeago, David S. "Gnosticism, Antinomianism, and Reformation Theology: Reflections on the Costs of a Construal." *Pro Ecclesia* 2, no. 1 (1993): 37–49.

———. "Martin Luther on Grace, Law and Moral Life: Prolegomena to an Ecumenical Discussion of *Veritatis Splendor.*" *The Thomist* 61, no. 2 (1998): 163–91.

Zachman, Randall C. *The Assurance of Faith: Conscience in the Theology of Martin Luther and John Calvin.* Minneapolis: Augsburg Fortress, 1993.

Index